WITHOUT WARNING

WITHOUT WARNING

DAMIEN THOMLINSON

WITH MICHAEL COWLEY

HarperCollins*Publishers*

HarperCollins*Publishers*

First published in Australia in 2013
by HarperCollins*Publishers* Australia Pty Limited
ABN 36 009 913 517
harpercollins.com.au

HarperCollins*Publishers*
Level 13, 201 Elizabeth Street, Sydney NSW 2000, Australia
31 View Road, Glenfield, Auckland 0627, New Zealand
A 53, Sector 57, Noida, UP, India
77–85 Fulham Palace Road, London W6 8JB, United Kingdom
2 Bloor Street East, 20th floor, Toronto, Ontario M4W 1A8, Canada
10 East 53rd Street, New York NY 10022, USA

National Library of Australia Cataloguing-in-Publication entry:

Thomlinson, Damien, author.
  Without warning / Damien Thomlinson & Michael Cowley.
  ISBN: 978 0 7322 9716 9 (paperback)
  ISBN: 978 1 7430 9980 3 (ebook)
  Thomlinson, Damien.
  Australia. Army.—Commando troops—Biography.
  Afghan War, 2001—Participation, Australian—Biography.
  Afghan War, 2001—Personal narratives, Australian.
  Afghan War, 2001—Medical care.
  War wounds—Patients—Rehabilitation.
  Amputees—Rehabilitation.
  People with disabilities—Rehabilitation.
  Soldiers—Australia—Biography.
  Cowley, Michael, author.
355.0092

Cover design by Philip Campbell Design
Cover images by Tim Bauer
All internal photographs provided by Damien Thomlinson, unless otherwise credited
Typeset in Plantin by Kirby Jones
Printed and bound in Australia by Griffin Press
The papers used by HarperCollins in the manufacture of this book are a natural, recyclable
product made from wood grown in sustainable plantation forests. The fibre source and
manufacturing processes meet recognised international environmental standards, and carry
certification.

5 4 3 2 1   13 14 15 16

This is a tribute to those people who,
on so many different levels,
have helped to keep me here.

This book is dedicated to each of those
who have been part of this journey:
family, friends, surgeons, medical staff,
fellow amputees, and most importantly
the guys on the ground that fateful night.
You are, and always will be, my inspiration.

And finally this book is dedicated to
the proud soldiers who have served in any
Australian Defence Force, and to their families
who make their service possible.

Foreword

by Ray Martin

I first met Damo down at Perisher, riding a runaway snowboard like a mad thing — taking on the mountain and anything else that got in his way. Getting to know Damien Thomlinson was about as tricky as opening a blizzardly cold VB on a hot Sunday afternoon. Getting to like him was even easier. There he was sporting a technicolour thermal top, a smile as big as Coogee Beach and a twinkle in the eye that was downright dangerous. He was clearly one of those blokes you would never dare, because he'd probably do it — whatever the dare.

It's a weird thing to say — given the cards that life has dealt him lately — but he still has the essence of an athlete, moving a bit like a football player who's done a hamstring and may be 'out for a month'. It's no surprise to learn that the Iceman's childhood was a cocktail of cricket, surfing, bikes, adrenalin and risk.

'I'm not handicapped,' he laughed, 'I just don't have any legs.'

(How he came to be named 'Iceman' is a very funny yarn in itself.)

His surgeon Andrew Ellis told me that after the IED blast Damien was 'as close to death as you can get'. I had met Dr Ellis, an army reserve officer, in the blood 'n' gore of

Aceh after the 2005 Boxing Day tsunami hit the Indonesia archipelago. (He's not just a top surgeon but a top bloke, too.) I asked Ellis what Damo's shattered body would have looked like in the dust and chaos of that wild Afghan night. Ellis paused for a moment then said thoughtfully, 'Like he'd just been attacked by a mad axe-murderer.' That seemed to answer my question.

Yet here was Damo — not that long after having his body savagely chopped and broken — scooting down the snow, falling over in a barrel of laughter and refusing to let anyone help him back on his board. (You could almost hear him muttering, 'Piss off,' under his breath.)

Damien is the classic alpha male, always a commando 'in the beret that says he's bulletproof', an absolute army pin-up boy — despite the fact that this elite soldier left the battlefield on a stretcher and has given away his dreams of ever being deployed again.

What makes this story so compelling is its honesty and its inspirational outlook, in which 'love finds a way', as Tin Pan Alley songwriters put it.

It's also a novel way to tell a story — through not just the eyes of the main player, but also from the perspective of his parents, sister, surgeon, fellow soldier, coach, childhood mate and his devoted partner in recovery. It's quite a revelation and highly personal.

Damien Thomlinson never whinges or asks for your pity. It's simply not in his DNA. He just makes you wonder how the hell he survived his Afghanistan hell — and its aftermath, with all the pain and prosthetics.

Still, it comes as no surprise to learn that while taking on everything from the glaring spotlight of *60 Minutes* to the agony of the Kokoda Track (with the dad of a soldier-boy who never returned), this warrior tripped over his mounting anxieties, his misplaced guilt and the emptiness of what he poetically calls his 'self-destruct phase'. Damien doesn't think it's PTSD, but clearly 'stress' and 'disorder' were major speed bumps on his road to recovery.

I must admit that when reading his story, I felt a little guilty that although we kept in touch I didn't realise how badly Damo was travelling, especially in 2011 and 2012. Mind you, he worked hard at covering it up from all those who loved him. Thankfully, now he's opened that door.

This book is more than just a rollicking saga about a young hero, who without warning has had to beat impossible odds. Writing about the trauma I suspect has been great therapy for Damien — an important part of his recovery. It's also been a journey of personal 'truth and reconciliation' for everyone close to him. You can't go to the dark place he has been and not suffer some collateral damage.

Still, by any definition, Damien Thomlinson is a remarkable young bloke. Now he's come to terms with who he used to be, and how he got to where he is, get ready for the next exciting phase of his life. Because it will be exciting and exhilarating.

I am so glad Damo decided to tell his story so far.

PROLOGUE

I call it 'my luxury'. I might get the occasional flash, an image of blood, but I don't know if that's a realistic memory. I suspect it's simply a vision that arrives in my head because I've heard so many versions of what happened that night, in the dead of night, on April 3, 2009, in Helmand province in Afghanistan. I have no memory of that day. I have no memory of the day before. When people ask, I simply say that the sun came up, but I only know that because it always does. And that hole in my memory is my luxury. I can't remember the accident, so I can't relive it.

I had never experienced a prouder moment than the day I was handed my commando beret. Commandos are the elite of the elite in the army, and I had earned the right to become one of them. I was a month into my first deployment to Afghanistan, a time I had visualised throughout my four years of army life. This was what all the intense years of training had been about, to get here and do our job. But my world, and the worlds of my loved ones, were about to be dramatically altered forever. On that night, my tour was over. My life almost was, too.

A bomb had exploded below me. The car I was driving was completely destroyed. It would be another entire month before I fully realised what had happened.

From my first moment of consciousness, all I knew was that I was alive and it was the only thing that mattered. I had no emotional connection to the fact that I had lost both my legs and that my body was severely shattered. My head was completely rattled and my brain felt bruised. I was dosed up on painkillers and continually being injected with drugs that were keeping me alive. I was permanently confused, and while it might sound odd, the last thing I thought about was the damage.

Weeks later, on the other side of the world, I finally understood my new reality.

There was a guy at school who was obsessed with the military, but I wasn't him. He used to absolutely love the army. Lived and breathed it. He knew everything there was to know about being a soldier. He even wore a pair of army boots as his school shoes. At different stages later in my adolescence, my thoughts drifted to life in the military, but I certainly wasn't one of those young kids who would spend all his waking hours playing war games and dressing in army combat clothing.

I had a fun childhood growing up on the New South Wales Central Coast. The beach and sport were my things.

Like most kids I was also influenced by television. My grandma, Dad's mum, used to love westerns. We would watch every John Wayne picture, and all the old midday movies introduced by Bill Collins. I remember watching them with Grandma and seeing the cowboy ride into town, high on a horse, looking larger than life.

When I was six or seven, friends of ours had a donkey. I was intent on convincing them that it could be ridden, and that I was the boy for the job. They tried hard to talk me out of it, but eventually both families collectively decided it would be a great idea if I learned what it was like to fall off and hit my head on the ground. Sure enough, their plan succeeded, and I hit my head pretty hard. But that wouldn't be the last time. There would be plenty of falls from skateboards and motorbikes to come.

I was really into team sports, and wouldn't discriminate against any. I played just about every single team sport at some stage. In that 80s era, martial arts, Bruce Lee movies and the Rocky movies were all huge, so I liked boxing and other forms of fighting, too. I had a boxing bag which was hung up downstairs in a rumpus room and I would beat the crap out of it regularly, causing the whole house to vibrate. But my bread and butter were sports that required good hand-eye co-ordination, like cricket and baseball, and those were the sports I dedicated myself to.

I played baseball from when I was around 12. I was strictly a hitter back then, but I always wanted to be a pitcher and got to do that when I was 14 or 15, when I could actually start to control where my fastball went. I had a great time playing baseball. In the under 12s, our Central Coast representative baseball team won the country championship, then we headed down to Silverwater in Sydney to play all the city teams, and we won the State Cup.

Back then, I played with another left-hander, a kid from Toukley named Chris Snelling. He was always a brilliant player. He was one of those guys who was a cut above everyone else. All the other players in the rep teams would have moments of brilliance, but Chris had freakish talent. In 2000 I got to go to the Olympics in Sydney and watch him play centrefield for Australia, and that was a huge deal for me. A couple of years later he was playing in the Majors in America with Seattle, and also ended up playing with a few clubs during his professional career. We don't see each other much nowadays, but I did run into his dad on the Central Coast a while ago.

When I was 13 or 14, I had a video compilation of great home runs, which also had interviews with some of the players on it. I remember seeing an interview with another Seattle baseballer, a legend of the game, Ken Griffey Jr, who at the time was one of the highest paid players in the game, and his words of wisdom stuck with me. He said that from the time he was a kid through to the Majors, he always had the approach to the game that it was fun. He said when you grew up playing it, it was supposed to be fun, and that's why you played. You never grew up saying, 'I want to make millions of dollars playing this game,' you played the game because you loved it. Maybe that was easy to say for a guy who had already made millions from playing, but it hit home with me.

While I enjoyed my baseball, cricket was the family game. I really looked up to my mum's brother, Uncle Mike, who was a successful cricketer and made decent scores at a high level. My pop was apparently a fantastic bowler, too, and Nan used to tell us the story about him splitting a bail with a ball. He also had a memento of a ball he took a hat-trick with. As I started to develop physically, I spent more time training and got more serious about cricket. Things started to click for me when I reached the under 15s and suddenly had some strength. I just wanted to hit the ball hard. I was really, really aggressive and that was my thing. When I was young, I got taught different things about technique, and my technique was decent, but at some point the coach decided to kind of take the reins off and said to me, 'Just hit the ball as hard as you want. Play your own game, but whatever you do, concentrate for your whole innings and you'll be fine.' After that everything fell into place.

I went on to play in the Hunter Valley Cup, which is sort of like the representative B side for Central Coast teams. The A side played against teams in Sydney, the B side against teams from the Hunter Valley. I also went on to play in the St George Bank Cup team, which was made up of all junior players on the Central Coast, from the under 16s down. As a 16-year-old I won the Central Coast junior player of the year, and despite my age, I was in the Central Coast under 21s rep team. This all happened in one huge year, but I still only viewed cricket as a way to have fun.

I had people pushing me, asking me about taking the next step, and trying to get me to play for our sister club in the Sydney Grade Competition, Northern Districts, but I never looked at cricket that way. I never looked at any great cricketers and aspired to be like them. There were guys I looked up to on my teams during that time who were successful vets, doctors or other professionals. I remember speaking to my dad about it. He's definitely not an optimist, but he is by no means a pessimist, and he pointed out that Australia had been playing cricket for around 120 years, but only 300-odd people had played for the country during that time. He asked if it was really what I wanted to do, career-wise. I saw his logic, and those numbers showed exactly how tough it was.

The most successful player I ever played with was Aaron O'Brien. He was much better than me and a great guy as well. He ended up moving to South Australia in 2008 so he could reignite his cricketing career. When I met Mark

Taylor, former Australian cricket captain, later in life, I asked about Aaron and whether Mark thought he was ever going to play for Australia. Mark said the fact that he had to change States to get a run in a State team suggested he was unlikely to take that next step. Mark's words validated what my dad had said.

While I have, and always will, respect my dad's opinion on things, and his advice on how tough a cricketing career would have been was backed up by Mark Taylor, it was also around this time that I thought about how much weight I put on people's opinions and advice. Whether their opinions are right or wrong, I don't ever want to get to the stage where I blame someone's advice for something that happens to me. I make the decision. It's all on me.

I certainly never regretted not trying to go further in cricket. My dad says that my biggest strength is that I can walk through doors, close them behind me and not look back and think 'what if'. In the end, I remember going to Dad one day and just saying, 'I'm not going to play cricket this year,' and with that, it was done. That ability to look forward with complete steadiness would prove to be very important later in my life, and I probably wouldn't be here without it.

I had four really close mates, friendships which have stood the test of time. We all surfed together, although none of us was good at it. I am still closest to Andrew Sauvage, or Freddo. The nickname Freddo came from some teachers calling him Andrew Savage, like the kid from *The Wonder Years*, Fred Savage, so we called him Fred, then Fred became Freddo and it stuck. There was also Dean Connelly, who had a loft out the back of his house, where we would go after surfing and play music; and there was Nathan Murray, who actually ended up in a band called Kid Confucius, playing two Big Day Outs and touring Australia three times; and there was Chris Marsh. I would go on to be best man at Marshy's wedding. We all had our own ideals, which weren't necessarily the mainstream, and despite being very different people with contrasting goals, we're all still mates today.

I went to Terrigal High School during the classic grunge era where the underachiever was king, and everybody either surfed or rode a bodyboard. The guys who could do the biggest moves in the surf, or tell the teachers to go and fuck themselves, were our idols. At school, like in sport, I played to my strengths. Maths, science and the logic side of things felt easier to me. English was a skill I needed to learn.

I remember one time I got into trouble in science class because I was paying way more attention to the girls than the lesson. The teacher asked what I thought was a simple question: 'Can a green plant grow in a room that only has green light in it?' The answer is obviously not. The plant will die because it will reflect the light, rather than absorbing any, and if it can't absorb light, it can't do what it should do, which is process light and grow. It seemed pretty obvious to me, but apparently it wasn't supposed to be that easy a question to answer, and my comfortable response led to a five-minute rant on how much of a waste of talent I was as a student.

I knew I wasn't dumb — I even topped my year in science in Year 7 — but I was more interested in fitting in than reaching my academic potential. On my report cards there would be comments like: 'What could Damien do if he put his mind to it for five minutes? He's got the talent, he just refuses to apply himself to his work.' That was the consistent theme and it must have been frustrating for Mum and Dad. But at that age, school was really just about trying to find my place.

I still had no aspiration to become a soldier. I think I wanted to become a doctor, because one of our family friends was a doctor and I saw him as a successful and intelligent man. His name was Lawrie Ransom and he and his wife Kerry played tennis with my parents. They had three boys, Andrew, Luke and Chris, and we all got on really well. They had a great house, he drove a BMW, which on the Central Coast was a big deal then, and to me he represented exactly what success looked like.

But the older I got the more I thought my skill set was geared towards the physical, and that I probably would fall into a different sort of realm, rather than sitting behind a desk. It was a bit concerning that I didn't know where my future lay. I knew it was a problem, but I had no idea how to solve it. During Year 10 my marks were really good, and I was taking steps in the right direction. Then in Years 11 and 12 there was too much fun to be had. School started to become a secondary concern. It was a lot of hard work, and so was partying. But one was far more enjoyable. I went out with one of the more popular girls when I was in Year 12 and that took precedence over study, too. That lifestyle was everything I had dreamed of when I was in Year 8 or 9, and I thought I would just worry about the rest later.

I had a year off when I left school and didn't really do too much, but then one of my mates got a job labouring for a tiler. He was earning $500 a week, which seemed like a truckload of money. You could get three longnecks for $10 and by the end of the second one you were off your face anyway. So I quickly decided I wouldn't mind getting in on the money train. I worked as a labourer for brickies and I also worked behind a counter in a service station. My focus was just getting work where I could. There was nothing too stable, but I was quite comfortable about where I was and what I was doing. I didn't know enough about anything to know that what I was doing was going nowhere.

At one point I went to live in Coleambally, a small country town in south-western New South Wales, for six months just for a taste of something different. My cousins — four brothers — owned a pub down there. It was great. I enjoyed it, and it was the first time I started to explore different ways of doing things, and how it felt to be independent. One of their big things down there was cricket, and I was asked if I wanted to play. I said sure, and was recruited to the Bs. I scored the first hundred that had been scored in the club for something like 30 years and was instantly promoted. While I was there, one of the guys I played cricket with took me shooting. That was the first time I ever shot a gun, and the last time until I joined the army.

Down there I worked in a rice mill as a cleaner, sweeping floors and stuff like that, but earning good money, around $600 a week, which seemed great at first. But the novelty of it wore off after a few months, and there were things like running along the beach and fishing that I missed from my home on the Central Coast. So after about six months I decided it was time to move back, but sadly the work opportunities weren't the same.

On the coast I tried to pursue work in IT, which was what Dad was in. I thought I had the maths skills and that I'd give it a shot. The first step was a Certificate III in information technology at TAFE. I enrolled there, but just wasn't into it. It didn't interest me enough to make me want to put in the effort required. Even at that stage I still wasn't thinking far ahead. And I couldn't be told what to do.

I had a problem with authority and whenever someone with authority told me what to do with my life I would just dismiss it. I thought that regardless of what happens, I'd be fine because I always succeeded when I chose my own path. The penny started to drop when people I went to school with began to graduate from university and get a start on careers, not simply jobs. That was the first time I realised that maybe I didn't know everything. I finally started to dig deeper and ask some serious questions. I had been having a good time, but now things were happening for other people. I said to myself, 'Now you really need something. Come on, your ego has been telling you for so long you're great or you are going to be great, but what have you got to justify that?' I thought, right now, what have I got? What is my direction?

I knew I had to start from square one and get things rolling. I got on the computer and thought that it would be simple — I'd do the things required, and I'd put myself in the right position to start looking for a job, or even a career. As I was reading the paper, and looking online for work, I came to the blinding realisation that this wasn't nearly as easy as I'd expected. I didn't understand how the world really worked at that stage and there wasn't a whole stack of work going on the Central Coast.

I could have gone to Sydney to get my RSA (responsible service of alcohol qualifications) or I could have worked in McDonald's. But it just wasn't me. My dad has always held me in high regard despite the consummate disappointment

I felt I was to him as a kid. He would ask me, 'Do you want to be flipping burgers? Do you want to do that? Really?' He always saw something a little more in me. He pushed, 'Do you want to be pulling beers in a bar? Do you want to be the guy pulling beers or the guy on the other side of the bar?' I loved being the guy on the other side of the bar, so I kept looking.

I'd been working my whole life to impress my dad; it's one of those father–son things. Seeing him proud of me when I'd make a team meant so much. When I was wandering aimlessly in the 'lost years', as he called them, he would say, 'I'm not mad at you, I'm just disappointed.' I knew I was the kid with all the ability in the world but with no drive and I was always getting into trouble. It was never anything too major, just silly things, often brought about by saying too much and not knowing when to shut my mouth. People would come up to him and say, 'Oh, you're Damien's dad?' And Dad would say, 'Oh yeah, what's he done now?' Sons always want to make their fathers proud, whether it's by following in their footsteps or achieving something new. I finally wanted to start working for that respect because my father's pride meant everything to me.

STEVE THOMLINSON — Dad

I call the period between school and the army Damien's 'lost years'. He was labouring, working in a chicken factory and even had an apprenticeship as a mechanic for six months. He was doing this and that, but was nowhere near fulfilling the potential he had. I used to say all the time to both Damien and his sister, Naomi, that if you aim at the top and miss it, you're still going to end up somewhere good, but if you aim at the bottom and miss, you're in the shit.

The kid is very intelligent. Whenever he would do any IQ tests, he always scored highly. I thought he could do anything he put his mind to. That was also the case when it came to sport, and we saw signs very early on. At about three, we bought him one of those Totem Tennis sets. I stuck it in the backyard and I was sitting up on the back verandah when out he waddles, and picks up the bat and goes whack, and as the ball comes around the other way, he goes whack again, and the ball went back and forward, never getting past him to do a full circle. I counted 50-something times in succession the ball went around before he got bored and put the bat down and walked away. I thought, gee, this must be easy … I got three hits.

Both Di, his mother, and I are golfers, have been all our lives, and we took him out to the driving range at Bateau Bay when he was around five or six years old. I showed him how to hold the club but that's about it, and he was hitting a few out there, when the pro said, 'I bet you a can of Coke you can't hit it between those two trees out there.' Damien asked which two trees, and was shown a pair about 220 metres in the distance. He said OK, and went whack — straight between the trees. 'Where's my can of Coke?' This from a kid who doesn't play.

His hand-eye co-ordination with bats and balls is unbelievable. He can do anything. He could have done anything in cricket, but he just didn't want it. He came to me one day and said, 'Dad, I'm not playing cricket this year,' and that was it.

He even stood out as a swimmer. He never trained — we didn't have a pool — and he went in the school swimming carnival and got beaten by a fingertip, by Ky Hurst, who'd go on to become a champion ironman and Olympic swimmer. They were only about eight or nine, but Ky was in the nippers at Terrigal and was one of their star swimmers. I told Damien that it was a great effort, but his reply was, 'Yeah, but I got beaten.'

I don't know why he ever thought he was a disappointment to me, and I know he is sensitive to what I'm thinking, but it's always been the same. As long as he was happy, we never really cared. Of course it used to frustrate the hell out of us when he didn't want to achieve what we thought he was capable of, but that's what kids are like, and he eventually found his niche. At times I thought I was subtly hinting to him that there were some great careers in the army, but despite him sending away for some information on the air force, I really didn't think my hints were getting through.

for those soldiers. I remember visiting him at one of those old people's homes out at Wyoming. I can vaguely recall that every time we would go out there with my mum to visit him, he would say, 'Finally, pack my bags, we're going home. Finally!' Apparently he said the same thing right up until he passed away. And I can understand his mindset, it's something I would be able to later testify to. The body may be weak, but the mind hasn't lost much. All he wanted to do was get out of there and go home where he belonged.

Fred Bowditch, my pop, served during World War II. He was a member of the 2/17th Infantry Battalion. The unit saw service in the Middle East in 1941–42, taking part in the fighting at Tobruk and El Alamein before returning to Australia early in 1943. In 1943–44 the battalion took part in the Salamaua–Lae and Huon Peninsula campaigns fought in New Guinea against the Japanese, before its final campaign in Borneo in June 1945. Following the end of hostilities, the demobilisation process began and personnel were repatriated to Australia, where my pop was discharged and returned to civilian life. During the course of the war, the battalion lost 188 men who were killed in action or died on active service; a further 573 were wounded. My grandfather was one of those wounded, a leg wound, while in the Middle East. Members of the 2/17th Battalion received one Victoria Cross, four Distinguished Service Orders and one bar, three Officers of the Order of the British Empire, one Member of the Order of the British Empire, one British Empire Medal, 11 Military Crosses, three Distinguished Conduct Medals, 11 Military Medals and 46 Mentioned in Despatches. Pop was awarded three separate stars — the 1939–45 Star, the Africa Star and the Pacific Star — for the conflicts he had been involved in.

He was also awarded the Defence Medal, the War Medal, the Australian Service Medal and a medal for the Tobruk Siege.

I never knew any of that when I was young. All I knew was that Pop went to the war. I didn't know any details and I probably wouldn't have been able to comprehend them if I did. I was just too young. War was a game you played as a kid. That was all I knew. When I was in primary school, we learned about World War I and World War II, and there was a part of me that could relate to those lessons and stories in class through my pop. After he passed away, Legacy looked after my nan as a war widow and provided her with great support. That triggered my curiosity. As a young kid it made me think, wow, if Nan's getting all that help, Pop must have done a fair bit for the army.

But it was only curiosity at that time. Pop's service history was never really spoken about, at least not in front of me. It was just common knowledge that 'Pop was in the war'. Also, he never spoke about it himself. Knowing what I do now, I can see why.

At the same time, it was difficult to imagine his experience because, as I was growing up, there weren't any high-profile wars going on, and none which involved Australian troops in combat. Australia's military — particularly the navy — had a role in the Gulf War in the early 1990s, but as it was a non-combat role, it didn't seem to have a major impact on me or most of my generation. It wasn't until the disasters of 9/11 in the United States, and then the subsequent wars in Afghanistan and Iraq, that Australia's military contributions became newsworthy again, and part of our everyday lives.

There was, and still is, a photo of my grandfather in the study at our home. He's standing there in a jacket with a chestful of medals, with the hint of a proud grin. I used to look at it almost without thinking, but it's possible that this picture was the start of things for me. I could see how proud of him everyone was, the way everyone referred to him and reinforced the role that the war played. It was easy to see his own pride in that photo taken at a Rats of Tobruk reunion in 1983, and other photos of him with a chestful of medals and those three separate stars marching on Anzac Day. I was looking at a kind face that had done so much to ensure that our lives in Australia were secure and happy. I admit at times I thought about how good it would feel for people I cared about to have that same sort of pride in me. I wanted to be that proud old digger in the photo. If I could carry myself with half the class of the man in that photo, I would be content.

But as I moved into my 20s, I realised I wasn't even going nowhere — I was going backwards. I was disgruntled with my lack of progress, and still searching for my place in society. I was prone to taking things to the next level just to see how far things could be pushed. Sometimes I would say too much or go too far for no reason other than a compulsion to do so. This was a trait that would come back to bite me in the army, where I had the same compulsion to talk back, but the consequences were much more severe. Up to that point I felt like I had been a constant disappointment, and wondered whether anything I did would make the whole family proud. I didn't realise it yet, but that was kind of the ideal situation for me. I seem to have an ability to fight my way out of any corner, no matter how tight, and grow with the challenges I am faced with.

I was sick of being the one who let everyone down. I was sick of the way people looked at me, spoke to me and judged me. It may sound narcissistic, but I'd always seen myself as capable of doing something better than average. Yet there I was, the kid who had all this talent and potential, now a full-time labourer, scraping money together to go out with friends and party and drink and do whatever he liked.

But I knew I had something extraordinary inside me.

On this particular day, I was sitting at the computer in my dad's study, browsing through jobs and seeing all the qualifications required for various positions. Qualifications, I thought, yeah, that takes time. I was naive. I didn't understand the principles of networking or building relationships. How do I get a job? What do I do? How can I convince someone, with nothing to back it, that I am their man? I had confidence I could do anything that came up, it was just finding that specific thing, and convincing whoever was in charge that I could do it.

I had looked at the air force, but the reality was I wouldn't be happy unless I was a fighter pilot, and to be a fighter pilot, I'd have to go to university. Was that the path I truly wanted to go down? No. The whole idea of joining the military had come about not only because of Pop's photo, but also because of my growing fascination with the military. I loved watching the documentaries on wars that would screen on the History Channel. By that time, too, in the middle of 2003, the Iraq War had been going for a number of months and had now gone ballistic, so the patriotism of our military was starting to float around my subconscious. Sitting at the computer that day, with my pop's photo staring at me, I saw the home page of the army's website. They were direct recruiting for the Special Forces. The website asked: 'Do you have what it takes?' I looked at it and suddenly thought, yeah, I do. Every last bit of it. I was arrogant, self-confident and narcissistic, but when I looked up again and saw that picture of Pop across the room from me, I was sure this was what I wanted to do.

I wasn't just interested in army recruitment; I knew I belonged in the Special Forces.

They were trying to build the regiment. It had been re-rolled nine years before, then rolled back to being a normal unit for a deployment in Timor, then re-rolled back to a Special Forces unit and they were basically building on that when I came across the website. They were looking for a specific type of person. You couldn't learn to become the person they wanted; you just had to be that person. I knew I had what it took. I was confident.

I looked at some other sites, then went back and visited the army website again. I got that same feeling of pride about what it would be like to be able to represent my country. I think I knew that my many menial jobs were only things to pass the time, and pay for the fun. When it came to doing something more serious and more permanent as a career, the last thing I wanted was something ordinary. That just wasn't in the picture I had of myself. It might have been who I was at that time, but it wasn't the person I wanted to be. As a kid I wanted to be the best at what I did. I think that's why the Special Forces appealed instantly. It was the answer I was looking for in my life. I could work out physically, it would be tough and mentally challenging, but I would get to do so many amazing things that civilians would never get to do. I wanted that adrenalin buzz.

Up until then I had been taking the advice of others. My choice of role models was far from perfect and overall that wasn't going well for me. I'd take 10 per cent of their advice and then make 90 per cent of a bad decision, and blame it on the advice each time. And that was where it was all going wrong. Listening to other people's opinions of me was not my thing. I decided I needed to take responsibility, and do something that I wanted to focus on, and do it my way. That was one of the major moments in my life. I'm really stubborn and defiant and if I want to do something, I want to do it on my terms. The army gave me the perfect opportunity for that, and there was the added prestige that goes with the position — commandos are immortalised in stone. It's rare to have a really fresh beginning at something that will put you in a very elite group of people. I had been presented with that opportunity and I thought I would be so proud to be one of a select few.

But it was more than just being a good fit for me or making others proud, it was about being able to do something meaningful for my country, and for my fellow Australians. Ultimately, I wanted to stand up for each Australian against those who wanted to harm others. As I said, I used to watch a lot of documentaries on the History Channel, and seeing the problems in the Middle East, for example, or how the Nazis treated Jews, and similar things through time made me angry at the sheer brutality. It's not just what has occurred in the past that inspired me, though; there are injustices happening today, in Africa, the Middle East, everywhere. I have never liked people picking on others who are unarmed or weaker than them. I still have an extreme reaction to seeing people get whipped. It makes me go white. The guy has got no chance. Someone is tied down, and is not just being hit by another, they are being hit by another with a weapon. All

I want is to be put in the room with the guy holding the whip. If there's someone being oppressed by someone else, you want to fight the oppressor. It's an Aussie thing. You back the underdog. If you are watching an old lady getting mugged on a bus, are you the guy who looks the other way, or are you the guy who makes that an even fight for her? I was the second guy, and I wanted to do more.

At that stage I honestly didn't think about putting my life on the line in Afghanistan. The prestige side of it was a big attraction for me, and of course the money. That was all part of the army's advertising campaign. Commandos, along with the SAS, are amongst the highest paid soldiers in the Australian Army. The money they were offering as a carrot to join wasn't going to change my life, but it would make me completely independent, and as such it probably played a small part in my decision. I decided, this was it. This was for me. I was going to be a commando.

I went to tell my dad about the decision. He was sitting out on our balcony with Lawrie Ransom. I was pretty excited about it, and I pointed out that I thought I had all the attributes that were described as required on the army website. I told them I thought I had what it would take. To this day I can still remember Lawrie kind of giggling, then sarcastically saying, 'I bet you are exactly what they are looking for.'

Considering what I had done since school and up until that time, Lawrie probably had every reason to say that. And while Dad sort of approved, in the back of his mind he knew there was a big gulf between rattling around doing menial labouring jobs, and being one of Australia's elite soldiers. Parents are always supportive, but Lawrie just said it the way it was.

As I had done all my life, if you told me I couldn't do something, I just made sure I did it. It had always been dangerous to tell me I couldn't do something. Not that I needed any more convincing or motivation, but Lawrie's comment was like poking a tiger. I would prove all those wrong who thought I was just a lost soul going aimlessly down the wrong path. For me right then, there was no doubt, I would be a commando.

3

Special Forces isn't for the faint-hearted. You're told that you've got to expect you could be dropped over the horizon, out to sea, at night, where you can't see a thing and that you're going to have to put a boat together, then rendezvous with another boat. You're told your boat will then not inflate, so you'll have to spend four hours in the pitch black bobbing out at sea with no way of communicating with anyone, and that when you eventually start paddling towards shore, you won't know where the shore actually is. They tell you: 'If this scares anyone, you're sitting in the wrong room, wasting your time in this aptitude test. You are not who we are looking for.'

They still hadn't lost me.

My first step towards the Special Forces was a trip up to Newcastle for what they call a Joe's Day. It's where you meet with the recruiters and explain to them what you want to do and why you want to do it. They let you know a little bit about what you need to go through to get there. I guess that way they lay it all out so that if you have any doubts that this is for you, you can change your mind there and then before getting involved in all the testing. That wasn't going to happen to me, I wasn't going to change my mind, and I went back to the Central Coast and kept up my personal training, preparing to go back to Newcastle for testing.

A couple of months later I got a letter telling me my aptitude test would be on a certain day, and that if I passed that phase, I would go back for physical testing. Suddenly it all seemed real, and I was full of anticipation and excitement when I headed to Newcastle for that first written exam. I was one of around 20 or so hopefuls there for the aptitude test, and standing in front of us was the first Special Forces soldier I had ever actually seen. Before that, because of security, I had only heard about them, or seen photos of men with black stripes over their eyes to hide their identities. Other than that, the only time you would see a photo of a Special Forces soldier was if he had been killed. This one started to tell us about what would be involved in our recruitment and training. I remember thinking that this was the start of the tests. They were already trying to strategically scratch away at us, and see if they could put us off balance. I kept thinking, regardless of what he is saying, don't be distracted from the goal.

When I was younger, I was always susceptible to sledging in cricket. I loved talking, so if someone said something to me, I would feel compelled to talk back. I eventually realised it was all about them getting into my head — and I couldn't allow that to happen. Sport is 90 per cent what happens above the shoulders and it took me a long time to learn that. I needed to call upon that experience now, and just focus on the job without distraction. When they tried to terrify us with the thing about the boat stranded in the dead of night, I didn't let it affect me. I did the aptitude test, which was similar to an IQ test with logic-based problems, some maths and basic mechanics, and I thought it all seemed to go well for me. I walked out of there confident that step one was complete, and knowing that getting through the physical shouldn't be any major problem for me.

It was a fairly basic test to see what you could do, and to make sure all your moving parts were working well. We had to run a 10 on the beep test, do 45 or 60 push-ups, and maybe 80 or 100 sit-ups. It was just entry-level stuff. We had to do blood and urine tests as well, and a psych test. The basic questions included things like: 'When you are standing on the edge of a building, do you consider jumping off?' This was not the best question to ask an adrenalin junkie — 'Yes, I do, I'd want to jump off.' Of course I said no because I didn't want to come across as a lunatic.

Again, I thought it all went well, and the next step was to go into a room and chat with an officer. I sat there across the desk from him, and he told me, 'Come back in 12 months and we will give you another go.' They wanted me to come back in a year when I was more mature. I was 23 then and thought I was a lot more mature than I had been a few months earlier when I embarked on this. I walked out of that office fuming. I had put the last four months into preparing for this and I assumed that I had done enough. I had every tool I needed. I went back in to speak to the guy again.

Apparently my problem stemmed from the response I gave to the question about drug use. They asked me what drugs I had done in my life. I told them I was just being a kid, no different from many others, and drug use is just what happens. I named them all. It wasn't yesterday. It wasn't last year. It was when I was a kid. My beef was that I had come to them with honesty. I had respect for the guy sitting across the table from me. He was wearing a beret. He had already done it all. He was not just a desk guy. When I went back in, I said to him that 80 per cent of Australian people have at one stage at least tried drugs, and so I was just being honest about it. I thought it said something about my integrity. I read all the attributes on the website and I saw integrity. He said, 'Look, it's done. Come back in 12 months and prove your dedication.'

Someone had said no and it meant no. Not 'you can try a bit harder and get in', or you can talk them into it, or find another way around it. No meant no. That was it. Over. I was a cocky kid in complete shock. The decision was made and that was the first time I hadn't been able to do anything about it. He didn't buy the pressed shirt and suit slacks. People had said things about my maturity before, but only casual digs like, 'Pull your head in, you idiot.' I used to think I was pretty good, but I was nowhere near as good as I thought I was. Now, I'd been told no, I wasn't quite good enough. I couldn't get into the Special Forces, and there was nothing I could do about it. It was out of my hands. I could stand there and dance and jump up and down. I could do whatever I wanted, but it wasn't going to change this dude's attitude. The reality was, I had to accept that I wasn't going to be a commando — well, not then anyway.

This was not the picture I'd painted for myself. I knew I had all the tools required, physically and mentally, otherwise they wouldn't have bothered saying come back in 12 months. You don't get smarter over 12 months. I was so disappointed as I headed back to the Central Coast. I got home and my parents had thought the same thing I did. They had confidence in me and saw how dedicated I had become.

They thought I'd get through. I was standing at the door, telling them what happened, when my sister, Naomi, and her husband, Andrew, rocked up with big grins on their faces, ready to congratulate me on the great achievement. They had come over for a celebratory family dinner. That's how confident everyone was, and it was shattering to have to tell them the news and see how disappointed they were.

For all my stuffing around, I didn't like letting people down and I still don't. As a sports person, that was one of the things Dad instilled in me. When I was a kid, sometimes I would get to a stage where I said, 'Oh, I don't want to today,' and Dad would always say, 'You'll be letting the team down, it's not about you, it's about a team of people. You don't want to be that let-down guy, do you?' That night I felt like the guy who lets everyone down. I was crushed and even my ability to talk my way out of problems couldn't change the situation. That might be why I pushed forward so hard. I really cared about this.

My family obviously cushioned it as best they could, but I couldn't help but feel disappointment at that moment. A small part of making the decision to join the Special Forces was not just to prove to other people I could do it, but to prove it to myself. I wanted to prove I could do something meaningful. But I wavered and thought that maybe those people were right to doubt me. Maybe I was never as good as I thought I was. Those thoughts consistently argued with the part of my brain that still believed I had what it would take.

I sat there that night on the balcony on my own, and half a bottle of scotch later, tears just started flowing, not because I'd missed out, but because I'd disappointed the whole family. In my mind I had placed the weight on my shoulders and couldn't handle it. What happened? Even though I felt so gutted, I never contemplated throwing it in right there, and my family wouldn't have thought that either. Firstly, I told myself, that's not happening again, and secondly, I'm going to prove to that guy who sat across that table that I'm better than he ever thought.

It was a wake-up call. I was not invincible, I was not as good as I thought I was, I had to work harder and I had to be that much better than I already was. I had needed someone to kick me in the head and say, 'Look at you, you are an arrogant kid who thinks he's red-hot stuff. You think you are going to waltz through everything? You think you are going to get through everything on natural ability alone?' That's pretty much what my approach had been up until that moment. I now had 12 months to get it right and then I was going to go back there and make sure they couldn't say no again. Finally I had some perspective on my situation and my character. That feeling of disappointment was a good thing. To be honest, it was one of the best things that could have happened to me. If I had got in first time, I would have got my arse kicked and probably wouldn't have lasted. I really wasn't mature enough. I didn't have it upstairs. I just wasn't at the level I needed to be.

Despite the morning-after effects of the scotch, I started training the next day. I'd always pushed myself a little bit beyond what was expected, but now I was motivated more than ever. To be a level better you have to go a step further. I had to train harder than every other guy who was going for that role. At that stage I didn't know anything about who they were taking, what other people had done, or what their histories were like. All I knew was that they were taking

29

guys off the street and training them up to be the best of the army's elite. I would be up against guys who were worthy adversaries.

The Special Forces only accepted a certain number of people each year to the scheme. Then it was two intakes of 42, but soon became one annually, and now there are only spots for 12 or so, from what I understand. I read through the attributes on the website again and again. I had to concentrate on being 'that guy'. I spent the next 12 months being the disciplined soldier I imagined they wanted. The countdown started from day one. I actually rang them after two months and said, 'I'm ready, can I come back now?' and they said, 'No, you were told 12 months and there is nothing we can do about it.' After six months I rang again. Same response.

It was never just about proving someone wrong, or showing them I could be the guy they desired. I often thought about the photograph of my grandfather and about how much pride I had in what Australians soldiers did. I thought about the Anzac tradition and what a big deal it is in Australia, and about how much of Australia's history revolves around our participation in wars. It would be a big thing to be part of that. To think that I was going to be pushing forward towards that bigger picture was another thing to spur me on.

I trained as hard as I could, and I saved up as much money as I could. Three months before the year was up, I started training with a personal trainer. I wanted to leave no stone unturned. I saw a note on the wall at my gym advertising a physical training instructor named Scott Burnham. It turned out he was a reservist. He had a military background, and had been deployed in Iraq, so he gave me the perfect preparation specific for the Special Forces. I think he fed off my enthusiasm as well, and he would randomly ring me towards the end of the three months to see if I felt like doing an extra session. I had a huge amount of respect for him and loved those sessions. He trained like no-one else at the gym. He was clearly a few years ahead of the curve and was very inspirational.

My concept of training through that entire period was all about pushing through my comfort zone. If I was in my comfort zone, I wasn't training. I might as well have been walking down the street. I loved running on the beach, but I would do different things to push my stamina, like running down the beach on the hard sand, then coming back on the soft. Many people do 12 sets, and then rest for a minute and a half, because that's the way you are supposed to do it. In that 90 seconds, I'd do push-ups. Through simple things like that, I pre-fatigued myself.

Scott taught me a lot about training that I didn't know. I was really one-dimensional when it came to fitness until he started to open my eyes. The work we did together taught me so much. I had complete confidence in what he said, but he had completely unique ideas regarding training. Out the door went chest and triceps day, back and biceps also became a thing of the past. Things I thought were conventional thinking were gone. Slowly the immature kid inside of me was being beaten out. It was 12 months to the day that I went back to Newcastle to try again. Not thinking but knowing I had what they wanted. I was ready.

4

The 12 months after my initial army rejection seemed like forever, and in the end I lost count of the number of times I tried or thought about trying to convince them to give me a shot earlier. When the day arrived, I was on the road early, up to Newcastle, and as focused as I had ever been. I kept telling myself that what happened a year ago wasn't going to happen again. They would want me and they would take me this time. I had been trying to live, think and act like a Special Forces soldier for the past year. With my 1000-yard stare, I knew my fate was inevitable.

My aptitude test result must have been fine the first time around because I didn't need to do that again. That might just be the way it works, but it added further confidence to my bid. I went and did my physical and fitness test, the bloods and urine, then a week later I had to go back and do the psych test and the face-to-face session where it all had come apart for me the year before. I wished the first conversation had had no effect on me, but it was definitely in the back of my mind as I sat there, as straight as I have since kindergarten. Everything seemed to go well, but history told me not to be complacent or overly confident when I entered and found myself in front of that same officer, at that same desk. I went in there with the attitude I expected army people to have — I sat bolt upright in the chair and just stared directly into the officer's eyes.

The mind games continued, though. The officer gave me a spiel about whether I thought I was really ready, but then he picked up the phone to call someone and I heard him saying, 'Oh yeah, blah, blah, blah, yeah, Thomlinson, blah, blah, blah,' and he was staring at me while he was saying it. I think I realised at that stage he was going to say yes.

I sat there trying not to show any emotion, but inside I was bubbling, wanting to release this massive high. He got off the phone and just said, 'Well, look, how soon can you be back up here?' I told him I lived on the Central Coast, so give me three hours and I'll be packed and back, ready to go. This was in December, and he laughed, and told me not to rush, but to be back in January to start my training.

I was in — cleared to enlist into the army anyway. I still had some very tough times ahead of me if I was going to be a Special Forces soldier, but I had taken the first substantial step towards my goal.

It was a much more pleasant drive back to the coast than it had been 12 months earlier. I never wanted to face my family with disappointment again. I now felt extreme pride. I had finally taken the first step towards doing exactly what I wanted to do. When I got home, I think my family were a little bit tense after what had transpired the year before. I'm sure they believed in me, and Dad and Mum would have seen the change in me over that period, but still, until I told them I was in, nobody wanted to say anything to jinx it. That night we had the celebratory dinner we were supposed to have had back in December 2003.

On January 17, 2005, I officially signed the contract and was enlisted into the Australian Army for the next four years of my life. It was a proud moment, but it only lasted a moment. We were immediately driven away by bus to the recruitment training centre at Kapooka, down in the Riverina. At that stage we went through Kapooka for 49 days doing basic training. The next step was to go to Singleton and do six months' initial employment training — which is where you learn your base trade, in my case infantry, and in which you must qualify before you can progress — and then there was two months of advanced infantry training. After a week off, we would do the barrier test, a fairly brutal physical test of fitness, and then we would go onto the three-and-a-half-week Special Forces selection course. If I was successful, I would get posted to 4RAR (which stands for the 4th Battalion, Royal Australian Regiment, but has since been renamed the 2nd Commando Regiment). You still weren't a commando, but you were posted to that unit for more training, more courses and the Special Forces reinforcement cycle, which is the initial collection of courses that are required to qualify you for your beret, even though the training continues. Alternatively, if a soldier failed the Special Forces entry test, they would either be transferred immediately to other units, or put into a 'holding cell' at 4RAR and transferred later. That soldier remained in the army, but instead of becoming a commando, he would become a conventional rifleman. I have huge respect for riflemen, but this was never an option for me.

I was in the last group at Kapooka that only had to spend 49 days there. It's a three-month course now. This is where we were shaped into soldiers. We learned the basics, and how to pay attention to detail. There was a boatload of yelling, which I loved and thrived on. I was extremely determined when I got to Kapooka. I thought I was a soldier before I got there, but reality is a little different to the over-dramatised television shows I had been influenced by. The dead-straight stare, standing to attention and other typical army clichés were all familiar to me thanks to TV, and as a result I arrived mentally ready to do stuff like that. But, it's not exactly like that, although my perceptions definitely prepared me in some ways for what I was in for.

Kapooka was super competitive, with 50 alpha males all compressed into one environment, trying to do our best and out-soldier one another for a position in the Special Forces. While it's not like the Special Forces training course, there's no breezing through Kapooka. It's hard no matter who you are, or who you think you are, but you get through it. It's mentally challenging, and the entire thing feels like a selection process. In the back of my mind I wondered, is this being recorded, is it being written down, what's being said about me? I thought that if I took a wrong step, I could be removed. I discovered later that wasn't the case.

Kapooka is a high-level course and they try to keep the shock factor very intense. We were constantly forced out of our comfort zones and our patience was tested again and again. A lot of it was about learning the concept of chain of command and coping with Sense of Urgency training.

People who knew me were concerned with how I would cope with the authority side of the army. But I was fine with it. I think at that time I just thought this is what it is, it's what I want to do, and this is all a part of it, so just live with it. I'd always respected rank. I admit that in time my tolerance for it definitely wavered a bit, but at the start I didn't have any problems. It was about playing the game.

Sense of Urgency training is an important attribute for your military career, not just Kapooka, and is essential to progress. It's about learning how to react promptly to any situation which may arise on the battlefield. But also, since all instructions are given by staff, it reinforces that you don't question what a superior says. We were kept awake until we were exhausted, moving all day, marching places with everyone always in step — that uniformity builds a bond.

I was in 11 Platoon, and in the mornings, at 6am, we would hear the shout: 'Hallway 11!' Everyone would have to respond immediately, and run out to the front of the room with our sheets over our shoulders, in our army-issue pyjama pants. That was the introduction to the day.

On about day six or seven, we were all exhausted physically and mentally. No-one was used to working and functioning at that level. Everyone was dreaming of sleeping. At 5pm, they sent us to bed. I looked around and saw so many smiles, but I kind of knew something was going on because Scott Burnham had warned me about this exact incident.

We went to bed, and three minutes later we heard the shout: 'Hallway 11!' Bang, we're up, sheets over the shoulder, going through the morning routine, shaving, cleaning our teeth and making our beds with a bayonet-length fold at the top and hospital corners on all points of the bed. We stood out in the hallway, everyone at attention, before being told: 'Alright, everyone back to bed.'

There were still guys who thought they would now get to go to sleep. Two minutes later, another yell: 'Hallway 11!'

This happened four or five times as part of our Sense of Urgency training. Simple little things like that teach you a sense of urgency. But also, because everyone hates the same thing, it creates a good distance between the new soldiers and the directing staff. The staff would never be in a personal relationship with us. They had to assert their authority and the effect is exactly as intended. The system works. It makes people behave in a particular way.

I had a great time at Kapooka, but the most frustrating thing was being told to do things within time limits that were virtually unachievable. We were told: 'You have three minutes to get ready to go to lunch.' Naturally, it takes three and a half — nobody had a watch, so nobody knew how we were going. And then we would be told: 'I was going to give you 21 minutes, now I'm going to be generous … you have 14 minutes to go down, eat and be back standing in the corridor.' From there we would join the back of a line that is a mile long, get our food, scoff as much as we could because we were so hungry, and charge back. We were always late. That means: 'You need Sense of Urgency training.'

It's not for everyone, but that's Kapooka, and it works. It does teach you some very important lessons. Is it easy? No. Does it break people? Yes. But it's a necessary part of the machine.

I was extremely competitive with one guy in particular, more focused on everything being right, and because of that it seemed like my Platoon Commander at Kapooka, Sergeant Roach, was out to hassle me. I also had a virtual flat-top at the time, and he said in front of everyone, 'Look at him, it's fucking Iceman off *Top Gun*.' I didn't realise at the time, because he was taking the piss, but his comment related to the competitive attitude I held towards this other soldier — a guy called '50' whose dad had spent 30 years in the SAS — who was a little bit looser than I was. He is a great guy and I ended up becoming close to him, along with the 48 others who were there at that time. We just had one of those rivalries, 50 and me. We both had similar sort of builds, similar everything really, but I was much more serious at that stage. And when it came to being competitive, the race everyone wanted to see was the one between us two.

When we went to Singleton after Kapooka for our next phase of training, we were all filling out a form called a PM Keys form, which is your basic details for your army file. It is the first form you fill out when you march into a unit and basically it starts your record. I just thought it was another random form we had to fill in. I didn't realise at the time it gets entered on computers as part of your unit's record. It's permanent and your officers get to see it. Our platoon from Kapooka obviously knew about the Iceman joke, and when there was a spot on the form that said 'Nickname or Preferred Name', everyone told me to put down 'Iceman'. I thought if someone mentioned it, we would tell them the story, and everyone would laugh. So I put the name down. What I didn't realise was that this decision would paint me with a specific brush before I even got to the unit.

This fantastic little joke blew right up. I heard a Platoon Sergeant say, 'Who the fuck is this Iceman guy? Who says they are that?' It got back to the unit and I copped it. The first time I walked into the mess, everyone said, 'Is that the Iceman?' I got whaled for it. When you first walk into the mess with a group of fit, good-looking alpha males, it's intimidating already. We would get what's affectionately known as 'Mess Checked'. I fought tooth and nail against the taunting at the start, thinking this thing is just monstering me. I couldn't go anywhere without running into guys who would whale into me. And these were guys I respected. 'Who are you, a young buck coming here thinking you are something? Iceman!' It was horrible.

Everyone gets hassled about something or other; it's a boys' club and that's the way it works. But one guy saw that I was getting really upset about it. He sat me down one night when we were out having a drink and gave me what turned out to be really good advice. He said, 'You've got to take it on the chin. Like it or not, you are the Iceman, that's the way it is now.' I did listen to his advice, but I thought I knew better. I thought fighting my way out of it would prove how tough I was. I figured the best way out was to fight the biggest guy who said it. I would have got destroyed, but I was prepared to do anything to take the heat off. Through the initial part of training it would have been wise to fly under the radar and be the grey man, but already I was tarred with a brush I would rather have had nothing to do with. The character of Iceman was a douchebag and absolute idiot. How could I embrace that? I didn't want to show any of the characteristics of that guy, but it's true that I had always been way too much of a hothead. The cruel irony was that I had a little of the Val Kilmer look about me at that stage, and had also acted like a dickhead. Looking back, I probably deserved the name and the shit that came with it.

To this day, people still call me Iceman. I've got two get-well cards from after the incident in Afghanistan that are addressed to Ice and Iceman. If only it was my cool, calm and collected attitude that spawned the name, but of course it was quite the opposite. I have Sergeant Roach to thank for it. I always got along well with him, even on a personal level. We had the same bar-fight attitude. He was one of those rough and tumble types, with ideals as well. He was an interesting character and a fantastic person, and I do thank him for that name. Iceman … it was something that grew legs and it took me a while to catch up.

Not everyone who went to Kapooka made it to the entry test. Some were being cut, some were pulling the pin. They wanted the best, the elite, and if you weren't showing a propensity to fit into that category, it was pointless to have you there. When I got to Singleton, I was given a piece of paper. It was the piece of paper you hand in when you want to quit, when you've had enough. It was mine to hand in any time. One guy who was doing the course for the second time called it halfway through at Singo. I couldn't believe that another soldier called it on day 10 of the course after that one, the selection course. To have gone so far, to get so close, and to then call it, wow … but that was what the course did to you. It was tough.

There was a big group of them, including four or five guys I was close to through our initial training, who decided to hand in the piece of paper and call it. I just didn't understand. We had been getting our arses handed to us for months. This is what we had been training for, what we wanted to do, and this was our moment. It didn't make sense to me, but the course is designed around breaking people and you can break any time. Success rate is around 30 per cent of those who begin the course.

Before moving on from Singleton at the completion of basic infantry training (basic navigation, basic medical, standard weapons training), and the advanced infantry training course, to the three-and-a-half-week selection course, we had to pass the barrier test. This is the fitness test that determines whether you can undertake the selection course. In the barrier test you do 60 Basic Fitness Assessment push-ups, 100 Basic Fitness Assessment sit-ups, 10 heaves, a 3.2-kilometre run in patrol order (carrying seven kilograms plus a weapon) in 16 and a half minutes, a four-hour endurance march (carrying 28 kilograms plus weapon) completing a minimum of 22 kilometres, tread water for two minutes, swim 400 metres in 18 minutes in combat uniform, then do a navigation and weapons test. I got through all that, which meant I could have a go at the selection course.

The selection course is incredibly tough and punishing from day one. It is designed to test a soldier's resilience and ability to think logically in different extreme conditions. During one part of the course, I didn't eat or sleep for 48 hours and was carrying my pack, webbing and rifle for four-hour stands, all of which involved different scenarios. There is rescue, intelligence gathering, and exercises in your ability to think and deliver on your feet with no preparation. We were told that three people out of our 12-man section were going to be picked to deliver a 10-minute talk to the group. Of course I was one of the lucky souls, and got picked first and was given the topic on a piece of paper: 'What creates good karma?' Thankfully I have never had a problem talking in front of people and what followed were 10 of my best minutes. I started by asking what is karma and what does it mean, and just went from there. It's a bit of a blur now as we all hadn't slept for a few days, and precise memories from that time are understandably a little scratchy. But I'm sure my old man would have been proud of my delivery, especially given that maths was my thing and English was his.

We were also taught particular skills and then assessed on our ability to retain the information. We were driven to the point of physical exhaustion and then would have to learn something mental, to show we could learn and retain things under duress. Could we think rationally even when we were completely exhausted? I found out later why you really need that ability. My survival in Afghanistan is a testament to the fact that the selection system works. But it's hard for anyone to do. Try staying up for two days, then going for a run. After you've gone for a run, do five heaves and 10 push-ups every minute on the minute for half an hour, then sit down and try and learn from a map, and complete a complex plan. We were told to go to sleep only to be woken up three hours later with the instruction, 'Go for a walk with the Colonel's cows,' which involved a 10-kilometre route march with our houses on our backs. During that physical session guys would walk around, trying to psych us out: 'You think it's cherries and lollipops? You think you're going to get paid $100,000 a year that easily? This is exactly what it's going to be like. It's not a job for pretenders.' The whole selection process is about how bad you really want it.

I never really got close to breaking point. I viewed everything as a test, so while I knew it was going to be hard, I just had to keep doing it. Rather than feeling broken, I felt like I knew what I could handle and that I'd give it my best. Could they ask for anything more? I thought about the type of guy I'd like to have by my side. That guy is about to fall over and he's still walking forward. Having got to this stage in our training, I knew we all had the aptitude to do it. Now it was about being the person who doesn't break. I couldn't stop and think about it, I had to get it done. I went into this phase of my training with no preconceived ideas and only expecting it would be tough. I needed to be ready for everything and anything and be ready to roll with the punches. It was a good approach to have. I kept saying to myself, 'Come on, just keep going, just keep going, just keep going.'

I had mates who got two weeks through that three-week selection course and then got injured. It was tough. Put simply, after doing it once, I would hate to do it again. Even though a lot has happened since that day, I can vividly remember the last day of that course.

We had washed all of our gear, had officially finished everything, but still didn't know if we'd made it or not. There was a formal briefing where we would find out.

Everyone goes in and the selection panel is sitting there. A little spiel is given before they read names from a list. Those who are called are told they have not been successful and are asked to please leave the room. My name wasn't called. There were about 25 guys left in the room, but there was a whole lot more who had just been asked to leave.

I started to look around the room and tried to figure out what might happen. I knew some things in training had gone wrong for a few of the people in the group left around me, and that there were other things where I hadn't done so well. But the reality was something goes wrong for everyone at some stage. No-one in that room thought they had made it all the way yet.

At that stage most of my confidence had been beaten out of me. It's true that I had to be confident in everything I did, but I started to ask myself, did I do enough?

A guy called Hans Fleer, who went on to become honorary Colonel of 2 Commando Regiment, and also likes walking with his 'cows' at four in the morning, was standing in front of us. We were ready to get the news, and he stood there with a perfect steely face, and started speaking: 'So far over the last three weeks you've been through this, this, this and this …' He gave it a real build-up, before saying, 'In this room, I am proud to say, you men are the exact type of men we are looking for to enter the role of the Special Forces.'

Wow. I felt exhausted euphoria followed by shock. But I was actually thinking about the guys outside. I knew how many of them were out there, and I had spent a lot of close, intimate time with many of them, but they hadn't made it. The good part was that Axe (another Kapooka name, for being built like a battle axe) and Changi (appropriately named because he looked like he had just left the prisoner-of-war camp that carried the same name) were still in the room with me. These were guys I had grown close to over the past weeks. Even though they were in a different section, seeing them succeed gave me an extra bit of oomph.

Mates are a really huge thing in the army. It would be impossible to get through the Special Forces selection course without guys around you, driving you. We would feed off each other's energy when we felt weak, because everyone has moments where they are near breaking point. It's at that point you look at the guy next to you, and think, I'm doing it for them just as much as myself. It's a weird mentality and it's hard to describe to people who haven't been through it. But it explains why, at a time I should have been over the moon, I couldn't stop thinking about who hadn't made it.

When I walked out of there, it was the first time in three and a half weeks that I was able to turn my phone on, and the messages started to pour in. People were wishing me luck, asking how it was going, and so forth. I rang the home phone at Terrigal, my mother answered and I didn't have much time, so I simply said, 'Mum, I made it. I got through. It's just happened, and it's amazing.' She was naturally pretty excited, but it wasn't a long detailed conversation. I was still exhausted and just so relieved it was over. In the weeks after, when I got to visit home, I saw Dad, and I could see how happy he was and when he shook my hand, he had a big grin. I felt like I had finally given him something to be proud of. I had never seen him as enthusiastic as he was when he shook my hand that day. That was a great moment. After years of disappointment I could see the pride in his eyes. He was about to go from the father who said, 'Yeah, I'm Damien's dad, what has he done now?' to having people say, 'You're Damien's dad, I heard he's joined the army, and doing great things.'

Getting through the selection course was huge, and also a poignant moment, but that was just the start. There were many more courses to come which were selection processes in themselves. You have to pass each of them and you are under pressure for the whole time. The next stage was a reinforcement cycle, which went for around 12 months or so and at times was known to be very intense. During that reinforcement cycle you underwent such courses as: Commando Urban Operations, Advanced Close Quarter Battle, Close Quarters Fighting, Commando Roping Course, Commando Amphibious Operations Course, Basic Parachute Course, Basic Demolitions Course, Special Forces Weapons

Course and Communications Specialist Course. So, as you can see, there was a long, long way still to go. But right then, I wasn't thinking too far ahead. I was just happy and proud that I had got this far.

STEVE THOMLINSON

He was devastated when he missed out the first time, and that's probably the first time in his life he has really, truly wanted to do something, and it didn't work out. But I think it was a turning point and rather than turning him off, it made him more determined to succeed the next time, as usual. I took the view that if Damien got into the army, it would be good for him. The discipline would be great. I didn't know exactly how he'd cope, but I knew it would be good for him. And, if he didn't get in, we would close that door and go through the next one.

We were both very proud of him when he got in, as any parent would be. Only 18 months before he was a lost soul. It was an astounding transformation to see him devote 12 months of his life to making it after the disappointment of being knocked back. During that year it was like living with a different person, because of the focus he had. When he told us he had made it, Di and I both thought, wow, he's really achieved something that only a very, very small section of the population could ever achieve. But, even though he had reached that stage, there was still plenty of work and plenty of courses and tests he had to get through to be fully qualified. When he eventually made it through to Special Forces training, we were very proud of what he had been able to achieve, and of how his life would now essentially be about helping to keep Australia a safe place for us all to live.

Having your occupation as one of the world's most highly trained killers did come in useful one afternoon at home when we got a visit from the Jehovah's Witnesses. Damien decided he would answer the door when they knocked and I instantly thought, oh, here we go. They were chatting away and Damien was being really nice to them. They went on and on and on, and after a long conversation they then made the mistake of asking him what he did for a living. Without missing a beat he said, 'I kill people,' and technically he was right. I reckon you could see the burn marks from their scuffs all the way up the driveway as they scampered to get away from the 'killer'.

5

After I got into the Special Forces I probably expected that the hardest part had been successfully negotiated. By no means, though, did I think it would be time to put my feet up and bask in the glory of becoming one of the Australian Army's elite soldiers. I knew there was still much to be done in terms of training and preparation for eventually going into combat.

At that stage it wasn't an absolute given that we would be heading to Afghanistan. The third rotation from 4RAR was currently over there, but after that rotation returned, there would be a gap, and rotations to Afghanistan had effectively finished; we had been stood down. That would later change, but at the time, I wasn't thinking about Afghanistan or the Taliban or combat. All I was worried about was making sure I continued to get through all the training courses I still required.

There was course after course after course. If I went into details, it would fill a good slice of this book. One that people are often most curious about is the Conduct After Capture Course. I can't say where or when it was done, but I can tell you it's not a fun experience. They call it 'getting bagged' and it really sucks. It's based on sensory deprivation, and is conducted according to the rules of the Geneva and Hague Conventions, which deal with combatants and non-combatants. If I did happen to get captured in Afghanistan, I'm sure the story would be completely different. Morally the Taliban are very different from us, so I'm sure the situation would not look like what we went through in the course. I tell you, if someone put my cock on a chopping block or balls in a vice, I would start to sing like a bird. Wouldn't you?

In the Conduct After Capture Course we were blindfolded a lot of the time. You wear a set of goggles that are blacked out, and earmuffs, so you can't hear anything. As well as being blacked out, we were stripped naked and given a hospital gown which was done up so tight that it ripped as soon as we were forced to sit on the industrial matting. The course is designed to train you to only say the things you are allowed to: name, rank, date of birth, serial number. There is music that is played repeatedly which you can hear through your earmuffs. The first song, and one I will never forget, was called 'Schnappi das kleine Krokodil' and lasted for six hours. It's a children's song about a crocodile and has a rhythm section that is distinctly childlike. The humour comes when you are ordered to stand and it is explained that the song is the national anthem of the country which has abducted you and you will sing it each morning.

The whole time I was sitting on the mat with crossed legs, which is a position that causes a fair bit of stress on your back. I was cuffed, initially in zip ties which caused some damage, but then with cuffs similar to a seatbelt of a car, wrapped round your wrist with a buckle in the middle keeping your wrists tight. My wrists were tied palm to palm with what felt like an inch and a half of separation, restricting your ability to bend your arms and what you could do with them. At times I would try to lift my legs up and wrap the cuffs I was wearing over them to relieve stress. After a while, apparently because I was being 'recalcitrant', my cuffs were tightened and it was uncomfortable to put them over. At one stage I had my legs up and felt hands pushing my knees back down. I grabbed the wrist of the hand that was touching me and said, 'Touch me again and I will fucking kill you.'

A few more hours passed until I was led outside for what I thought was the next session of interrogation. But once outside I had my legs kicked out from under me and was told to kneel. So I kneeled, and as I did I felt one of my earmuffs being raised. Then softly in my ear I heard the words: 'Do you think you are in a position to kill anyone?' I said, 'I can't answer that question …' He repeated it and I responded again. I was then met with the words: 'This is cold water.'

Too fucking right it was cold water, in what felt like the middle of the night.

This obviously pissed me off quite badly and I was then taken back to my mat. After a while I said my back was struggling so my accommodation was upgraded to a milk crate. I could feel my temperature dropping and I began to shake. Again my earmuffs were raised and I was informed by a female voice that she was a medic and had to check my temperature. I asked her to lift my goggles so I could see her uniform, which would mean she was out of the exercise. I asked her this so I could look around and get an idea of my surroundings. But the female voice said she couldn't, so I told her to go fuck herself. She left without another word.

Half an hour or so later I was beginning to struggle more severely and the same voice came in and said, a bit more forcefully now, that she was out of the exercise, she couldn't lift my goggles, but had serious concerns for my wellbeing. I obliged and let her take my temperature. Then I was immediately lifted up and taken to a bed and had hot-water bottles put under my arms and between my legs with blankets over the top. My earmuffs at this stage were lifted and I was still suspicious that they would try to get something out of me while I was on that bed. Though no-one said a thing to me, I heard in the background a male voice saying that this was his second one and it made him sick. This was strangely reassuring because it reminded me that the guys doing this are human. A few minutes later I was back on my mat.

By the time it was over, there were 56 hours I could have definitely done without.

Because I was training so hard the whole while, I didn't have time to stop and think about too many outside influences. I pretty much had tunnel vision. I didn't have time to think about any external things, or just let my mind wander. It would be like asking a footy player: 'Did you think about this or that while you were running around in the grand final?' When you are intently focused on something, you can't focus on anything outside of that.

By the time we finished up our nine months at Singleton, it was nearing Christmas 2005. We had a break then we headed to the barracks at Holsworthy down in Sydney to start our courses. When I got to Holsworthy, it was nothing like what I thought it would be. I guess I had expected something a little more Hollywood-like, more like what the unit looks like now after the buildings were upgraded. Back then, though, it didn't exactly live up to the picture I had envisaged. I think the whole process through Singleton built me up to something. I had always wondered what it would be like after Singleton when I became part of the unit, and how everything would work. There was a moment of massive shock when I got there and learned the reality. It was like walking straight back into kindergarten. That's how that chain of command sits.

When you walk through the doors at Holsworthy, it's a new world. While I felt I was like a new kid in kindergarten, I also had a feeling of achievement, and that I'd earned my stripes. I was one of the boys, and suddenly people would speak to me normally. It was really easy to fall into the trap of thinking that all I had to do was what people told me. Without warning, I went from being told everything I had to do, not really having to think for myself, to suddenly being expected to know what to do, just simple things like paperwork and how to apply for leave or the process that is necessary to keep the administrative side of the house in order.

Because the style of person who has what it takes to be in the unit tends to have a fairly strong sense of themselves, there is a lot of ego that runs around the place. Think about the change room of a football team that has just won a premiership and then multiply it by about 500, and you've got an idea of the level I'm talking about. There is a lot of dick measuring, so to speak, at Holsworthy. It was a little odd to me because I wasn't used to so many people walking around with a sense of arrogance about them. Back in the day, for me that meant: 'You squaring up? OK, let's do it.' But I soon realised that's just the way it is. I learned that it's all about making those things that are unbearable, bearable.

The mess hall at Holsworthy is where you find out who's who in the zoo and where the respect lies. 'Did you hear what he did?' 'He did this and that.' 'He's been on that many rotations?' A guy may not be the funniest or the loudest or whatever, but what he's done carries huge respect. That's how that world operates.

Part of getting through is about feeding off each other. You are your job; it's a lifestyle as well. You are with these guys for so long that, even if you don't like them, you respect them and they are your family. In so many ways it's not like other jobs. If anyone gets into trouble at the pub, regardless of who it is, if it's one of the boys from your unit, you are there. You've got to make sure your arm is over him, and you're with him. Naturally we also had falling-outs, as happens with family sometimes, but we go through so much hard shit together and respect each other so much that it's a very strong bond. When you do get deployed and find yourself in a contact (the term we use for when you get involved in a battle and get shot at), you've got to know what everyone around you is doing — your first thought can't be a selfish one. If you think about yourself, the next thing you know, one of your mates could be dead. I knew I would be looking out for the other five lives in my specific team, not just my own, but there were also five looking after me as well, so the chances of survival have just increased fivefold. I don't give a shit who you are; if there are five people looking out for you and you are looking out for five people, all six of you have a better chance than one does looking after himself.

There was always something happening at Holsworthy. I was always getting sent away for something or doing different tasks, such as guard duty or a statistics course.

When I started, I was nervous the whole time, thinking, is this what I'm supposed to be doing now? The courses, the training, it's all about preparing for those exact same things to happen away from training. It's all about being totally prepared before getting involved in any conflicts. The preparations, the rehearsals and the contingency plans were all to get us ready for when it really mattered.

One of those courses we did was the RIO, or reinforcement cycle. As I said, we all make mistakes sometimes, and the one I made towards the end of that cycle nearly cost me becoming a commando. At that point we still hadn't received our berets, and wouldn't until we completed this cycle, which ran for several months. It was the end of the third last course we had to complete and we were down in Melbourne for it. We were warned before we got on the drink the night before that if we turned up late the next morning, our career in the Special Forces was over. Our course would get torn up.

I won't go into specific details, but I woke up in a room in a random house with a girl — she was quite attractive, but I'm not sure if she was completely worth the fallout that would happen — at 7.10am, which was 10 minutes before we were scheduled to leave the base. With those words of warning ringing in my ears, I just thought, fuck, my life is ending. The girl offered to call a cab, but I said I didn't have time. 'Seriously, I have to get to this place, just outside Melbourne, where are we?' She said she didn't even know where the place was. I told her if she could drive me back to the city, I could find it from there, but we'd have to start driving — now!

We got in the car and started driving towards Melbourne and ultimately to the base where we had done the training. I was getting phone call after phone call. 'Dude, you've fucked up badly,' one of my mates told me. 'We're 15 minutes out, stall them somehow,' I begged. But then he just said, 'Dude, I've done all I can.'

We arrived and I ran out to where they were parading, not knowing if someone had packed up my room or not, and made my apologies to the Corporal. 'Get on the bus,' I was told.

At that stage I thought that was it. I'm gone. I had made it to the third last course, and had turned up 30 minutes late. That's it. It was over. There was another guy who was in the same boat; looking back, that kind of cushioned the fallout for me. His name is Cato and he's a really good guy. He was asleep in his room, missed his alarm, and the other guy in the room left without him. They woke him up to tell him he'd missed the parade time. He was done.

Sitting there on the bus, waiting to make the long drive back from Melbourne to Holsworthy, with everyone having been out on the drink the night before and feeling a bit seedy, I started falling asleep in my seat. Suddenly I heard this guy, one of the shooters who was running the course, yell, 'Thomlinson, if you go to fucking sleep, then no-one on this bus is sleeping!' So I was responsible for everyone on the bus and I wanted them to be able to sleep, because they were going to be pissed off enough with whatever fallout there would be for me and Cato not making parade. I spent a 14-hour bus trip staying awake, thinking it was all over and about what I had wasted.

We got back and a guy called Dusty walked out and tore up both Cato's and my course reports in front of us, then told everyone to 'fuck off to bed'. The next day we got up to go to the mess at Holsworthy and I could see five guys sitting there with their reports in front of them: they had all failed the course. One was fighting back tears. When mine was put on the table in front of me, it said: 'Commando Urban Operations — Passed.'

But I thought, hang on, I saw him tear up my course report. What the hell is going on?

I was perplexed. We were told to wait behind if we had a question, so I did, along with three of the five guys who had failed. 'Sir, I saw you tear up my course report,' I said and he told me, 'No, you passed the course. What happens beyond that … You passed the course, you did enough to pass the course, but you fucked up. Here's your course report, now get the fuck out of my sight.' I didn't understand until the next day when the Captain pulled me into his office and told me that Cato and I were being sent across the road to 3RAR and would be parading there.

When you cross the road to 3RAR, all of a sudden you are one of those guys looking through the fence at our unit. Effectively we were back to square one, getting yelled at and treated just like we used to back in infantry training. We were told we would have to wait for the next RIO and make up the courses we still hadn't completed. Only then would we be awarded our berets.

I'd met a lot of guys who had transitioned across from 3RAR, the parachute battalion, to 4RAR, and they were great guys. It's a proud unit as well, and I ended up having a really interesting time there, but it just wasn't where either Cato or I wanted to be.

When it happened, we had to fill out and sign the charge form, which is a military legal document. When we looked back into it, the charge we should have had to fill a form out for was 'absent from place of parade'. But we didn't know any better and were advised to fill out and sign an AWOL form, so, without question, we did. The AWOL form has much more gravity and carries much more serious consequences. It was just a mistake, but we didn't realise it then. We were both just worried about getting posted to another unit.

We had Christmas holidays soon after we moved over and then two months after we had been back at 3RAR, Cato decided to call the SCMA (Soldier Career Management Agency) to find out how much longer we were going to have to be there. He rang and told the woman on the end of the line that he had joined as part of the DRS (Direct Recruitment Scheme), and that he had got through a certain amount of the course. He said, 'I know I had to be slapped on the wrist, but why am I posted at 3RAR? I want to get back to 4RAR.' The woman from SCMA said, 'Excuse me?' He said, 'I want to get back to 4RAR. That's why I joined the army, either that, or I want to leave the army.' She replied, 'What I mean by excuse me is that we had you down as parading at Alpha Company at 4RAR. Where are you exactly?' Cato told her he was at Bravo Company at 3RAR. She said she would call him back.

Cato then got a call from a Colonel who asked, 'Excuse me, where are you?' Cato told him he was at 3RAR, then the Colonel said that he had us at 4RAR, 'which is where you are going to be in six days. I'll have this cleaned up and someone will receive a please explain.' Cato rang to tell me the awesome news. I was on a training exercise at the time, and when I finally got to my phone, I had five voicemail messages: 'Pick up your fucking phone. You fucking idiot, can you pick up your phone? Man, I obviously have something important to tell you, come on.' When I finally called him back, he said, 'We're going back to where we should be. It's a mistake. I'll tell you about it when you get back, but next Monday we parade at 4RAR.'

Six days later we were sent back to our regiment, which was fantastic, but the reality was we were behind the eight ball, having been away for around four months, and I had to catch up on the two courses I had missed: the Commando Amphibious Operations Course and the Basic Parachute Course. The amphibious course was a disastrously terrible course. It just never seemed to want to let up. It was freezing, and we never got any sleep. One guy actually got frostbite so badly his fingers swelled up like Italian sausages. Then I had to do my Communications Specialist Course. All of these were required before I could be awarded my beret. Until we were awarded them, Cato and I were walking around with our bush hats on, while everyone else was walking around with their berets. Finally, without too much fanfare or hoopla, I was given my beret. Putting it on for the first time remains one of the proudest moments I've ever had.

But I still haven't shaken off the feeling of sleeping in that morning in Melbourne. You know when you wake up and you know you've slept in, you just think to yourself 'oh shit'? Since sleeping in that day, I still get that feeling really badly from time to time, and it's still a terrible feeling.

6

As a Special Forces soldier you operate on a need-to-know basis. This concept was explained to me really well by a guy I have a great respect for. It's very clichéd, but he said if you need to know, you are told; if you don't need to know, don't fucking ask.

There is a simple pride in Special Operations which I never will compromise, and its training, tactics and procedures are a major part of what makes Special Operations work. Keeping that information sort of locked down as much as we can keeps our mates alive. It's not quite one of those 'I could tell you, but I'd have to kill you' scenarios; it's more a matter of once a commando, always a commando, even though I no longer wear the beret. Little details, like not naming people who are still serving, can be very important. I admit it's upsetting to me when I read detailed descriptions of operations written in books. It's not the way I would do it. Does it change the chance of someone getting a lucky shot away, or someone being in a bad position? No, but the less that's known about what goes on, the intricacies of the Special Forces, the safer those guys are.

On an overall scale of things, I have done nothing compared to some of these guys who have done five or so rotations. I still have a shitload of respect for what those guys do and I wouldn't compromise the security of what they do by saying anything directly about their operations or explaining how specific things work, for anything. It's a small thing they deserve. Each and every one of them has given up enough to not have that compromised. You could walk down the street, past three commandos who have sacrificed so much for their country, and you would have no idea. I don't know how many times the Star of Gallantry has been awarded to guys in our unit — again, that's publicly anonymous. You may see 'Private A or Sergeant S was awarded ...' but that's about it. I have served with guys with Stars of Gallantry, and as far as I'm concerned, the difference between that and a Victoria Cross is minimal, and only in the wording of the document. There is an honour roll at our unit that's 80 people long.

But anonymity is the way it is, and the way it has to be. In this book I have mentioned some people by name. They no longer serve in the military and as such their identities are no longer protected. Others, however, are still serving, and as a result they cannot be named and are referred to by rank and letter. None of us does the job for public recognition. Unfortunately the only time the public sees an identified Special Forces soldier is when their photo appears in the newspaper after they have been killed. I have been somewhat of an exception to that rule, and that in itself has led to lots of ups and downs.

In 2006 we were in Townsville while the coup was unfolding in Fiji. HMAS *Kanimbla* was to be sent to sit off the coast, ready if Australians needed to be emergency evacuated. I thought we would just hang around in Townsville and be the quick-reaction force. If needed, we would fly over, parachute in, do the job and then get out of there. I remember we all got called into a room and our Captain — who coincidentally would be my Captain in Afghanistan later on — asked if there was any reason why anyone couldn't do this job. Everyone said no, and the Captain said, 'Good, because we are on the boat this afternoon.'

That's when we did all the last-minute phone calls, and made sure we had everything to take with us, because we were going to be sitting off the coast of Fiji, in the box pattern, or as it was satirically known, 'Battle Box' — where the boat must sit so that the location of that 'box' can be used during the planning process of the operation — waiting, waiting and waiting, for who knew how long. I made a classic rookie mistake in not taking anything to read, or even my iPod, and the lack of activity nearly drove me insane. I very quickly went off everything. The living quarters were disgraceful. They were originally used to house soldiers decades ago during transport from one country to another, and were never meant to be living quarters for an extended period of time. I had a classic case of ADD, and a small living space combined with restricted movement, squared by no entertainment, made Jack a restless boy.

I would later realise that this was the nature of Special Operations. Things are put together really quickly, and sometimes conditions are just a bit challenging. I don't think it was a particularly comfortable environment for anyone. Because of our training we were used to things not being comfortable, but only for specific amounts of time. Plus, I was having trouble back home with a girl. This may become a theme with me, but hey, at least I'm consistent. I guess that despite all my training, I really hadn't been totally ready for my first mission. This was not a reflection on the army's training or preparation, just my own inexperience. I wasn't thinking rationally. Very soon all I could think was 'get me off this fucking boat' — I just wanted to jump overboard and swim.

I had a great set-up back home. I was living in Randwick, just out of Coogee, and was getting used to having a free and independent life and being an adult. To be torn away from that and trapped on a boat was a really difficult thing for me at the time. I was thinking a lot about how much difference the little things make, such as day-to-day things like paying bills, owning furniture, renting a nice unit and slowly saving for a house deposit, and it was an opportunity to reassess what I took for granted.

We thought we would only be stuck on that boat in those mentally challenging conditions for five days or however long it would take to travel over there. But it was a complex political environment and we were going to be on that boat for a while. If bunks stacked four high, along with the smell of 120 solid men and ventilation that was no doubt cutting edge in the 1960s sounds like your bag, then you would have loved it. We were on there for six weeks — precisely five weeks and six days too long.

I have a huge amount of respect for the guys in the navy who spend so much time on those things. It was groundhog day on the *Kanimbla*. I let it get to me and I lost it. I hadn't been in the Special Forces for long at that stage and the mission, which was my first, could have easily been the end of a very brief commando career. Did I mention that for the first five days the navy chaps in charge of the entertainment repeatedly played the movie *Groundhog Day*? It was a great joke for anyone who was not relying on a movie to keep them entertained.

I have a heap of respect for the Major who was in charge of our company then, and he was also very approachable. He saw me as an immature kid who had got all of his confidence handed back to him now he was qualified, and who was being driven to the edge of insanity on this cruise from hell. It was about four weeks in and we had just finished a briefing where it was made clear to everyone what was happening. We weren't going anywhere, nothing was happening, but we were staying put.

I was mentally unprepared to be in the position I was now in. Things had built up inside me and I made a rookie mistake. I waited after the meeting for the Major, and said something like, 'Look, boss, what are we doing here? Where, during briefs and everything else we have learned, does this even go close to fitting into our role?' He said something like, 'I know it's unfortunate, but this is the army. We fit into a small specific part of a big machine and sometimes the ball doesn't bounce your way.' He was extremely good at wording things. My response to that was incredibly childish. I complained: 'What can I do? This whole thing is really driving me in a bad direction.' He told me, in a very friendly way, to be patient, and that there were good things on the horizon.

Another year down the track with that same face saying the same thing, I would have understood what he meant and what I needed to do. But at that stage I was entirely too selfish and immature. I didn't snap or blow up, I was just frustrated.

There are ways you can speak to a Major, especially one like him, and there are ways you can't. Our voices were never raised, but the way I spoke was insubordinate. I said something like, 'Oh alright, there is nothing we can do. Whatever.' I pulled a face and then walked off.

Looking back, I can't believe I did something like that to someone I have so much respect for now. It seems ridiculous and I'm still extremely embarrassed at how disrespectful I was. I think he understood how I was feeling, but I did need to be taught a lesson, quickly. Things like that wouldn't be tolerated, and nor should they be. But at that time, I didn't care. I was ready to swim to Fiji.

Of course I regret the incident 100 per cent. If I had the chance to do that entire trip differently, there are a number of things I would do, starting with taking a book. It could have ended much worse than it did. I was being insubordinate.

The problem I had on the *Kanimbla* was figuring out when my colleagues were my mates and when they were my superiors. It was an inherent feature of the unit. Soldiers always respect their superiors, but it's inevitable that sometimes they will be good mates as well. A superior doesn't have to be a prick to get you to do something. They can just say, 'Dude, we need this done,' and you're happy to do it. It is just like mates having a conversation. But I was also just being a deadshit. I wasn't giving the job I was in, the position I had, or the army as a whole the respect it deserved. I was that same arrogant kid again who needed a punch in the face, and luckily for me my Major was the guy who would eventually give it to me, so to speak. It would turn out to be one of the best things that could have happened to me.

But my personal problems were far from the worst part of that trip. It wasn't long after my incident with the Major that I was on the balcony of the ship, the smokers' deck, about 10.30pm, and — *BOOM*. We couldn't tell exactly what was happening at first, but we could see rotor blades flying in the air. A Black Hawk chopper had hit the deck. I knew they were doing sniper drills out of the chopper, but then I heard something I hadn't expected to hear on the open sea: 'TAKE COVER!' It was coming from the Warrant Officer standing next to me, a larger-than-life character — who had a great way of telling stories and entertaining his soldiers around the mess table — with a massive voice, straight out of a Hollywood war movie. We all ducked. There were rotor blades and debris flying through the air. The officer took off up a set of stairs to the Communications deck and I just ran after him. Then we looked over the side of the boat — I was scared at that stage. We couldn't see anything except for a bit of foam where the chopper had entered the water.

I remember thinking that the aircraft had disappeared a lot quicker than Helo Escape Training had suggested. The officer then proceeded to count, holding his hand out behind his back, and raising fingers to relay the number of soldiers we had sighted popping up one by one from the foam ball created by the chopper entering the salt water. 'We've got three, four ...' and he got to six, and there was a long pause. A long time had passed between the rotor blades hitting the boat, us running up the stairs, and seeing that the chopper had sunk. The count was still only six. I knew there were more guys on board the helicopter than that. My heart sank as shock set in. I'm not sure how much time passed. It was a matter of minutes probably, but time slows down when adrenalin kicks in.

The chopper had sunk very quickly, and it turned out that by the time two of the guys got out, they were so deep that when they emerged, the current had taken them over the other side of the *Kanimbla*. Luckily, the SAS divers were doing drills at the time and had a boat in the water, so that helped with the rescue. They got nine people out in total, but tragically, Captain Mark Bingley later died on board the *Kanimbla*, from his injuries. Trooper Josh Porter's body was trapped in the wreckage and sank to the ocean floor. It was recovered more than three months later and he was finally laid to rest.

I actually spoke with Josh a week before it happened. I recognised him, but couldn't quite place his face. I had a feeling it was from the Central Coast, though, so picked one of my two main sports and asked him if he played baseball there. He told me no, but he used to play cricket for Toukley on the coast. He said, 'Yeah, you used to have long blond hair, didn't you? Good to see you got it cut.' Turned out he was working in the SAS, which I'd had no idea about until we spoke that day.

That accident was a real wake-up call for me. I began to feel a little bit embarrassed about my conversation with the Major and the parts of my behaviour on the *Kanimbla* which weren't exactly up to the expected standard.

When we eventually got back to Australia, we had six weeks of summer leave. But the *Kanimbla* had left a sour taste for me and I didn't want to go back. I asked to use more of my recreational leave, but the boss said no. Soon after the break, every company was asked to send two people to the boat platoon as part of their rotation system. It was a regular allocation of personnel, but when I was one of those chosen to go across, the rest of the unit saw it as a punishment for my behaviour on the *Kanimbla*. If it hadn't been me, it would have still been someone from our unit, but I probably stuck in the Major's mind because of my actions.

I was moved out of my company and across to a section where they drive RHIBs (Rigid Hull Inflatable Boats). I spent the next nine months driving around Sydney Harbour and Jervis Bay, basically preparing for the APEC Summit. They were nine of the best months of my army career, as it turned out. Although I was a beret-qualified commando, the weight of that responsibility had effectively been taken off my shoulders.

I had a great time with some interesting people in the boat platoon. I think this particular job came right when I needed it. The *Kanimbla* wasn't that long after the 12-month RIO course, and I never really got time to mentally unwind from that. Looking back on it, the warning signs — anxiety causing a physical reaction (or, more to the point, having a physical reaction as well as an emotional one to stress) — were there for me, but I never paid any attention to them and doubt if I ever will.

During those nine months with the boat platoon, I would spend my days learning the ins and outs of driving RHIBs. It was just perfect being in Sydney Harbour, Georges River and around the heads. Everyone thought this was punishment, and there I was looking across at Maroubra, where I surfed, and then out at Coogee. Driving past in the formation of five boats, I thought, wow, this is amazing and this is really my job. It was one of those moments where I was glad not to be stuck in an office and felt completely content with the direction I had chosen.

I still had my job, but the mindset required wasn't as constantly tough and gruelling as it had been. The pressure had also been lifted because I knew exactly when the work day would end and that I would soon be running down towards the surf I had been eyeing off the whole way up the coast. I am pretty stoked that the *Kanimbla* didn't steal my love for the water. I still loved sitting out in the ocean, letting go of any problems and being content with where I was and what I was doing. Being with that group gave me a real taste of what army life could be like and that was the mix I needed.

What I didn't realise at the time was that this stint with the RHIBs would obviously change my route in the Special Forces. Had I avoided the *Kanimbla* problem and stayed with my unit, I probably would have gone to Afghanistan a year earlier than I did. I didn't realise the gravity of that when I got moved.

In a funny way, being moved to the boat platoon taught me to be a commando. It gave me enough of a rest, enough time off, and let me watch what happened around me. I got to a point where I could say, 'Right, so it doesn't matter who the toughest guy is, it matters that you are going to be there when you say you are going to be there.' It was having the time to reflect on simple things like that. The training had been so intense, for so long, and in the end the move to a slower pace taught me to sit back and really realise what I had to do.

I had been switched on since Kapooka. It took that whole incident with the Major, and moving platoons, to realise that, while I would never be totally switched off, I could tone it down a little. That wasn't how I thought it was supposed to be. I thought it was all about being the toughest alpha male on the planet. It wasn't. I didn't have to fight every battle.

While I enjoyed the RHIBs, I did ask about when I would be going back. It wasn't anything to do with getting into a rotation again, which would see me go to Afghanistan; it was more that I wanted to become part of a close-knit team again.

Finally, on a Wednesday, I got a call asking if I wanted to go to Timor. I said sure, and was told I'd be leaving Friday. I was a little shocked and said something like, 'It's Wednesday, Sir.' He replied, 'I know, Friday it is. Are you still in?' I thought, hell yeah, let's do this.

Timor would be great for me. It was good to be back in the unit again, and I felt like my Special Forces career was back on track. But as a fully fledged commando, relationships were difficult to juggle, and I had some interesting times in the romance department. It's not like I could use my job as a pick-up tool at the pub. Because of the sensitive nature of the situation, and protected identities, I actually had to go the other way and try to conceal my true job, which can be a heap of fun but is not the most solid start to a relationship. If I started dating a girl, I would tell her I was in the army, and if there were any more questions about what I specifically did, then I'd say something like, 'I drive trucks.' The circle of family and friends who knew the truth had to be kept as small as possible, and let's face it, when you start dating, you never know whether it will last a week or a lifetime.

Once I established more of a serious relationship with a girl, I started to give a few more specific details about what

I actually did in the army. Once they knew a bit more about the job, they understood a little better some of the things I might be doing. Still, some found it strange that I would tell them I was going to be in Townsville, for instance, and then I would ring and simply say, 'My phone is going to be off for a while. I'll contact you when I can. See ya,' which is what happened with the *Kanimbla*.

In Timor I found out just how tough it could be. I was doing a training session one day with a great guy who was always very tough and steely. We were sitting there, and he wasn't himself. He was clearly bothered about something, so I asked him about it. It wasn't often that he broke his resolve, but he said to me, 'It's my son's birthday today.' I said, 'Obviously I don't have a son, I mean, man, I would say something if I could but … well, you know.' He said, 'Nah, mate, you don't get it. It's his fourth birthday today and I haven't seen one of them.' That moment was my first real experience of what people sacrifice. It made me even prouder to be associated with that guy.

Sure, we could call home when we got the chance, but it's not the same as being there for occasions like a son's birthday. We aren't machines. I think that trip on the *Kanimbla* and then to Timor made me draw a line in the sand. Anyone who was going to get close to me would have to accept some of the realities of my world. There would be sudden departures and periods where I couldn't say where I was going or what I was doing. There would be times when I couldn't make contact at all. It's true that this is the most dangerous job, in the most dangerous places. It is what it is and that's what I was doing. Any girl I was with would have to come to grips with that and if she couldn't, I would understand where she was coming from. It took me a couple of failed relationships to realise that's just how it had to be. I had to stay focused or it could cost me my life, or worse yet, that of one of my mates. I have so much respect for the wives and children who have to spend so much time away from their loved ones and still hold it together. Without their support the machine just wouldn't function.

While we were in Timor, in November 2007, we also learned of the first death of someone from our company: Private Luke Worsley, who was shot and killed in Afghanistan. It wasn't the rotation I would have been in even had I not been sent to the RHIBs for my *Kanimbla* outburst, but it came as another reality check, and a major shock. We all knew something had happened, but we didn't know what. Then our team commander pulled us all into a room and read out the statement about Luke's death. We were told there would be no communication about it and that 'lines will be down here so there will be no internet'. That's just standard procedure out of respect for his family. Unfortunately there are journalists out there who care more about getting the story first than about whether the soldier's mother knows yet.

Timor was the best three-month trip that I had been on. We had a great team, an awesome platoon, and I couldn't have asked for better people. At that stage in Timor it was quiet, and we got to train a lot in a sunny environment. It was eye-opening but an enjoyable experience from a cultural perspective, to see the day-to-day happenings in a young country. From a professional viewpoint, until you deploy you do not have the same respect from your peers. I was happy to have the chance to prove myself and I learned a lot from the more experienced guys on that trip. It was a really good feeling there, and I thought everything was falling into place for me in the army. I was starting to find my position and figure out how the real dynamics of being in a team worked. I came back home in the best shape of my life, and was ready to make the most of the summer party life in my home town, Terrigal. In the aftermath of the *Kanimbla*, I had at times doubted if I had made the right choice in being part of the Special Forces. This trip to Timor reaffirmed that I had.

7

As soon as I got re-posted back into the company, I knew that unless I had any more serious hiccups, brain explosions or any other stuff-ups, it would be only a matter of time before I would get deployed to Afghanistan. By the time I got back from Timor, I was raring to go.

I came back as physically fit as I think I had ever been. But more than that, I came back motivated. While I was on the RHIBs, some of the guys at the unit I had done my training with were starting to deploy, and when I returned home from Timor, some of the guys were coming back and had great stories to tell about their time over in Afghanistan.

Before anyone goes on deployment, though, you need to do 12 months of lead-up training with the company you will be away with. We didn't know exactly the date we would be leaving, but we knew it would be our turn in the rotation in early 2009.

That 12 months' training was a good period, and it made us realise our time was nearing, which was exciting. For every commando, this was the ultimate. We had spent our time to date in the army preparing for this moment, training like madmen and equipping ourselves with all the tools we needed to make sure that when we got there, we had all the game we needed.

The best part of the training for me was that I was doing things with a lot of the guys in the company who had been there before, some getting ready for their second rotation, some their third. I loved hearing about their experiences. It's all well and good for people who had never been there telling you 'exactly' how things were going to be, and 'when this happens, you'll be ...' But to be hearing directly from guys who knew precisely what it was like, having experienced it themselves, describing things such as being involved in a 13-hour contact, that's completely different. Of course it's hard to imagine what a 13-hour gun battle with the enemy would be like. There is no set time for a contact, but consider having shots firing around you, or jockeying for position, continuously for 13 hours.

They would explain different things that happened on different trips, and what could happen and how to deal with it. They also knew from firsthand experience what to do if things go wrong — the company I deployed with, Bravo Company, was the one that lost our first guy (Luke Worsley) over there during a raid.

While you are made aware of what can go wrong, it's not something you linger on. I never spent very much time thinking about what could happen or going through worst-case scenarios. It's just negativity that isn't worth the energy. Sure, it's a numbers game. There's a possibility that you might die or be injured. There's always that possibility, but I had a real underlying confidence that I would be fine. The attitude I took was, we are better trained and better equipped than the enemy, and most importantly, I knew I could totally rely on the guys I would have around me. As a group, you are extremely confident.

I was excited to be finally going. After all, this is what you join for. And it was also about earning some respect amongst the unit. At a normal unit, it's about getting some time up, whereas at my unit, it's like, 'Well, what have you done?' It's like you've got to earn your stripes.

Telling my parents I was going wasn't a big deal, and I don't think they were too concerned. It was always going to happen, so it wasn't as if it was something I threw at them out of the blue. I think they were pretty confident and realised there was no point thinking about the worst-case scenarios, either. If you give in to that kind of fear, you'll avoid everything, and sit in a plastic bubble all your life. Are you going to cross the road? No, a car might hit you — it's an off-chance, but it might happen.

I naturally have a positive outlook on life; it's the way I've always been. And I think with all the things we'd done together as a company, and all the training we'd been through — it's such a long process — we were all as prepared as we could humanly be by the time we arrived in Afghanistan.

Special Operations are how these wars are fought. It's a guerrilla war, with highly trained operatives. And our enemy are trained a lot better than people think. These guys can shoot, they have been fighting for 30 years and they know what they are doing. They are born and bred fighters. Before we went to Afghanistan, we were told: 'Don't make the mistake of thinking you are going over there to fight against untrained idiots. These guys know the ins and outs of it, they are fucking fighters. We know where we have the advantage, let's use that.'

75

As for worrying about what might happen, I learned the best way to approach things was by taking them in bite-sized portions. Rather than worrying about what is going to happen in two days' time, I believe you need to focus on what's going to happen in the next 10 minutes, and then what happens in the 10 minutes after that. Just take it step by step — that's how you deal with what ultimately might happen in two days' time. Training in the army taught me that and I still use that philosophy today.

DI THOMLINSON — Mum

Sure, we knew he was in the army and would more than likely be heading to war in Afghanistan, but you don't focus on those things until they happen. I think also, until recently, we had not heard too much about what really goes on over there. We're so protected from what happens and most Australians really have no idea of what it's like for the troops. I think for us the reality and enormity of what Damien was doing really hit home when he was on the *Kanimbla*.

He can't tell you where he is going or what he is doing, and that not-knowing is difficult as a parent, but you realise it's the way it is and has to be. You know they have protected identities and they go to great lengths to protect them. It's funny, I never thought he could keep secrets, but clearly he can.

The *Kanimbla* was really secret, too. Until the helicopter crashed, no-one knew there were Special Forces on board. I remember it came over on the news that night that a helicopter had crashed and it was Special Forces. I sat up and listened to every news bulletin and went constantly trawling through the internet until we knew he wasn't one of the dead or injured. We had also met a lot of his mates who had come to our house, and so we wondered, was it him, or was it him? You immediately think is it someone you know.

At that time we didn't know how the system worked — which is that if he was involved, we would get a call, and if he wasn't, then we wouldn't. When the time came, he didn't say, 'I'm off to Afghanistan.' He said, 'I'm packing my bags and I might not be in contact. I can't tell you any other details.' So, we did kind of know that he was going away.

DAMIEN

It was late October, early November in 2008 and I was out with some friends for a drink at a pub called The Rose in Chippendale. I met an attractive girl at the bar, as you do, and we had a quick joke about something, then went off in separate directions until later in the night. She was from Brazil, a country not only known for its attractive girls, but for good Mixed Martial Arts fighters, a sport which to this day I love, and its professional surfers. I'd always been intrigued by and interested in Brazil, and soon I also became intrigued by and interested in Tisha.

There was just something about her. Soon after we began dating, we had plans to meet at the beach at Coogee. I vividly remember standing across the road as she walked down towards me, with this wonderful grin on her face that she still wears today, and I don't think she even knows she does it. I just wanted to spend time with her, and that's what we did.

That day we went from Coogee to the Royal Hotel at Randwick and spent the afternoon chatting away. Back then, Tisha's English wasn't as good as it is now, and she wrote down some Portuguese words for me on the back of a coaster, and we had some interesting conversations about them. I was not only learning about Tisha the person, I was also learning about her culture. Every time I was with her it was exciting. And she was, and still is, so patient with everything.

After a few dates I met her group of friends and there was a great family-like feeling when I was there with them. They also party with the best of them. One night in particular I remember we were in her apartment in Chippendale and all the Brazilians had a singalong with a guitar, which lasted for three hours.

Until I met Tisha, everyone I knew was focused on the things like work. She was the polar opposite. The thing that mattered most to her and all her friends was Sunday afternoon when they would all sit down and everyone would have a beer and tell stories about different things they had done that week. None of it was commercial or materialistic. After intense weeks at work, it was the perfect environment for me to be in.

I knew she worked at a pharmacy, but at that stage she hadn't dropped the bomb on me that she had a Master's degree in biochemistry. I kept thinking, what is wrong with this girl? Why is she speaking to *me*? I don't get it.

Things progressed, and I told her exactly what I did. As my deployment to Afghanistan approached, I decided that I would introduce Tisha to my parents. While I again couldn't spell out where I was going, they all knew. And as hard as it is on a girl to have her man away in a place like Afghanistan, Tisha said she would have no problem waiting for me. I have never doubted Leticia's loyalty, and that trait is very important to me. One thing I didn't want was for her to be getting any confronting phone calls, so I asked my parents if they would let Tisha know if anything happened, so she would not be stressed out. I didn't think that anything bad would happen and especially never thought that she would get the call she ended up getting.

MARIA LETICIA DE PAIVA AGOSTINI — or as she is known, TISHA

I remember the night we met. It was at The Rose. I was getting a drink at the bar and because I had only been in Australia for a year I still had a very strong accent. I think I was ordering a drink and the guy who was serving me couldn't get what I was saying. I had to repeat what I wanted 10 times, and then I was pointing at things behind the bar. This guy, who turned out to be Damien, was next to me and he started laughing. I asked him, 'What are you laughing about?' We had a little chat at the bar and he teased me about my accent. I got my drink and went back to my friends and he did as well … but he had caught my attention.

He was obviously attracted to me as well and at the end of the night we caught up again, kept talking and then we exchanged phone numbers. He rang me and we went to the movies, then we caught up for a few beers, and then we started dating. He told me he was in the army but he wasn't specific about what he did, and to be honest I didn't really ask, either. In Brazil the army is not such a big thing. Now I understand how big a deal it is in Australia and how important it is, but in Brazil it's just like, 'Oh yeah, you're in the army … whatever.' It's like being a policeman.

I think it was around January, after we had been dating a few months, and getting a bit more serious, when he told me he was going away with the army. I couldn't believe it. You're what? Excuse me? In Brazil nobody goes to war. War for me was something you see in movies and on TV. I was really surprised and shocked, and then he kind of explained to me exactly what he did, although he couldn't tell me much. He just said he was in the Special Forces, and he was going to Afghanistan, and he would be there for a while.

I was stunned. When the shock subsided a little, we had the 'will you wait for me' conversation. He said, 'I have to be sincere with you, I'm going to be away for several months, we need to see if you are keen to do it or not.' We were still really in the honeymoon period of our relationship, and now this. But I felt something genuine for Damien, and I said, 'No, I'll be waiting for you. I like you and I like being with you. I will wait for you.' When I had time to think more about it, obviously I was concerned about what might happen. He was going to war. He could be killed at any time. Anything could happen at any time, so it was a massive worry. But I just took a deep breath and thought, well, it has to happen, it will happen and hopefully he'll be fine and he'll be back and we'll be fine. That's all you can do, hope things will be fine. I am one for fate and destiny. I really believe if something has to happen it will happen, it doesn't matter where you are … but that didn't stop me from worrying.

ANDREW SAVAUGE — or as he is known, FREDDO
I knew Damien was heading to Afghanistan because he actually came over and visited me in January before he was deployed. I was doing a snow season in Whistler in Canada, and he came over for a few weeks. I must admit I thought at the time it was a little bit out of character for him. Apart

from the trip to see me in Canada, he had also done a couple of other 'catch-up' trips, including a trip with another mate. I wondered if it was the 'just in case something happens to me' trip. If you think you're invincible, you don't do those sorts of things. Maybe in the forefront of his mind he wasn't thinking along those lines, but in the back of his mind he might have been thinking, if something happens, at least I want to have seen my mates.

Obviously you've always got it in your head that he might not come back because you see that from time to time, but you don't want to think about it too much because it's self-destructive. Earlier on, Australia had quite a low level of involvement in Afghanistan and then as more people went over, there were more high-risk missions, and it's basically a numbers game. The Special Forces soldiers look at their missions in the same way we think about driving a car out on the road. But the numbers are just a little bit shorter.

DAMIEN

Freddo was right that I knew it was a dangerous trip, and before I went I wanted to spend time with my mates. Not that I was concerned about not seeing them again or not coming home, I just wanted that time, a good time, before I got involved in the most intense and stressful situation I was ever going to find myself in. I had New Year's at Dean's, and I was with Marshy for a week before I went to see Freddo in Canada. While I was over there I roomed with a guy called Pete Cooledge, who Freddo had lived with while he was in the UK, and we had the time of our lives.

And I fell in love with snowboarding. Whistler was a gorgeous location with great people and I loved the feeling of freedom snowboarding gives you. It was the break I needed before Afghanistan.

We had some great times there, sitting and chatting in a hot tub with our beers being cooled by snow, telling stories and planning for nights out on the town. What was also handy was that for the previous four years I had always had to have my phone on and be checking if the call had come in that a job was on, which just quietly keeps you at a specific level of arousal. This was the first trip I had been on where I turned my mobile off on arrival and kept it off until two days before I left. This was the first overwhelming experience of relaxation I had had in such a long time, and coincidentally it was while on a snowboard.

Guys like Freddo, Marshy and Dean were also my grounding to the 'real world', the world that didn't involve the stress associated with working in Special Forces. They could no doubt see that my job was no walk in the park and that my carefree attitude was the flipside of being wound tight through my occupation. Despite the stress, though, I loved what I did and have never regretted choosing that path, regardless of what was about to happen.

8

It doesn't matter where you go, a place is never exactly the same as what you see in photos or on television, and that was my initial impression of Afghanistan. The harsh reality of a place like that is that it is a lot like a land that time forgot. It's not until you go there and walk through some of these places — where families have lived on farms for so many generations and continued to build extra rooms onto what was initially a big square compound — that you have the history rammed home. The whole time it's such a sensory overload of information — every minute you are trying to get used to the terrain and adapt to everything happening around you. You're moving through hills where spotters can be, wondering what they're doing, what they're listening out for. It's a different world, and one you have to be fully focused on the entire time. You certainly don't have enough time to sit there and think, shit, this is dangerous.

While we didn't sit around soaking it up, we also didn't charge straight into a contact, either. We had to prep everything and make sure every piece of equipment was ready to go. We would go to the base, make sure all our weapons were zeroed, do some test firing, and we would do everything twice. At that stage we were still vehicle mounted, so we had to prep the vehicles as well. And that's where collaboration comes in, with the experienced guys helping the less experienced with the set-up of vehicles. It's how you find out 'this is what worked the last time they used it', and 'this is part of the set-up procedure'. As someone who is new, you are constantly trying to pick little tricks up from other more experienced people and you're always wondering if you are doing everything right. The first six or seven days were all centred on this preparation, making sure everyone was ready, then getting orders, learning about the place. Over those days we could certainly feel our anxiety levels start to creep up a little bit.

We had our teams. There are three in a vehicle: me as the driver, my second in charge beside me, and our gunner behind us in a turret on a MK19 grenade launcher. That's your team and you've trained with them for ages, and your team trains with another team as a section, and then all together in your platoon. You are used to working with all the people who are around you.

I often get asked if it was like I thought it was going to be. When it came time to head out on our first operation, we didn't really have time to daydream about it. For most things you do in your life, you have that luxury of those couple of minutes to think, is this what I really expected this to be like? But when you're sitting in a car like that, driving through unfamiliar terrain, you are way more focused on what is happening in front of you and around you. I never even tried to associate it with the way I had pictured things.

For the reasons I gave earlier, I can't go into specific details about what the Special Forces do in Afghanistan, but it's a major misconception that we just go in and clear out whole towns with all guns blazing. The Taliban run on a spotter network, so they know when we are coming, and we would sometimes see all the women and children leaving the town in droves — really big groups — before we got there. When we saw that, it was a signal that we needed to really switch on.

It's not like we would move into a town and there would instantly be a gun battle. I think it was a lot worse when we would go into a place and find a ghost town. It's incredibly eerie, especially when we had just seen a whole lot of people leaving that town very quickly. When that happened, we were expecting something; it was just a mystery to us where that something was going to come from. We had been briefed before we went to Afghanistan that the improvised explosive device (IED) threat was extremely high now as the Taliban were starting to get smarter with their use of them. They had watched from a distance how we would go through anything to get into buildings, and so they started putting IEDs in walls and various other spots. As I said, we were not up against untrained idiots.

Part of our preparation involved working with members of the Incident Response Regiment (IRR) — which is now the Special Operations Engineers Regiment (SOER). We studied what weapons and explosives the Taliban were using, what they were likely to use and how their tactics were evolving against us. For example, the Taliban were weaker in firefights, but had a huge advantage when it came to IEDs at particular choke points. This was their way of gaining a guerrilla advantage.

At one point, I actually met and spoke to a guy who had been in the Taliban in Tarin Kowt. He joined and served in the Taliban for 12 years so that his wife and daughter didn't get raped and murdered. Threatening to rape and kill young girls is just a part of their recruitment drive. He served with them long enough to get his family away from where they were so they would be safe. He then asked if he could leave and the Taliban said, 'Yes, you can leave,' and then they cut his fucking eye out. Think about that.

Now that I've had some exposure in the media, I often get asked by people who recognise me — and some do try to bait me — about whether or not we should have troops in Afghanistan. Usually I say something along these lines: 'I understand there are terrible things happening in Africa and in other places around the world, but let's face it, Afghanistan harbours a group called Al Qaeda, who are at the centre of groups who have directly attacked Australians. I'm sure you have heard of the Bali nightclub bombings back in 2002? Now just sit in front of any of the families of Bali bombing victims and ask them whether we should be there.'

I was personally affected by those acts of terrorism. One of my mates is friends with some of the guys from the Coogee Bay Dolphins — he used to play footy with them — and a number of the Dolphin players were over in Bali at the time of the bombing and they lost some of their boys. It wasn't until a year and a bit through my service that I really got to meet some of them. We got along well. We always used to go down and drink at Coogee with them and have a great time, but then when that time of year came around for their memorial service, that's when it really hit home what it does to people on a deep personal level. I think that's when I started to look at the situation differently. What the Taliban do in these far-off places — be it Bali, New York or Tarin Kowt — does affect us.

Back to my deployment in Afghanistan, one of the more important things we get trained for as commandos is to be able to work in extreme situations when we are tired and exhausted, having been awake for a day or two or three. We're trained to put the tiredness behind us. Everyone feels exactly the same, extremely exhausted, but everyone must also be operating on a particularly high level. Your body really does adapt to it, and I think your body's recovery time just shortens as it gets used to having to recover at a quicker rate. That might be the reason why Special Forces guys recover in hospital so quickly compared to others, too. Our bodies are used to recovering in short periods of time and not having a regular sleep pattern. A normal person gets up at a particular hour and their body clock is set. Our clocks never are. When we get sleep, we might only get three hours, but because of the nature of the job, we can't spend hours peering through bleary eyes. If we're awake, we're alert and ready for anything. Sometimes more ready than we might need to be.

You can't see a mortar coming, but you can hear its whistle, and the closer it gets to you the louder that whistle gets. It is actually very Hollywood-like, and just in case you needed any convincing of how real it is, that noise does the trick. It was mid-afternoon one particular day, we had been driving for a couple of days, and I heard this whistle and it was getting closer. Then I heard this boom, and there was a dust cloud — not too far from us — and I said, 'Why are our mortars firing? Why are our guys ...' That thought lasted about a second before I realised: fuck, it's not one of ours!

I instantly realised the gravity of the situation. I heard a couple more rounds coming in with that whistle, which is hard to forget, and I put my helmet and armour on, because you never know where the next one might hit.

I was still freaking out while I took cover, but when I looked across from the side of the car, I saw the team next to us sitting there in singlets, playing cards and eating. 'You can take that armour off now, Iceman, we're good!' one of them yelled to me. I was wondering why no-one else seemed worried at all. How could they be so cavalier? I would soon discover that after a while you really do get used to things like that, and the more experienced guys are a bit looser with the way things are. They explained that if it was going to be something major, we would have heard about it before now. So, back to cards.

We had a couple of close calls before the night of my incident, including having a Bushmaster (a protected mobility vehicle) blown up by an IED. Thankfully the guys in the car escaped serious injury. Bushmasters are usually good like that. When that happened I thought, oh yeah, that's another little reality check. We also had a couple of big contacts, but that was all part of the experience of war. Sadly, so, too, are casualties and death.

Just two weeks before my own incident, we had been part of a disruption operation and had identified an IED in front of our position. Standard operating procedure was to blow it up in place. During this process, there was an explosion. I can still remember the call coming through to one of the teams up front: 'We've got a KIA' — a soldier killed in action.

Sergeant Brett Till — JT as we knew him — was an EOD, an explosive ordnance disposal technician, one of the guys who sweep for and defuse IEDs. He was defusing an IED buried in the road on Chambarak Pass, and it was booby-trapped.

I didn't know JT that well. We had done a small bit of training with him about how to use the mine sweeper, where he taught us the basic stuff about them. Although I didn't know him well, he was one of us. We had just lost one of us, and that really hit me. The guys who do that job do amazing work. They work their arses off in the position they are in, and for the life of me I couldn't imagine stepping out in front of everyone like they do. That's a really ballsy thing. I can handle barging through doors and doing stuff like that, but those guys might as well have targets on their backs. They work for days on end, too, with minimal breaks, and have to stay extremely focused, just for us to be able to get to where we're going. At that particular stage, they had been sweeping for at least two days. And because they are using their detection equipment, it doesn't give them the chance to patrol like infantry. It's just a man with a metal detector, which is a daunting thought, but they are just doing all they can to keep us all alive.

After it happened, we held up for a while. I don't remember the amount of time, maybe an hour or two, and then they were back out there sweeping, moving everyone forward, doing their job. That's fucking tough.

I don't care how tough you think the toughest guy you know is, what the EODs do, that's a solid effort. It was hard not to be proud being behind them.

9

CORPORAL B — the commando sitting alongside Damien when he drove over the IED

The first time I met Damien was when I was a part of the Team Command/Direction Staff (DS) on Damien's advanced infantry course, run at Singleton, as part of the direct-entry scheme. He came across as very immature — which doesn't mean a lot coming from me — but he was keen to put the work into what he was doing. One of the reasons he came across as immature was because the bloody idiot put 'Iceman' down as his preferred name on one of his personal documents. After that it stuck forever, and it also made him known to all the DS.

I did follow his progress through his RIO cycle and saw that he had made a few mistakes over the various courses, but was successful on completion. We deployed together on the operation where we sat on HMAS *Kanimbla* for six weeks. We didn't do a lot on the boat, apart from going stir-crazy. Damien was sent to the RHIBs upon our return and we didn't see each other for quite some time.

Then, in 2008, we were placed in the same team — I was the 2IC and Iceman was the gunner. These two positions go hand in hand throughout the combat world. Once I found out I would be getting him in my team, I wasn't sure what to think and was reluctant about taking him. After seeing him work for a few months, though, I realised that he was not the same soldier I had once known. Someone had given him a kick in the arse. We struck up a friendship, which wasn't hard given we grew up in the same place and shared common interests such as golf and surfing. Because of that, a lot of our afternoon PT (Physical Training) sessions would be surfing at one of Sydney's perfect beaches.

When we deployed to Afghanistan, while it was Damien's first rotation, it was my third trip. I can't remember clearly what my thoughts were at the time. I guess it felt like any other trip: I was excited, nervous and anxious. When I get those feelings, I recall previous deployments. I know that the boys I have trained with are there to look after me as much as I would look after them.

The night the incident happened was very, very cold. We were wearing all of our Softiegear — jumpers and beanies. The ground was still quite wet from all the rain over the previous weeks. Yep, it still rains in the desert. It was quite a bright night; the moon was big and full, although we still needed to use our night-vision goggles for driving. My memory is that it was very quiet and calm. We were moving up to an overwatch position and I remember watching the BM (Bushmaster) and the SRV (Special Reconnaissance Vehicle), which were in front of us, proceeding to the top of the hill. We were just shy of cresting the hill when I believe I heard the primer of the IED pop.

The next thing I felt was something hitting me in the face and the rest of my body pushing through the passenger door. All this felt like it happened in slow motion.

I was thrown through the passenger door, but I was not knocked out. I found myself about two metres from where the car ended up. Something had landed on top of me. At the time I thought it was a pack or something from the car. I can remember my ears were ringing and my face was sore and wet. The smell of diesel was all around me. We were covered in it from the two 20-litre jerries on the front of our SRV.

That smell still has a lasting association. I can't stand the smell of diesel now. When I do smell it, it always reminds me of that night.

I heard someone at the rear of the car stumbling, so I moved towards that noise, at the same time shrugging off what I thought was the piece of equipment that had landed on me. It was the gunner stumbling around and I grabbed him to stop him moving so I could make sure he was OK. He had a few bumps and bruises and one of his eardrums had popped. We heard some gurgling and moaning coming from where I was thrown and we made our way back there. It was then that I realised it wasn't equipment that had landed on me, it was Damo. He had been thrown up in the air, and had come down on top of me.

I thought, holy shit, I hope Damo's alright, but as we got closer to him, we realised he was in trouble. One leg was completely gone, leaving the femur exposed. The other was not in the position that a leg should be in and was held on by a piece of skin. So straight away I knew at least one leg was gone and there wasn't much hope for the other one. I kneeled down beside him and got out my torch to see what we were dealing with. The gunner was on Damo's other side. We then pulled out our trauma shears and started cutting off his pants. We got to his waist and began placing three tourniquets on his legs. When we were tightening one of the tourniquets, we caught one of his balls under the strap and he let us know about it — so he was responsive.

The rest of the platoon, with the engineers, were making their way to us, ensuring there were no secondary devices. We removed the rest of Damo's clothes, including his helmet and body armour. Once we exposed him, we realised that his legs were not his only injuries. His face was quite swollen and bloody and there was blood in his eyes. Both his arms were broken. One arm was an open fracture with the bone exposed and the other one was sitting at about 90 degrees from where it should be.

At this stage Damo was trying to fight us. All he wanted to do was sit up. That was when I lay on top of him to hold him down and keep him warm. I do remember how strong his stomach muscles were that night, because he was pretty much doing sit-ups with me lying on top of him. As you would expect, he was very distraught and it didn't matter what I was saying, he was doing whatever he wanted to do and it took all my strength to hold him there.

To be honest, I don't know how he survived the explosion. We were sure he was going to die. His legs were pretty much gone, his arms were broken and he had lost so much blood, but we just kept working on him and holding him down. Once the tourniquets were on, we put a morphine pen into his upper thigh.

Everyone started to rock up, including the medic, Platoon Commander, Scott Palmer and the people in the Bushmaster that was behind us. I believe Scotty worked on Damo's open arm fracture, while the medic got an IV running and gave him some more morphine and fluids to help replace the lost blood.

For the majority of the time we worked under white light (torches, not the Infrared or night vision), so it wasn't too bad. We were not under fire, but were worried that we would come under fire. We could see insurgents moving in the distance and we knew they would want to exploit the situation, so we needed to go 'no-light' in order to keep us safe.

Damo's arms were splinted to the side of his body and we wrote a capital 'M' and 'TQ' on his forehead to make all the nursing staff and doctors aware that morphine had been administered and tourniquets applied. He was then placed on a stretcher, lashed in and covered in puff jackets and space blankets to keep him warm. From there I stayed with our vehicle while Damo was moved down to another Bushmaster and transported to a secure helicopter landing zone for evacuation. Until I was asked about the '56 minutes we spent working on Damo', I had no idea it had taken 56 minutes. To me it went in an instant.

On previous deployments I got to work in the Tarin Kowt US medical facility, working on major trauma casualties, so I had seen a fair bit of that sort of stuff before, but it's a little different when the guy you go for a surf with is lying there with his legs pretty much missing. I didn't really think about it until after, when I had time to sit down and gather my thoughts. When the chopper arrived, we had done all we could do. I still didn't think that he would make it, though. I just don't understand how someone with so many injuries could survive.

The very next day we heard he was still critical and, once stable, they would fly him to Germany. A little after that the OP (operation) we were in was contacted over the phone by Damo from the hospital in Germany, and that was when we really knew he was good to go. He was still very drugged up and probably doesn't remember.

One thing I do think about was that the vehicle we were driving had actually been on tow for a few days because we had blown the gearbox. We had put in a new one a couple days prior. If it wasn't for a gearbox being there and taking the brunt of that explosion, I would probably be in the same situation as Damo, or worse. To give you an idea of the effect the IED had on the car, the gearbox was pushed into the passenger seat through the firewall and floor pan. On the driver's side, there was nothing left from the back of the seat to the dashboard. The bonnet was missing, as was the front driver-side tyre. What really stood out was that the steering column and wheel were pushed forward over the front of the car. I wish we'd taken a photo just so everyone could understand the power of the explosion that Damo was sitting on.

DAMIEN

It took a while before I heard about everything that happened that night. It was never told to me as one story from start to finish, just voices, around a dozen or so — including Corporal B — each providing a piece in the jigsaw puzzle of my missing memory. Many of those fragments were recollected eight beers into the evening, when inhibitions had finally relaxed. When someone says something, it often feels kind of familiar, but finding memories from there is hard. Maybe the memories are locked in there somewhere, not ready to come out. I'm not sure. While I cannot write here my recollections of that April night, what I can do is relay what I have been told by the sources involved. This is what my jigsaw puzzle looks like.

In war, decisions have to be made. What separates good leaders from the ordinary is the fact that they make tough decisions. Commanders have to allocate resources and support roles, and on this particular night the Platoon Commander made the call that his resources would not be best used by sweeping the hill we would travel. In a perfect world we would have had every path we could take swept, but it was deemed it was a greater danger for the platoon walking in that night. Though it's easy to assume that mistakes were made on the night of my accident, I am sure my Commander would make the same decision again. Operation first. I understand it and don't question it. It's impossible to go into too much detail, but there are a lot of moving parts which create the bigger picture of each operation. What we did that night was what we did regularly.

Our attachments were moving into an overwatch position on a mountain range that overlooked a south-eastern corner of a particular town. We were moving up there to cover another platoon who were going in. They had an intelligence-based target identified and knew where the building was. All the information was confirmed and we were basically covering them on their way to that compound. We were driving in a convoy and our marching order that night had our vehicle as number five. I was driving, and as usual we were following in the tracks already made by the vehicles ahead, to ensure we were on clear ground.

In war, just like life, centimetres can be the difference between life and death. The guys were moving up to get better cover. Somehow my vehicle was a fraction over from where I should have been in the wheel tracks. My wheel hit a rock, and it bounced onto an IED. *BOOM.*

The other platoon heard the explosion from where they were, and aborted the mission immediately. If a massive firefight had started at that stage, and everyone was ready for this to happen, a chopper would not have been able to come and get me and I would have died. For the next 56 minutes my mates looked beyond the gruesome scene which confronted them. There were limbs hanging off, blood everywhere and hideous sounds as life drained out of my body. With death standing there, waiting to take me away, they fought to save my life. As I have already said, I have no memory of the event, and that is a luxury. Unlike my brave mates, I don't have to relive that horrible night.

One of the most vivid stories I have heard over the past four or so years about that night was from a mate who was controlling the scene. He was a Lance Corporal who had served for a long time and whose commendation for gallantry still has me asking what more you need to do to win a Victoria Cross. He mentioned a few things about control on the night and looking out for more attacks and pulling the guys around, but his main recollection was when I let out a God-awful screech and in his words, all he could think was: 'Fuck, the poor bastard. He's dying.'

Our gunner, 22-year-old Private Daniel Landt-Isley, or Spork as we called him, had been blown out of the vehicle. When he came to, he had rushed over to help me. I was being held down but was trying to get up and run, and apparently I was trying to punch my way out of it, albeit with two shattered arms and my elbow hanging out, which resulted in very soft slaps.

Spork applied a tourniquet to my leg to stop the bleeding, but had got my balls stuck in the tourniquet. Despite all the duress my body was under at that point, it was still looking after the good bits. That was the cause of the screech. That Lance Corporal and I used to box a bit together, but to see his face when he told me that story, to see dudes starting to break a bit, makes you realise just how heavy it was at that moment.

Spork was a tough kid. He got his nickname after he sliced his finger through to the bone while he was trying to make a spork out of a spoon. After doing it, he strapped it with electrical tape and walked out with us on the job that night. From that moment on he was known as Spork, and he, too, did a phenomenal job on that April night. All the guys did, and it's the only reason I am here today. Spork and I had an interesting relationship, though. We didn't really like each other too much before we were deployed. I had pretty much offered to knock him out a couple of times at Holsworthy, just because he was a smart-arse. 'Come on, kid, you're a straight left away from being on the ground,' I would say. He knew how to get under my skin and I knew how to kickbox, so eventually we were going to work it out some way or another. We were usually at each other's throats. He would start saying smart stuff to me and I would say, 'Do it again and I'm going to fucking hurt you.' I would also say to whoever else was present, 'You are going to have to tell him to shut his mouth, or I'll do it.' That was the relationship we had.

He had been over to Afghanistan on two tours before this one, but he was still relatively new to our company. When we arrived in Afghanistan, the kid proved how professional he was. As soon as we got there, everyone in our team was instantly shocked by the fact that our relationship changed so dramatically. The things that used to get under my skin ceased, my physical threats stopped, and we both spent our time dealing with stuff to do with our cars. We worked really well together. It was like: 'OK, it's time for business now and we're doing this shit.'

The rest of our six-man team couldn't believe it. They would say, 'Look at you two, when are you getting married?' I think it was just shocking that both of us, with how stubborn I am and how loose he is, had just dropped all of that when we got overseas. When you put the helmet on, all of a sudden you have got to be that guy, and he did it really well. I remember he taught me how to Melbourne Shuffle dance, which is notable because the only place I have ever been able to do it was in a room with five guys in Tarin Kowt in Afghanistan, rather than in the Ivy nightclub in Sydney.

He was a great shooter. I remember one time he had a window pointed out to him, about 400 metres away, and about a metre by a metre. He leans back, fires one round — one round. Now firing one accurate round from an MK19 isn't the easiest thing. You have to get used to the trigger, and usually you would fire a burst of two or three or sometimes four rounds. But Spork fires a single round that goes through the window. He looks down at us and goes: 'That one?' We just looked at each other and thought, are you fucking kidding? Wow. That's awesome. We were happy enough for him to get the round near the window somewhere, just enough so it gets the heads of the enemies down, but no, it's bang, straight through it.

The first thing people I have spoken to about that night usually recall is Spork waking up screaming. To me that paints a picture. I think the kid is tough. There is no two ways about it. He was blown out of the turret, at least seven or eight feet in the air, landed on the ground and was knocked out by the equivalent of Goliath. He was concussed, had his eardrum blown out and he woke up screaming. What's his first instinctual reaction after that? He crawls over and starts helping and working on me. To be able to put everything that has happened to you behind you and go and do what you have to do for someone else … it's beyond words.

In that situation, every second is so valuable. Spork was our team medic, and his treatment and the treatment of others around me, like Scott Palmer, are why I am here now. For those guys to use their specific skills to focus on keeping me alive is just amazing. The good thing about Special Forces is that these are the types of guys who surround you. When I am told about what went on, all I can think is that it's superhuman how someone can still do their job so well under so much duress. Spork got a Special Operations Commander Commendation for Gallantry for that night. Guys like him and what they did became a big part of my driving motivation to walk again as soon as I could. Whenever I hear stories about the 56 minutes those guys worked on me, all I can say is 'fucking wow!' I still can't put words together to describe it.

A little over a year after my incident Spork himself ended up in hospital in Germany. Defence released details that he had been found in his room, at the barracks in Tarin Kowt, unconscious from a suspected overdose. What truly disappointed me, though, was that the army decided to release his name. I was really upset by that and I didn't think it was deserved. This was the same kid who had been blasted out of a vehicle, had his eardrum blown up, was knocked out, and came to with the first thought to crawl to me and start working to save my life. I don't know what happened over there in his case, but I did hear he was speaking a lot about my incident on the trip before the one where he was evacuated to Germany. Regardless of what happened, he is one of the toughest kids I have ever known, and along with the others, I owe him my life.

Long after the accident another commando from my unit, Private D, filled me in on his memories. He told me that he had approached our Platoon Commander that night, and suggested that we sweep the hill. In his opinion the hill we were moving up was a strategic position that would likely have an IED on it. The Platoon Commander responded, 'What's your fascination with sweeping hills?' That really got him going.

In the end it was the Platoon Commander's decision, but one which will no doubt haunt Private D for longer than I would like. The Platoon Commander was a few cars back from mine, so he would have instantly known the gravity of his decision, too.

Seeing Private D's passionate reaction when he was telling me about what happened really rammed home how this one incident affected so many people. My conversation with Private D was one of the rare moments in the Special Forces world when emotion was unavoidable. Showing emotion is generally regarded as a sign of weakness, whether it's just apologising for something or having any type of outburst. Because my injuries were so confronting, it was not possible to be desensitised to what had happened in front of everyone's eyes. There was no way to train for it and no matter how emotionally detached you become, you still feel the hit of seeing something like that.

Mine had been the second incident in two weeks. Our Recon Snipers had also been close to the other incident and this would have no doubt added to Private D's frustration. Watching his own prediction come to light before his eyes would have been incredibly tough. I still feel inadvertently responsible for the things other people had to see. But as I said, the Platoon Commander's decision doesn't really weigh on me. At the end of the day, it has turned my life around for the better.

10

DR ANDREW ELLIS — orthopaedic trauma surgeon at Royal North Shore Hospital, army reservist, and in 2008, Clinical Director of the Australian Medical Taskforce in Tarin Kowt, Afghanistan

I did not meet Private Damien Thomlinson until he arrived at Royal North Shore Hospital in Sydney, but I saw the medical reports and his records from Afghanistan, and I think it's a fair statement to make that he was as close to death as you can get. At the time I think he was the most wounded Australian soldier since Vietnam. The Americans and the British would have had some triple amputees and I think there are one or two quadruple amputees. There have been people who survived with that level of injury, and it's not a contest, but Damien was about as close to death as you could be amongst all those seriously injured patients. There is no question his mates who were there saved his life. We — meaning a team of ultimately around 150 that would cross his path during his treatment — rebuilt him, but those one or two in that small team saved him from dying.

They did great work, as they are trained to do, in what must have been pretty shitty conditions. They are beautiful, strong, good human beings and they have my full respect.

We, as doctors, come to it over years, and they come to it in a sudden, abrupt way. Soldiers don't work in hospitals all day long and they don't get the extensive training we get. They get trained in being Special Forces soldiers, and they get some hospital experience. A lot of those guys come to the operating room and resuscitation room to get experience, but nothing could have quite prepared them for what they faced that night. They would have seen things they had never seen before and wondered what to do. Working out how to move the patient without bits falling off, and deciding what was important and what was not important, and what to do if something dropped off, or wondering if they caused the leg to be amputated are some of the things that would have gone through their minds. But they saved his life.

He was taken to a Fort Operating Base Hospital, where he still had what they called near above knee amputation and a very bad left leg wound and near amputation. His right leg was blown off. These Fort Bases have surgical teams close by ready to move. The one Damien was taken to was British, but American surgeons worked on him. The injuries that people in those situations have, and I'm speaking in general terms here, having seen x-rays of what they are like at the time and having worked in Afghanistan, are very shredded; they are multiply injured with multiple puncture wounds. The bone can be in 40 or 50 parts and the soft tissue all mangled. They get an injury from the blast wave travelling through them, too, which can shock organs and the brain and is the cause of traumatic brain injury. Even if you don't have to have a brain operation, these kids get broken. Damien had facial lacerations as well, so he obviously took a fair blast on his head.

There's the fragmentation effect, which is when all the 100s of pieces that are part of the IED pass through them. Then there's the force pressure effect, where you've got your feet on the vehicle and the vehicle cops it, and it's as if someone with 25 jackhammers suddenly applied them to you. And then there can be effects from burning, and heat and fire from the projectiles as well. It's a very complex and serious injury which our colleagues the Americans have learned a lot about treating, and they have trained us to manage that sort of injury, so these people survive now.

When Damien arrived at the Fort Operating Base Hospital, he was, as I said, very seriously injured, and in that circumstance they have to work very quickly, to minimise the amount of time in the operating room. You must get the patient as fast as possible into a situation where they can have their body warmed and be resuscitated in the intensive care unit. Once upon a time we used to spend 15 or 16 hours trying to put all the pieces of the jigsaw back together without much chance of it being effective. The patient would get colder and sicker because you couldn't look after them as well in an operating room as you could in intensive care. Now, they work quickly and they stabilise the patient, and they did that in Damien's case.

What they did initially was complete these near amputations — those parts would have been pretty mangled. His medical reports say he was cold at this point and the body system designed to help stop his bleeding by clotting would have been seriously affected by this and the trauma he experienced, and they stopped surgery after just 30 minutes. Thirty minutes in an operating room is not very long. He was dying. He was hypothermic, meaning his temperature was low, he was bleeding, not just from the cuts but because his blood-clotting system had stopped working, and that's called the lethal triad. He was an example of a patient right in the middle of the lethal triad, which is like a death spiral and has to be arrested, which means stopping the bleeding. This is why they go for the amputation and other quick surgical wins, warming the patient up and giving him blood products, platelets and fresh frozen plasma that helps the blood to clot. All of that has to happen in intensive care. In there, they also had to fix his acid-base balance, which was very low, and showed he was very, very, very near death. He was fortunate he didn't have any major internal injuries. He might still have been saved, but possibly it could have knocked him over.

When *60 Minutes* did the story on Damien, Ray Martin asked me what his injuries were like. I had a flashback to some terrible injuries that I have seen and I thought, how can I put this in words without frightening the parents of all the kids who are over there? That was what I was thinking about. How can I explain what it looks like? It's a very graphic thing where all the parts are mangled. How can I put that in words and not frighten every mother of a 19-year-old doing their duty for their country? So in the end I said it was like he had been attacked by a mad axeman, and that's probably half of what it looked like. In reality, it's not even like something out of an abattoir; it's worse than that. It's something out of war and unless you have seen it, you can't really imagine it. It's what traumatises people in terrorist bombings when they see all the pieces of flesh.

We as surgeons are sort of used to it, but those guys, his mates, certainly wouldn't have been. So the first responders saved his life, then the people at the Fort Operating Base continued that. They gave him 16 units of blood and 16 units of fresh frozen plasma, and they treated everything they could to make him better. They used all the tricks in the playbook to get him out of death. A CT scan of his head and spine showed that everything was normal, but there were notable fractures in his face. They took him back to theatre four hours later, tidied up his fractures in both his face and arms, and stabilised them, and got him ready to fly to Landstuhl, in Germany.

The positive outcome of Damien's situation was the result of a few very critical medical strategies. The first was the use of tourniquets by the guys at the site to stop the bleeding. The second was what they did in the resuscitation room, not keeping him in the theatre too long, stopping the bleeding, getting his blood clotting right, and making sure he was warm. The next was the quick transportation from Afghanistan to Landstuhl. The ability to take those critically ill people, really quickly, from those little Fort Bases to somewhere better is absolutely critical in getting them to the next tier.

Landstuhl is said to be the biggest trauma centre outside the continental United States, and it puts the injured where they have all the specialists in the world and all the things they need to look after them. They usually only hold them there for two to three days, then they fly them back to their home country for definitive care. Damien was there for just under two weeks.

DI AND STEVE THOMLINSON
We were up at Magenta Shores playing golf that morning, and were on the 11th hole when a young guy from the pro

shop came out on a cart to tell us our daughter, Naomi, had been trying to get in contact with us. Etiquette and protocol on a golf course means you don't have your phone switched on, so effectively we hadn't been contactable out in the middle of the course.

We had no idea what Naomi wanted, and we very briefly thought about finishing the round and calling her afterwards, but there had already been a couple of missed calls on both of our phones. There was a message from someone with the army, asking us to call him back as soon as possible. Immediately we returned his call. He said he was at our front door and instantly we thought, if he's there, that's not good. During a family day at Holsworthy we were told that if you hear anything on the radio or television about something which had happened in Afghanistan, you'd know it's not your family member unless you have had a knock on the door. They prepare you for things like that, so you know if you get the knock on the door it's bad, and now we suddenly had that knock.

We asked straight away, 'Is he alive?' We were told, 'Yes, but there are some issues.' That was probably a stupid thing for us to ask anyway because if Damien had died they wouldn't have told us over the phone. We got home and the man waiting for us explained what had happened, and gave us all the details the army had at that stage. Damien was alive, but was far from being in any sort of stable condition. From that moment it was all about waiting for more updates, and praying he would survive.

NAOMI THOMLINSON-MUNN — sister
It was my husband Andrew's and my fifth wedding anniversary on that Saturday. We were just sitting around,

trying to work out what we would do to celebrate that night, when my phone rang. It was a Sergeant from the army who said he was at my parents' house, but that they were not home. He asked if I knew where they were. I had a mini panic attack. I was standing up at the time and I had to grab hold of something because I thought I was going to pass out. I said to him, 'Is he alright?' The Sergeant simply said, 'Yes.' Maybe that's what he had to say because he was on the phone. He said, 'Look, can we get in contact with your parents?'

I called the golf course and got hold of Mum and Dad, then we all headed back to Mum and Dad's house. Mum and Dad were pretty worried when we spoke on the phone. I think they realised the enormity of what was happening. I think I was a bit blasé about the fact that someone had actually come to the house, but Mum and Dad knew something serious had happened if it got to the point of the army sending someone to their front door with the news. For me, it didn't quite click. I had been told yes when I asked if Damien was alright. I just took it at face value. He's OK. It was a bit naive, but that's what my thoughts were at the time.

I remember when they first told us what had happened, I heard Mum make a shocked noise, a gasp. The main thing was obviously that he was still alive. It was strange, though, because I think it took me a little bit of time during the day for the news to really sink in. It's one thing to hear that he had lost a leg or both legs, but then I started actually thinking about it. Your legs. You use them all the time for everything. I was sitting there an hour later and for some reason I just thought, he will never be able to drive a car normally again. For me, that really hit home. Clearly there were more important things, but that was the one which hit me.

From there I was focused on just taking things as they came until we could get over there and see him. I ended up in shut-down mode. Not much else in the world mattered at that point in time. At the same time I was thinking, oh my God, how is he going to take it? He's always been so athletic, what's he going to do with this? Is he going to become intensely depressed? I don't think any of us can know how we would handle it.

TISHA

In the weeks leading up to Damien leaving for Afghanistan, he made a point of introducing me to his parents. We hadn't been together for that long, and I thought meeting the parents was something a bit serious, but then he explained to me that if anything happened to him in Afghanistan, the army would contact his parents, and then his parents would contact me. So while I'm sure he did want his parents to meet me to see what his girlfriend was like, one of the main purposes of the visit was the 'just in case something happened' scenario. Unfortunately that's exactly what happened.

I can vividly recall the morning. I don't think I'll ever forget it. It was a Saturday, and I was working at the time in a pharmacy and I remember I saw his mother Di's phone number come up on my phone. I froze. I instantly thought she would only ring for one reason. It wasn't like she would be just ringing to say hello or anything like that.

I immediately started freaking out, and I hadn't even answered the phone. It would be the worst phone call I had ever had.

I answered the call, and the first thing I noticed was that Di was breathing really heavily. 'Hi, Tisha, this is Di,

110

Damien's mum,' she said, and then there was a deep breath. You naturally think the worst straight away, that he has been killed.

She said there was an incident and Damien was involved in it. I think she said it was an incident involving a roadside bomb and I immediately asked, 'Did he survive? Is he alright? Is he alive? Is he alive?' She replied, 'Yes, he's alive, but the situation is bad. I think he is very badly injured, especially his limbs. He lost one of his legs, but apparently all the other limbs are badly injured. He's still unstable and he has to go through a lot of surgeries to save the other limbs, but he's not stable enough for surgery yet.'

It wasn't that I didn't comprehend all that she had said about his injuries and surgeries, it was just that the only way I looked at the news was that Damien had survived. He was alive. At times like that you need to grab the only positive thing you can find in amongst it all, and to me that was the important thing.

I left work and went home straight away in tears. I was living with my sister at the time and I got home and I was crying, and crying, and crying, and I was terribly worried and she kept asking me what was wrong. I just couldn't stop crying, though.

By then I had soaked up what Di had told me about his injuries and how he wasn't stable enough for the surgeries, but I just kept thinking if he survived, it's because he was going to survive. If he was going to die, he would have died, but he didn't. He survived. Eventually I told my sister that Damien had run over a bomb in Afghanistan. I told her he had lost a leg and there were bad injuries to the other limbs as well, but that was all we knew. The secrecy of the Special

Forces means that even when there is an incident they still don't tell you too much.

It was so nerve-wracking. I wanted to know what sort of condition he was in, but they would only give me little bits of information. On the Saturday night I spoke to his parents again, and Di told me they were organising all his documents and their own because they were going to fly over to Germany where Damien would be flown as soon as he was stable enough to fly. I immediately wanted to go as well. On the Sunday morning the army sent a padre to my place, and it was the padre who told me that Damien had now lost both his legs, and it was so terrible hearing that news, especially when the padre also said both arms were very badly injured as well.

It wasn't just the news of him losing both legs that was so terrible, it was what he had told me before he went away — something that was now really worrying me. I remembered before he left, he told me, 'If I lose one arm or one leg, it's fine, but if I lose both arms or both legs, I'm going to kill myself. I don't want to live.' After he told me that, I just responded, 'Oh shut up, nothing will happen to you.' So when the padre told me the news, I said to him straight away that they really need to look after him. When he wakes up and finds out he's lost both his legs, he'll try to kill himself. He won't want to live when he wakes up and finds out what happened. That was incredibly worrying.

I asked the padre if I would be able to fly over, but because we weren't married, I was effectively no-one to the army, which I can see was fair enough — we had met only four or five months ago. But that didn't stop me wanting to be there by his side. They told me they were flying his parents and sister to Germany. When he was stable enough to fly, he would be going to a big American hospital there, where they had more specialists to treat him.

So my focus went from he's survived, and he's going to survive, to telling myself that he will be stabilised — he *will* be stabilised. The padre rang me later and said that he was stable and would be moving to Germany soon. I went to the airport when his family flew out and I remember hugging his mother and saying, 'Don't worry, you are bringing him back with you.' We were all crying and I just kept saying, 'Di, don't worry, you will bring him back with you.'

Before Damien's family got over there, the padre remained in contact with me, giving me updated news on what was happening. Once they got there, they could then fill me in over the phone from Germany. Throughout the entire time it wasn't like I lived day by day waiting for news, I lived second by second. It was really about one step after another. He had survived, he was stable, he was stable enough to fly to Germany, he made it to Germany, his parents are there with him … It was all about small steps.

DI AND STEVE THOMLINSON

On the Sunday, four more army personnel — the acting CO (because the CO was in America), the padre, a Regimental Sergeant Major and a Defence community officer — arrived from Sydney. They came to our home to organise everything and ask if we wanted to go over to Germany and when we could go. We said right now. They spent most of the afternoon filling us in with whatever they could and they told us they had reserved tickets for us on a plane. They wouldn't confirm the booking, though, until Damien had landed in Germany. The fact was, there would be no point in going if he didn't get to Germany. The CO also rang us from America, and the army were great in that whatever information they had, they relayed it straight to us.

To be honest, we didn't have time to get anxious; we were just wondering when we could leave. We didn't know how long we would be going for, or what the procedure was, or how long they would keep him over there in Germany, whether he, and we, would be there for a month, two months, whatever. We had to organise everything here at home so we could just walk straight out the door when we were told it was time to go. And our passports had expired, too, so we had to get all that sorted out.

We were going to be no good to anybody if we just broke down in a blubbering mess, and we were incapable of doing anything to help Damien from the other side of the world. All we were concentrating and focusing on was going to get our son. We were going to Germany to get our son and bring him home.

He was still alive and where there is life, there is hope, and we just had to think that way. In terms of the information we were getting on his condition, the problem was, everything was still a bit sketchy. All they could really tell us was that he had lost both legs, had bad arm injuries, and had facial injuries, but they had no idea of their extent. We didn't know until much later, when we got the medical notes from the field hospital in Afghanistan, that they hadn't expected him to live.

His blood pressure had fallen to ridiculous levels, his temperature was going down, all his vital signs were negative and on his records they called him a 'DIC' — which means 'death is coming'. You have to read between the lines of the medical notes, but in effect they had given up on him. And then, all of a sudden, he came back. There was no explanation at all, he just came back. Later, we told him he went up to heaven and Saint Peter said, 'Piss off, we don't want blokes like you up here.'

Throughout, the army were very good, really supportive. They flew Naomi and her husband, Andrew, over, too. We were going over no matter what. If they hadn't flown us over, we still would have packed up everyone and gone — it was non-negotiable. We left Sydney at four o'clock on the Tuesday afternoon.

11

DI THOMLINSON

We had heard it before Damien's incident. An Australian soldier was injured in Afghanistan and they were 'going to Germany for further medical treatment'. We had no idea that it would be what it was. We just thought there is some hospital in Germany where they all go to be comfortably treated, away from the danger of Afghanistan. It wasn't until we landed and went to the hospital that we found out exactly what it was. I reckon there would be a big percentage of personnel serving in the Australian Defence Force who would have no idea what it's like over there at that hospital and what kind of facilities are available.

It's in Landstuhl, which is about a 10-minute drive from the United States' Ramstein Air Base. When we arrived, I got my camera out to take a photo and all these security people jumped on me. I was told I could take photos inside, but not outside. It's no big secret that the hospital is what it is, though. Each day, there was an ambulance bus from the air-force base to the hospital filled with all the latest casualties. You always knew when the bus was coming because there would be staff running everywhere.

It was an eye-opener for us. You had to show your passport to get into the compound, and inside the hospital it was all American. There was a McDonald's and a pizza place, and although we had changed all our money to Euros, inside we actually needed US dollars. One thing that was a real surprise for all of us was seeing the coverage on the television while we were in the compound. Naturally it was US TV, and when you turned it on first thing of a morning, you would be told how many casualties there were from the previous day. It wasn't as though there would be huge numbers every day, but there always appeared to be some casualties.

We in Australia are so sheltered from what goes on in Afghanistan. I'm sure there are still parents of kids in the army today who have no idea what they are in for when their kids are sent to Afghanistan. Having said that, even if we had known more before Damien joined or went, it wouldn't have changed a thing. If he was happy doing it, then you have just got to wear what your kids do.

Once we arrived at the hospital, all we wanted to do was see Damien, but we weren't allowed straight away. We had to get a briefing. We got to this place called Fisher House, a place built specifically for the families of patients or for soldiers who had to go to that hospital for treatment. Fisher House was staffed by German volunteers and we still keep in contact with one of them we met, a woman named Ulrike. I think the house had around 14 bedrooms and they provided everything for us.

Once there, we were met by hospital staff who explained everything to us and gave us the latest update on Damien's condition. Then we had to go to the hospital and have a meeting with all the doctors before they would let us go into the ward where he was. Even then we were only allowed to see him for 20 minutes or half an hour, because he was going back in for more surgery and they didn't want to get him too hyped up before he went to theatre.

To set eyes on him for that first time ... It was just the greatest feeling of relief — that's the best way to describe my feelings right then. We had been told he had facial injuries, but we didn't know what they were. He had driven over a bomb and been blown up. His face could have been disfigured beyond recognition.

Just to walk in there and see him, to see his face, to still recognise him. He was our son. There wasn't any shock about his injuries, just sheer relief. He was alive, and we were now there with him. Pain management was a real issue for Damien, but thankfully he doesn't remember any of it. They had this push button system — it's all computerised so you can't overdose or anything — but he couldn't press it because of his arms. So we stayed there with him from then on and did it for him in rotations, 24 hours a day. I just said, 'No, I'm not leaving him, he needs someone there.'

If he wasn't in theatre, one of us was there with him, doing a shift.

STEVE THOMLINSON

After all this big build-up, we walked into the hospital and looked through this porthole window into his room, not really knowing what we would see. What we saw was this big smile on his face, and he was motioning with his eyes for us to come in. They warned us he had some bad facial injuries, and his face looked a mess then because he had all these stitches in it, and his nose wasn't where it was supposed to be.

Later, there was actually a lot of discussion about what sort of nose he could have, whether to get Brad Pitt's nose, or whose nose would suit him the most. When we first saw him, though, his head was swollen, his arms were in braces and he was a real mess, but it wasn't confronting for us. You look beyond all that. I could just see my son there, he was injured and had no legs and his arms were in frames, but all I was thinking was: let's get him better and get him back home. It's not until I saw the x-rays that I understood the extent of the injuries. Before they took it off, the bones in his remaining leg were just splintered. And today, his arms seem like they have more metal in them than bone.

But there were also some horrendous experiences in that hospital. They were sensationally good doctors, but their way of operating is that after the patient comes out of the anaesthetic, they don't administer any painkillers, because they want to check the nerves are alright. I was with him after one of the operations on his arm, and when he came out of the anaesthetic, his blood pressure went through the roof, and his heart rate went off the map. He was in such incredible pain. I've never seen him like that, ever. If I could have traded my soul to the devil and taken Damien's place, I would have. That was the worst experience of the whole thing for me. I couldn't do anything and he was in such pain, it was just unbelievable. They did come in then and gave him painkillers, but it took a while for them to kick in — 15–20 minutes, maybe longer. It seemed like an eternity and there was nothing I could do but sit there and watch him in agony. I hated that.

But all that really mattered to us was that we were there, and we had our son. He had no legs and both of his arms were smashed up, as was his face, and he was in a pretty bad way, but still he had a smile on his face.

In Fisher House there was a woman who was grieving. She was American and had just flown over there. Her daughter had done two tours of Iraq, and had gone to Germany to visit her father. She slipped on soap in the shower, and hit her head, and they had kept her alive until her mother got there to say goodbye. She was brain dead, and had been in the room next to Damien.

All I could think was: we are lucky people. You know, we've still got a son. This poor woman was just devastated. It made us realise how lucky we are. It could have so easily been so much worse for us, too. We've still got a son and he's coping quite well. It's amazing how he has coped and it's remarkable what he can now do, and still does, and where he is going and all the rest of it. But from a parent's perspective, we've still got a son. Just a year later, a couple of his mates were involved in a training accident where they came out of a helicopter and died. It's moments like that when you think to yourself, well, he's only lost a couple of legs. As he says, 'I'm not handicapped, I just don't have any legs.'

Of course there have been a lot of frustrating times since the accident, but we just soldiered on. You only get one shot at being a parent, and you have got them for the rest of your life. You do what you've got to do regardless. If your kid's in trouble, you stop and go and help them and hope to get them out of trouble. People kept asking how I could cope. Well, it's easy to cope. There is no choice.

It depends on how you look at life and whether or not you dwell on what could have been or what came before. If you are always looking backwards, you're never going to go forward. You can't do the what ifs, and that's probably one of Damien's biggest strengths. He can walk through a door and shut that door and never ever go back and open that door again and think 'what if'. He's done it on everything.

DI THOMLINSON

As I said, we might have been in Germany, but it was like we were in the United States. The Americans would helicopter in all different types of entertainers to keep up the morale of the patients. Tony Orlando, the singer, was there one day, and he asked me, 'Do you know who I am?' I said, 'No, sorry.' And then he said, '"Tie a Yellow Ribbon" — I did that song, that's me.' And one of the Baldwin brothers met Damien there, too. I remember Damien said to him, 'Are you the forgotten Baldwin?'

While in the hospital, the Americans told Damien it would be at least 12 months before he could walk on prosthetics. It was a bit like the red rag to a bull again, and he was instantly determined it wouldn't be too long. We used to say to him in Germany, 'You've got to be up there walking as best man at Marshy's wedding.' Marshy had postponed it when Damien was deployed, so initially the focus was for him to walk down the aisle.

STEVE THOMLINSON

We were in Landstuhl for a week and a half, but before we left, the army sent a medical team of four people — two doctors and two nurses — from Australia to bring Damien back home. They arrived probably three or four days before we flew back to get everything sorted out and under control and they would fly back with him. There was some concern about how he would travel on the long trip home, and they told us they would pull the pin on the trip within half an hour of the plane leaving if something happened and they didn't think he was up to the flight.

We just got on a commercial flight with Qantas, and they were fantastic. He was in eight seats right at the back of the plane — eight double seats. They can flatten them out and then they put the stretcher on top of them. They pushed everyone in economy up to the front of economy so the back of the plane was just for Damien. We had a stop in Singapore, then flew on to Sydney, and we were the first plane to land at Mascot as soon as the curfew was lifted at 6am. From there it was off to North Shore Private Hospital.

TISHA

In the space of less than two weeks, I got the worst phone call and the best phone call of my life. My phone rang and I answered and I didn't know who it was. His voice was raspy and he said, 'Hi, darling, how are you?' I thought, who is this? I said, 'I think you might have the wrong number,' and then he said, 'No, no, it's Damien.' I just started crying. He had called me on his dad's mobile. We spoke for a while and then he told me, 'I will walk again, darling.' I said, 'I'm sure you will, I'm sure you will, I have no doubt.' It was just so amazing speaking to him.

While he had been doing well in Germany, I was worried about the long flight home. It was pretty nerve-wracking until the plane finally landed in Sydney, very early on that Saturday morning. His sister gave me a call to say they had landed and were heading straight to North Shore Hospital, and I told her I would head straight there myself.

When I got there, they were still prepping Damien in his bed and getting him settled and checking that everything had gone OK, so I couldn't see him. I was expecting the worst. He had driven over a bomb. I was expecting to see him in pieces and I was worried about his face, too, but his mum told me it didn't look too bad — a broken nose, something on his lips but not too bad.

I was chatting with his parents, the doctors and his sister, and then when he was organised in the bed, the first thing they said was, 'Tisha, come and see him.'

Finally!

I think because I was expecting to see him in a much worse condition, much more disfigured, that when I saw him I didn't think he was that bad. But he was asleep; they had sedated him. I didn't want to wake him up, but then his doctor, Dr Ellis, came in and I remember him saying, 'Damien, Damien, wake up, wake up.' I said, 'No, let him sleep.' But he woke up and when he saw me, he was in tears as well. It was a really special moment seeing him and I was so glad to have him back.

I didn't mention anything about him saying he would kill himself if he lost both limbs; he was so positive about it now, I didn't want to bring it up. When I had spoken to him on the phone and he had said, 'Darling, I will walk again,' I was so surprised, and so glad to hear that. I thought he would be losing it when he found out. But even his parents said that in the hospital in Germany he was always positive about it. It was amazing.

DAMIEN

When I said I would kill myself, it was really just a throwaway line. I can assure you there was no seriousness in it. It was arrogant confidence. I knew it wasn't going to happen and I think I just wanted to let Tisha know I was the tough guy she expected me to be. I had to give my family and loved ones confidence, too, so it was all about how I carried myself and how I spoke about things like that. Perception is reality. Truthfully, I knew that if it did happen, there would be nothing I could do about it. I would deal with it. In the end, that's exactly what I did.

As I've said, I don't have too many memories of Germany. I was on so many painkillers and had so many survival medicines going through my system. They took all of the emotional depth away from what was happening to me. What I did care about, though, was my nuts. I vaguely remember it was the first thing I asked the doctors in Germany when I was coherent. I woke up and they said, 'You've lost this and that, both your legs have been amputated and this and that,' and I said, 'OK, cool, but do I still have my nuts there?' I was told yes, I did, and with that I said, 'Sweet, I'm cool, I'm going back to sleep.' That was my primary concern. It was a relief as soon as I was told it was all good there.

At that time I didn't really have a concept of the extent of my injuries and I don't think I understood what I was up against until well after I arrived back in Sydney. Initially, my right leg was missing, my left leg was still attached but broken from midway down the shin, both bones in my left forearm were fractured, one bone in my left hand was fractured, two bones in my right hand were fractured, my right wrist was broken, I had a compound fracture and dislocation of the right elbow, my nose was broken — someone said it was up around my forehead — and I had lacerations to the face, as well as brain trauma. But hey, my nuts were good.

12

DR ANDREW ELLIS

When somebody like Damien gets wounded over there, the army tends to play a fairly close hand. Because I'm an orthopaedic trauma surgeon and at one time looked after a lot of the soldiers who had been wounded who were Sydney based, I heard probably a few days after the injury that Damien would be coming back to Australia and I was asked if I would be happy to look after him.

I knew he was pretty seriously injured, but because of the security side of things I didn't get too many details. That didn't really matter, though. It's not crucial for me to know exactly who it is, or exactly what it is, because when they get there and I see it, I work it out. In Damien's case we had some discussions with the doctors in Landstuhl about what they had done and what he needed, and I spoke with the Air Force AME (Aero-Medical Evacuation) team because moving someone in Damien's condition was very complex. He was being moved intercontinentally from one intensive care to another intensive care, with many different interventions going on at once. Those interventions included a lot of stuff associated with his injuries, antibiotics and also a lot of pain-relieving infusions and catheters. The Americans had done a great job. There are a lot of elements to a long-distance move and they were bringing him back on a civilian aircraft, which was unusual for that type of injury. They rang me from Singapore to let me know the time of arrival.

There were a couple of things I needed to do before he arrived, and the first was to determine where we would put someone so severely injured. Obviously they have to be at a hospital that manages trauma, so Defence usually, but not always, looks for a big hospital, often with a reserve member working in that hospital who can be the liaison contact, but sometimes that's not the case.

We opted to put him in North Shore Private Hospital for a couple of reasons. We knew we would always have a bed for him and we knew that his privacy could be protected. The hospital and their staff were fantastic. They had looked after a number of military patients before and they really tried to look after the family as well.

So on that day, April 18, 14 days after the accident, we waited for Damien to arrive in Sydney. He was picked up by a Defence ambulance and they rang from the airport to say he was on his way. I think there were a couple of notables waiting for him, his CO and possibly also the Commander of Special Forces. When he arrived at intensive care, despite the complexity of his condition, he was very stable; the retrieval team had looked after him beautifully.

It wasn't long before we took him to theatre and began the process of lots of rebuilding, with lots of operations. He had already undergone a lot in Landstuhl — they had operated on his right elbow and arm — but over in Germany it was more about getting him well enough to return to his home country to begin the reconstruction phase there. So when he came back, there was a lot of tension around him, and lots of people coming down to see him. There were many people involved in his care, particularly the intensive care unit. A lot of effort was put into getting him comfortable, but he wasn't very comfortable at the time. He was in a lot of pain, and things weren't working well.

He was very cranky to start with and you have to remember his last memory is being in a car, driving through the night, all aroused, waiting to contact the enemy. He may have been waking up in Sydney, but he was really waking up on the battlefield, and the people around him didn't necessarily understand that. It's not that injured soldiers get cranky with the people looking after them, it's just that they are irritable, they are very vigilant and they are having a stressed reaction. It's very different to post traumatic stress disorder (PTSD), but it's still a stress reaction. He wasn't panicking about losing his legs, he just wanted to know what was wrong with him. He was also in a 'leave me alone' state, and when people were doing things to him and for him, he was a bit uninhibited in the politeness department.

And there were a lot of people. We had a number of specialists who were consulted and the number of care teams was very large. Damien had the intensive care team, which consisted of probably two or three intensive care specialists, but also all their teams, all the nurses and all the registrars. He had a special infectious diseases physician who advised us on antibiotics and wound infection, because he had problems with infection in his elbow, which was very slow to settle. He had a shoulder and elbow surgeon who was looking at his elbow. It was critical to get that arm functioning right because he'd lost both his legs. He had a hand surgeon treating a metacarpal fracture and a nerve injury, a plastic surgeon for his skin grafts, and an ear, nose and throat surgeon saw him to make sure he didn't have any blast injuries. Then he had Professor Michael Cousins, the leading expert on pain management, and he was really good on providing information to Damien about his neuropathic pain, which is the pain people get after this sort of injury where they not only have sensations of reality in their limbs but also painful sensations from the nerves going to his lost limbs, and also other nerves that have been injured by the blast. There was a psychiatrist, a liaison psychiatrist, the army clinical psychologists, as well as the army doctors. Then there was the regional health director of New South Wales, who is the senior Defence doctor, making sure everything was alright and that Damien was being looked after. And I've probably forgotten a few in all that.

So the number of carers surrounding Damien and looking after him was huge. And everybody rose to the occasion in his health care, from the cleaner through to the theatre people, through to the anaesthetist and the wonderful nurses. Everybody thought it was such a privilege and honour to look after him.

That was the most amazing thing, to see that all the staff were proud as Australians to look after a soldier who had given so much. Damien came to theatre something like 14 times. He had lots of operations, some relatively minor, some of them big. We did plastic surgery to reset his nose, reconstructed his elbow and redid a little bit of surgery that had been done in Landstuhl. There were lots of things that went on with Damien, and everybody who did something was absolutely proud to do it.

I can't give you a dramatic statement like, 'This was the moment when he realised he'd lost his legs, and did this ...' I think it was an awareness that gradually surfaced. We certainly don't hide stuff from people nowadays. We tell patients straight up if they ask, but when they wake up, you don't say, 'Mate, you're cactus, the rest of your life is useless.' We want patients to wake up to friendliness and professionalism and gradually as they come through it, and want to know things, they are given the answers. One of the impressive things about Damien was that right from the word go, even when he was cranky and irritable, he was thinking about how he was going to conquer this; he was determined to just carry on as normal.

One of the challenges in looking after him was to make sure the people in his care team recognised that was his way of thinking. From a Defence perspective, we were told to give him the best, sort of an open cheque book, not that money was ever an issue at all. The things Defence has tried to do in looking after him have been quite remarkable. It was clear he was going to be very different from even the best young man who gets involved in a work accident. In some ways, he was like an elite athlete in terms of what his expectations were and what he wanted to do and working out how to get to that point.

One of the things I wanted to get him was the best prosthetics, so we looked around and I rang and spoke with half a dozen people about it. The consensus was that the particular company which does the Paralympic team were the best people to do it. I said very early on that we wanted to get a prosthetic person involved in Damien's care, who can show him as early as possible what it's going to be like.

Damien wanted to have the whole process driven as fast as it could be and we wanted to match that for him, so we did give him what we thought was the best. Damien wanted to get up, he wanted to be on the tarmac when his mates came home from Afghanistan, and he wanted to stand and salute them when they came home. He was going to do that. It was a big deal. So the prosthetic guys helped and we got him up early, and we couldn't slow him down. Once, he was found crawling around on the floor, having got himself out of bed without his prosthetics. We were worried that some of his wildness was a manifestation of delirium, a brain injury or a drug-related effect, but in fact his mum and dad said, 'Oh, that's Damien.' I remember the psychiatrist saying that he had spoken to his mum and he was reassured by her saying that's just him.

Apart from the amputations and fractures, Damien had a traumatic brain injury and the effect of that has been assessed by neuropsychologists. I don't feel I should discuss Damien's case, but in general terms it's a common thing in blast injuries and it sometimes leads to minor, and to a degree, persisting, short-term memory problems. It can also give the person logical thinking trouble, and sometimes other issues like headaches. Damien's done pretty well and is functioning at a very high level. He's very co-ordinated and speaks well.

He's lucky that he did not have the extreme form of head injury that leads to hemiplegia, a weakness on one side of the body, or balance disorders of a significant nature. He was protected a lot by his equipment and the things he was wearing, and by some good luck probably, as much as anything.

Was he a difficult patient? Maybe challenging! I never found him difficult because I related to what he did. That's why they try and put army patients around people who wear green at least some of the time. It's important for doctors and carers to understand a little bit about what's involved in army work and how the system works. I visited him twice a day, spoke to his parents every day and contacted his unit every day for the first few weeks. Every time we would do something we would speak to his parents about it and when we had done it we would tell them how it went. We tried to make sure the family knew everything that was going on. Trying to keep everybody informed was important.

He was with us here at North Shore Hospital until May 21, just over a month. Damien is a very likeable guy and everybody who comes across him thinks what a delightful ratbag he is. His resilient nature is a unique attribute in him as an individual, and I think it has helped him along the way.

The process has not been without its struggles and hurdles, but he's always bounced back.

13

From the murky and scattered memories of Germany, there is one incident that I can't really forget. An American three-star General came in to enquire about my treatment. I had just had a really bad experience with one of my operations. My right arm had been plated and it was not clear at that stage whether the doctor forgot or chose not to put a nerve block in. Dad was watching me through a window, wondering what was going to become of his son, when he saw my heart rate jump in a matter of seconds to 215bpm. My recollection of the situation is coming to, in the most intense pain I had ever felt (up until that point), then pulling my arm across my body before passing out from it. Dad almost had a heart attack and I know it was one of the hardest things he ever had to go through. I cited this incident to the General, and then asked him to leave my room until he could properly run the facility. He seemed to be forgiving after I explained what had happened. No doubt he has had to deal with confused, drugged-up, seriously injured soldiers who — not speaking for all of us but from my perspective — were not in the mood for authority figures. At that point, my responsibility as a soldier was the last thing I wanted anything to do with.

While I was lying in hospital, I wasn't spending all my time thinking about losing limbs, or injuries, or walking again. My thoughts were with my guys. What were they doing? I was alive and that's cool, but I was also a fucking soldier. I wanted to get back out there. I was being made to sleep and lie down all the time, eat regular food and stay in places with consistent temperatures. I think more than anything it was guilt getting the better of me. Team, not self, is something that is ingrained in you throughout the training cycle and that concept is one that keeps guys alive. In a team of six, that means you have five guys who are thinking of you and you are thinking about your five mates. We go through so many tough times in training and throughout our careers, which is part of what binds us together.

When I got back home, I got a couple of cards from over there. Everyone was giving me shit about it, making casual jokes — 'Oh, typical Iceman, lying on his back' — and unrelated comments about food — just the generic comments about how bad hospital food is, when they don't really know exactly what to write — mixed in with words of encouragement. It was a pretty heavy thing for our unit, and as I said earlier, I wasn't reliving it because I couldn't remember it, but who knows whether the guys who saved my life were? Based on the statistics, there was no reason that I should have been alive. Dr Ellis would later show other doctors my stats and ask what percentage chance a patient like that would have. They always said two, three, maybe four per cent. Then Dr Ellis would say, 'That's the guy, standing over there.'

Andrew Ellis was fantastic for me. The role he played in calming my mental state in hospital is impossible to put into words. He would come in every day after I'd been moved to the general ward. He would be there at six in the morning, and he would come in at around 10pm just before he left the hospital. He was the perfect man for the job — a patriot in the truest sense, with a deep family history of service to the country and unmistakeable respect for the sacrifices Special Forces soldiers make. His quirky mannerisms, although hard to describe without seeing them, just little things, were also a welcome change from the alpha male bonding that happens between shooters.

Every day he would spend time with me, asking for suggestions or complaints I had. He was my link to the hospital, but also to the army. It meant a lot to have someone like him come in, in a selfless way, every day. It's funny to look back on what should have been a traumatic experience and remember the smiling face of a man like Colonel Andrew Ellis. He and a multitude of my friends were there for me the whole time. And most importantly, day after day, my mother and father were there and so was Leticia, without fail.

I had plenty of motivation — not least from those regular visitors — to get my life started again, and get up on my new legs as soon as possible. But there were two particular upcoming events that were massive motivation for me to be up and walking. One was Marshy's wedding, and the other was that I wanted to be there when the guys got back from Afghanistan. Not there in a wheelchair, not propped up, but there, standing on my own, to meet their plane.

I met a lot of important, high-ranking people when I was in hospital, too, and one of those was Major General Tim McOwan. He was SOCAUST (Special Operations

Commander Australia). He was an enormously approachable man and a phenomenal leader. He was one of those guys who commands respect but not in a dominant way. That guy could tell me to win a high-jump award now and I'd do my best just because of the way he is. He can really relate to you, and never make it seem he is on a different level, even though the whole time you know he is. Every good leader I have met has had that quality and Tim McOwan certainly had it. The first time we met, he said if there was anything they could do for me, to let him know. I said, 'There is, I want to be there when the guys arrive back.' I thought about how hard it was for those guys and what they went through. I knew nothing about it, had no recollection, but they lived every moment of it, and it would have been fairly horrific for some.

I was told later that they had all sorts of stuff of mine, things that had to be pulled off me, bloody leftovers from my kit, and they put them in this pit we have where you burn all the rubbish. They didn't have a ceremony as such, just a couple of people from my team and from our sister team in the platoon. I was told it was a really solemn mood. Generally you would have someone say something clever to break the tension, but this was a very serious moment as they watched the stuff go up in smoke, kind of like a cremation for the gear. I think that was all part of them letting go of the whole thing.

But I thought that being there when they came back could be my way of repaying them. Maybe it would also help them get whatever images they had of that night out of their minds. There was just part of me that felt I really owed it to them. I wanted to show the guys that I didn't lose that much, and to reinforce how hard we are as soldiers. For me it was a simple thing: you can blow my fucking legs off, but I'm still going to be standing as soon as I fucking can, doing as much as I can to charge straight back at you. When I made my request to Tim McOwan, he didn't question it. Someone not in Special Forces might have said, 'Oh, OK, you just take it easy, bud,' but guys who deal with guys like us all the time know a bit better.

It was just willpower with me. I wasn't thinking: if I can, I'll be standing and walking when they get off the plane. It didn't matter what I would have to do, or how much it was going to hurt, I was going to stand there with a steely face and be the first thing they saw. These guys saved my life. I'm not going to get knocked down and not get up. I would be there.

I never wanted to sit in a wheelchair if I had the choice, and that's how I felt about being best man at Marshy's wedding. I had people saying, 'It doesn't matter, they can get a wheelchair there,' and I said, 'This is one of my best mates' weddings, I'm the best man, I'm standing the whole time and I'm walking down there.' Everyone said I didn't have to, but I wanted to be standing there and I wanted him to have the day he deserved. Part of that day would come from having his mates standing in a row behind him.

When I was at North Shore Private, my mum had the fantastic idea that everyone who came to visit should write an entry in my Yellow Book. The Yellow Book was just a notebook that looked like it was probably bought at the hospital lobby, but it remains something I am extremely grateful for. The book reminds me of the support I got from such a broad range of people. It was interesting to see the types of notes that people wrote and to try to put what they said in context. Some would crack a joke, some would give words of support and the majority would say, 'I know you will pull through.' I expected those sorts of supportive comments, but going through the book and seeing what friends wrote makes for some interesting reading. It still does today when I open it and reflect.

'Hi, darling, I'm still here and will be every day,' Tisha wrote on the second day I was back. In fact, Tisha has something on every page.

My regiment's CO at the time, Colonel Paul Kenny, wrote: 'Damien, glad to see you in such a positive mood. I am extremely proud to be your Commanding Officer. The unit will present you the 2 Commando Regiment badges with pride, and we all look forward to you returning back to work. All the best — Without Warning, Paul Kenny.'

'Without Warning' was our unit's motto.

And this: 'You are amazing. You are an inspiration to all of us. I find it unbelievable that you have come so far in your rehabilitation so quickly. In my view, the reason for this is quite simple — you demonstrated great courage and your single-minded attitude to meeting the challenge of your circumstances. Well done. I'm very proud of you. I wish you well — Angus Houston.'

I wondered how I would go about writing that type of thing to one of my close friends.

So many people came to visit me when I was in hospital. It's strange to say it, and my injuries are something that I wouldn't wish on anyone, but the amount of love I got from everyone was incredible. Every good friend I ever had came in to visit me, we would exchange stories and they were all so happy at that stage to see how happy I was. I actually had a great time and it was an amazing feeling.

But then I would have those little moments when no-one was in the room. Moments to reflect on the fact that Tisha, in particular, had had a really tough time. When I was in Afghanistan, she wrote to my Facebook account every day, and continued until I got back. I obviously didn't know anything about it over there, and only found out when I was recovering in North Shore Private. When I read the messages, I felt an uncontrollable wave rushing up my spine and tears rolling down my cheeks. There was no point trying to man up or hold my feelings back. She had me.

TISHA

It was a way of showing my feelings daily. It was a way of still being with him while he was away. I sent him a message on Facebook every day.

I knew he didn't have access to Facebook and he would only be able to see them when he came back, but he would see that every single day I was thinking about him.

It was a way of proving to him that I was with him every moment he was away. It was also a link for me. It's really hard being apart. When he first left, saying goodbye was really hard, because we were saying goodbye without knowing if it would be the last time we saw each other. And when he was over there, I just thought about him every day and hoped he was alright.

When the incident happened, I thought, I need to keep doing this. It sounds strange, but it was my way of still keeping in touch with him, and it helped me psychologically. Every day I would write, 'Hi, darling, how are you?' I told him things I did during the day, and when I got the message about what had happened, I kept going and wrote something like, 'I just got the message and you'll be alright, darling. I'm sure you'll be alright. You'll be back here soon.' Every single day until he came back to Australia, I kept writing to him.

He was back for maybe a few weeks before he saw all of my messages. When he first came home, he was obviously in ICU and didn't have a computer, but when he did finally see the messages, he messaged me straight away: 'I can't believe you did that.' He was so emotional. He really, really liked it and told me that he was reading my notes when a nurse came into the room and couldn't help tearing up. He's tough and he doesn't cry, so he was trying very hard to hide it.

It was naturally a difficult time for everyone involved. I was still working in the pharmacy at the time and was a casual worker, so I would only earn when I worked. I couldn't take any time off for anything, otherwise I wouldn't get paid and I wouldn't be able to pay my bills. So even after finding out about Damien's accident on that Saturday morning, I had to be at work the following Monday. I was still waiting to see if he would survive and I was in no psychological condition to work.

When he came back, I would wake at 6am, go to work and work all day, then at 6pm I would finish, take a bus, go to the hospital and stay there until 10.30pm or 11pm, get home around midnight, and then be back up at 6am. And of course I was dealing with everything that was happening to him as well and wanting to be there for him. I would get to the hospital right at the time everybody else would finish work and come to visit him as well, so quite often I wouldn't get to talk to him the whole time I was there. I just sat at the back, feeling like a bit of a decoration in the room.

I think I broke down once and told him, 'I come here every day and we don't even talk.' I wasn't blaming him, and I had nothing to complain about compared to what he was going through, but there was so much pressure, it was hard to deal with everything. Some days he was fine and some days he wasn't. He wanted to show everyone he was good, so in front of his friends he would be smiling and laughing, but when everybody left I'd get the real person. He would have breakdowns and explode and be rude, angry and at times over the top. One of the nurses in the hospital came to talk to me at one point, and asked, 'How do you stay with him?'

I said, 'He's just going through a lot.' I was always trying to understand how hard it must be for him to be going through what he was going through, but sometimes we would just argue. There were times when I wanted him to understand that it was difficult for me, too, and was hard for his mum and dad as well.

But I wanted to be there, I wanted to take care of him and I wanted to be with him. I never thought about leaving. Even on the worst days when we would have an argument in the hospital, and I would go home crying, I never thought, stuff this, I don't want to deal with that. I lost count of the number of times people asked why I was still with him. Everybody from strangers to people who knew him well would ask me about it. We had only been together a short time, and we had a major task ahead of us.

But I never considered leaving. Honestly, never. From the first day I knew about the accident, I didn't think about leaving for one second, even when I found out he had lost one leg, and then two. I can't explain why. At that time I didn't really think he would walk again. I knew people had prosthetic legs when they were missing one leg, but both of them? I thought I would have a boyfriend in a wheelchair, and that he would be in that chair for the rest of his life, and that was fine with me. It didn't worry me at all.

I just wanted him to survive so badly. I thought, as long as he survives, we can deal with anything that comes after that. We will work it out. Anything that happens, we will sort it out. Survival was a much bigger issue than anything else. I used to get so angry when people asked how I could still be with him. It seemed like an attack on me as a person. Did people think I was only with him because he was fine and perfect, and now he's had an accident, I'd turn my back and walk away? I can only imagine how hard it is not having legs. No, I can't even imagine. Damien's not lazy, he's not looking for sympathy, and he doesn't feel sorry for himself. He never thinks about what could have been, he just keeps going and does everything he can. He is the most determined person I've ever met in my whole life. I admire the way he deals with his problems. He would always have his ups and downs — everyone does.

And when I discovered you could actually walk with two prosthetics, I knew he would walk again.

DAMIEN

Tisha was always there and incredibly patient. I had so many people come to visit me, many of whom I hadn't seen for maybe a year or two because of the work I had been doing, and then I had some childhood friends come out of the woodwork, too. Apparently my story spread pretty quickly around the Central Coast on the weekend it happened, and everyone was so supportive of my parents, and offered to do whatever they could to help. That included showing their support by coming down to Sydney and visiting me.

I do remember Tisha saying to me at one stage, 'I know you're seeing everyone else, but I've been here every day and have hardly spoken to you.' We were both still figuring out how to deal with the situation. I hadn't taken her caring for granted; I had just unwittingly pushed her into the background while all these other faces came into my life again. It hit me when she said what she did. The stress had finally got the better of my rock and it was time she said something. If she knew how much it meant to just have her in the same room as me, things might have gone smoother, but I wasn't communicating very well at that time.

She asked why I wasn't paying attention to her and I didn't know what to say. There was so much going on with all my friends and family that it was true, I hadn't been paying her too much attention. I had a toilet in my room and I went in there while Tisha was outside with a nurse. Then it all hit me. I lost it and started crying uncontrollably. You can only be a tough guy for so long, and I'd cracked. I remember at the time I was giving it everything I had to show everyone that the situation wasn't bothering me and I got so caught up in the act that I had ignored Tisha. When that reality hit me, it became too much.

I was doing everything I could to make sure my family and friends knew I was fine. But was I fine? I didn't realise how loud I must have been, but when I came out of the toilet, I could tell that she knew I wasn't invincible any longer. That was the first time she had ever seen the tough exterior break. And she still didn't see it, only heard it. Her invincible boyfriend had become human.

I don't think she meant what she said the way I took it, but it made me realise a combination of things. So many friends were coming to visit, smiling at me and trying to lift my spirits. I would have long chats to them about all sorts of things. It was exciting, and it kept me on a bit of a high, at least on the outside. But the continual stream of visits and old friends was just masking what I felt underneath.

Knowing that I'd inadvertently hurt Tisha was the final straw. It was like I had been wrestling with my ego and finally I knew it was OK to let it out. I still remember it was a pretty tough emotional crash. Up to that point, I had cried with my parents in a three-way hug, which we had never done before, and I'd had my dad pour out his heart about how lucky we are that I'm still here. But it was taking time for me to realise that, while mentally I wanted things to be the same and felt like things could be so, it was never going to be the same. It was reality check time.

You have to remember that my mentality had recently developed from 'you need to do more', to 'you can do more', to 'you are superhuman', because that's how the military works. Every time I walked out of a course I was 10 feet tall and bulletproof. I have a beret that says I fucking am bulletproof. I was elite, proven, and had a feeling of self-worth that I had been looking for in all the wrong places through my youth. The surprising thing for me was that the aftermath of the incident was the best leveller for me and gave me so much perspective on things.

It may sound very weird, but the scary thing was, it showed how much of a cock I had been before it. You don't need to be a cock to be in the Special Forces. You need confidence. It is a very fine line and I do think a lot of it is arrogance; the trick is not to take it too far. The fact of the matter is that I was an arrogant narcissist. I was strong, I had always been strong, but I had never become mature enough to know what to do with that strength.

14

When I was in the ICU at North Shore Private, one thing happened that I really hadn't been taught to deal with. Because your body can quickly develop a tolerance to morphine and other opiates, the pain medication I was on wasn't enough for me and I was starting to get really aggressive towards hospital staff. Not too threatening, but really aggressive. I needed to calm the fuck down.

Professor Cousins, Australia's foremost expert in pain management, was brought in to help. Because I was in so much pain when I was in ICU, they changed the medication and the mixture of everything, then made me hallucinate for the first 10 minutes. Think *Fear and Loathing in Las Vegas* — it was awesome. It's fucking fantastic to begin with, but for the next three hours it's absolutely terrifying. There's nothing you can do to stop it. I didn't really know what was happening. I might have been dreaming, but I couldn't wake up. Then I would start to realise where I was and that I could see bizarre things in the room.

'Shit, I want to switch it off. I want to switch it off. I want to switch it off.'

Tisha came in and I remember saying to her, 'Look, baby, I can see things.' She said, 'Yeah, I know.' I explained to her, 'No, I'm fucking serious. There is a dog in the bed next to me, and a guy sitting there smoking.' I described the room as I saw it. Through a particular window, everyone outside my room was dressed like they were from the Old South in *Gone with the Wind*. Dresses with corsets and guys dressed like Southern gentlemen in three-piece suits and hats. I explained it to her, and alarm bells must have started to chime: he's gone insane, this is just what we need. I think everyone probably expected it of me, so I was just living up to the expectation.

Tisha raced out and, moments of terrifying wonder later, a psychiatrist came in. Well, he looked like one. All I can remember was his clipboard and for some reason my mind clicked and seemed to say to itself, 'Seems legit.' I began to explain the wonderful World of Oz that was surrounding me. Something told me it wasn't real, but I could see it, so I wasn't sure. The psych sat down with his clipboard and I said, 'I'm going to level with you. This is what's happening. There is shit all around me, there's a dog on the bed next to me, everyone outside that window is waltzing in Tara and a fat girl just walked past you.'

He looked at me, cool as a cucumber, apparently not shocked at all, and asked, 'Have you spoken to any of them?'

I said, 'That's the thing that shits me, none of them, not one of them, has said anything to me. They have all ignored me, as if I'm not here, just walk straight past.'

He said, 'Right, that's it then.' He stood and finalised whatever he was doodling on his clipboard, which may have had his shopping list on it for all I knew.

Later on, when I had been moved to a general ward and the hallucinations had stopped, Dr Ellis explained that having hallucinations would be normal considering the medication I was on at that stage. If I'd fallen into the zone of thinking the people were real or talking to me, I might have had a real problem. But I had never thought they were real; I was just freaked out and frustrated that they were ignoring me. To this day the whole thing is a mystery to me.

Another weird thing was that for the first two or three weeks I could still feel my legs. Any time I forgot they weren't there or got side-tracked with something else, signals that were still being passed through my brain would tell me that they were there. I remember one day Tisha went to sit on the bed where my legs should have been, and I moved the stumps as if she was going to sit on my legs. I just said, 'Sorry, force of habit,' and we both fell into laughter about it.

It was a really odd phenomenon, but I could still feel them. I would be lying there and suddenly feel an itch in between my toes. I would wake up and still be able to feel my legs down at the end of the bed. They were moving and then they weren't. It was very weird. I had to get used to these sensations, even though I was pretty stunned by them. I've lost my legs, but hang on, I can still feel them. What's going on? I would be looking down at them, my brain still coming out of huge amounts of painkillers, and I could see they weren't there, but I was still getting nerve pains that just jolted.

Imagine a bolt of lightning — bang. It cripples you from that moment. It shoots straight up to your head. It becomes a mental battle of who is tougher: the nerve pain, or you. I couldn't let it bother me, could I? I mean, it was coming from nowhere. But it wasn't that easy. I would grit my teeth and clench them as tight as I could. It was a debilitating pain.

I'd still get it when I went into rehab later on, at Lady Davidson, my recovery hospital, and it was so frustrating. Here I was, trying to work this whole thing out, and trying to walk on prosthetics, and still I could feel itches between my toes and underneath my feet. I could specifically feel a tingle coming from under my foot, but there was no foot there. I was angry about it — I wanted to beat this thing so badly.

The strategy I resorted to really hurt, but it was a means to an end. I sat there and slapped the part of my leg where the bundle of nerves was, just hitting it over and over and over, and telling the nerves: 'That's where your leg finishes, that's where your leg finishes ...' Then I would do the other side as well. I think in the end I convinced my brain to stop sending those signals to me. It took some time, but eventually it seemed to work. Once again, stubbornness prevailed.

When I was at North Shore Private, I had an issue with closing my left hand, which was a very strange sensation and one which gave me a small but powerful insight into the similar issues faced by those with spinal injuries and the reality behind what they go through. It is hard to describe what it feels like to look down at something that used to work but now refuses to. Losing legs was easy in that respect: they were gone altogether. Not being able to close my hand was frustrating on a completely different level, and I am pretty sure that during my efforts I was reminded of the scene in *Kill Bill* where Uma Thurman stares at her toe and says, 'Move your toe.' When I said the same thing, I no doubt did it with less finesse than Uma, but thankfully we both got the same result.

In hospital, one thing I had in large supply was time. I needed to keep my mind occupied as best I could, which was a challenging feat when I had ADD and hadn't yet built up the mental capacity to read a book. I did try, though it was frustrating when I realised I couldn't remember a thing that had happened on the previous page. I even tested it. I read a page, then closed the book, re-opened it and was genuinely surprised at the fact that Robert Langdon could see a strange symbol in one of da Vinci's works. When I was young, I had had some problems concentrating, but if I was interested in a topic, I could focus. That power seemed so distant at this stage.

My brain had taken a pretty big knock and I had to try to rewire it to the way it was before the incident. At the time I didn't realise how much had changed, but slowly, with time, it became clear that my brain wasn't the same. It might sound odd, but you have to learn to do a lot of things again. I had to teach myself to think again, which was a strange process. Part of it is memory and part of it is about getting your thought process in order. I didn't have to relearn how to remember things, it was more that I was still coming to grips with the fact that my memory had changed. I started using the stock market as a tool. My *Financial Review* was delivered every morning, and I began to settle into what seemed like my only option for the future … a desk job.

I was no stranger to stocks, having got involved in the stock market to pass my down time on my trip to Timor back in 2007. It was a great feeling and a boost for my confidence to know that I was making something of myself. I wasn't just getting qualified in the Special Forces, but I was now financially stable enough to invest. I would have a proud piece of common ground to converse on with my dad when I got back.

Above left: I might be too young to remember it, but it looked like fun getting a ride on Pop's back, at his and Nan's home at Green Point on the Central Coast.

Above right: Doesn't everyone have one of these 'butter wouldn't melt in my mouth' photos from their childhood? This is mine, as a three-year-old, wearing my all-time favourite shirt.

Below: Dad doing some work in the yard with his shadow. Little wonder I did a stint as a labourer with this training.

My first taste of snow with Mum and my sister, Naomi, down at Smiggins. The photo was taken coincidentally about 200 metres from where I had my first run on a snowboard, after my accident, in 2010.

The powerful photo I saw on the army's website, which came with a question asking if I thought I had what it took to be a Special Forces soldier. I did. (Photograph courtesy of Department of Defence)

This is the photo that sat next to the computer in the study at Mum and Dad's house. It is Pop at a Rats of Tobruk reunion back in 1983. You can see the pride on his face. I wanted to feel that.

Proudly wearing my beret out the front of the unit in Holsworthy. It was taken post injury. The way I can tell is I have a different nose here.

Bottom left: This was the first monkey I ever saw that wasn't caged. I was amazed by this in Timor. I thought everyone was joking when they said they were pets over there.

Bottom right: Nice view up here on top of the LandCruiser during my time in Timor in 2007. Hard work, wasn't it?

Always the entertainer. Playing the guitar for the kids in Timor. They loved it … at least they appeared to. They didn't speak English.

Left: Here I am at Christmas 2007, imparting my wisdom on my grandma about how to solve a Rubik's cube. It's an ability I actually learned in the army, during times of extreme boredom.

Right: At Crescent Head, my favourite break I have ever surfed in Australia and not far from where Dad grew up. This photo was taken the summer before I went to Afghanistan.

In Afghanistan, about 10 days before my incident, when changes of socks and smelly feet were an issue.

With the team in our car in Afghanistan. We decided we would pose for this photo, so in the front there's Corporal B pretending to be on the radio and me looking very serious, but our gunner in the back didn't want to participate. The only action he looks ready for is continuing to eat what he's got in his hand.

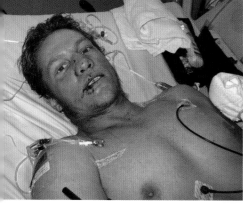

In hospital in Germany. This was taken around a week after my incident. You can see I'm still bleeding and there is blood on my teeth.

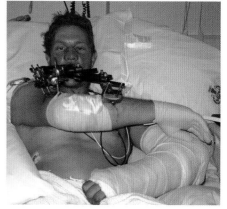

This is the salvage job the surgeons did on my right arm. It was a pretty severe compound fracture. My parents were originally told I was going to lose the arm.

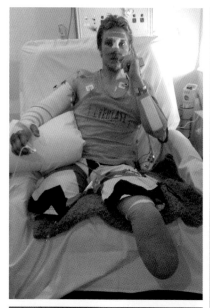

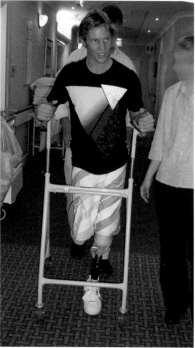

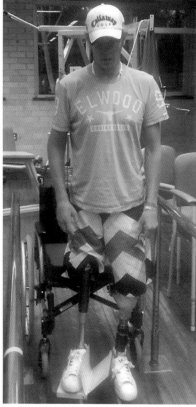

Above left: Back home in Sydney, at North Shore Private. I was just out of intensive care and into a private room. With everything that is happening in this photo, the thing that upset me the most is that due to the reconstruction of my nose, I had to wear this mask to breathe properly, and I looked like Hannibal Lecter.

Above right: Five weeks after the incident, with the first prosthetic leg I tried. They just wanted me to stand up and see how it fit and felt, but I was determined to get up on it, get that frame and get going.

Left: In the rehab centre at Lady Davidson Hospital, six weeks after my incident. You can see I had lost a dramatic amount of weight.

With the Governor-General Quentin Bryce. I'm not sure what I said, but judging by her reaction, I hope I wasn't too out of line. I was wearing my best board shorts, though. A truly wonderful woman.

The Royal Family — with Prince William. Dad, Mum, the Prince, me and Tisha when he dropped in for a visit on his trip to Australia. A great guy, and I think this was just about the moment when his backside cheek 'fell' into my hand.

Nice Autobot T-shirt, hey? At Mum and Dad's place with Tisha in late 2009.

With my coach Pete Higgins on my first snowboarding trip to Smiggins in August 2010. This was day one or two of my trip, but the big smile means I just had a great run.

With Ray and Pam Palmer — my adopted mum and dad — at the game of rugby that they organised up in Katherine in the Northern Territory. It was a tribute to their son Scott, Tim Aplin and Ben Chuck, all killed in a chopper accident in 2010, and raised $15,000 for Commando Welfare Trust.

In a hotel room in London during Tisha's and my European trip. I was doing my best not to draw attention to the fact I had prosthetic legs, and without the stick, would you know?

Above: Tisha and I in the customary 'selfie' outside Vatican City.

Left: Fore! At the Magenta Shores range. I don't worry any more about transfer of weight from leg to leg, twisting and bending of knees, and all those other things you are supposed to in your golf swing. I just belt the daylights out of the ball.

Below: My sea legs? I love this photo. It was taken in Thailand. I look like I've been locked down there and they have taken my legs away from me. Some also say: 'Damien, legless again, this time at sea.'

Left: Day one in the Canadian snow in early 2011 — not an outstanding testament to great prosthetic work. I had asked specifically for sockets that didn't spin, or to minimise that as much as possible, as this really affects my riding. I was told that was done. Now, when you look at what I am holding, notice the angle of the foot. The two fin-shaped parts coming up from the socket are supposed to be in direct alignment with the direction of the foot. As you can see, it's at about a 45-degree angle. Very frustrating to have this happen.

Right: Riding in Mount Washington, Canada, in 2011, with the Canadian Soldier On project. This was after I had done some prosthetic maintenance of my own, with the help of a fellow rider.

With former Prime Minister Bob Hawke during some promotional work for the Legacy car in the Targa rally.

On top of a mountain in New Zealand in 2011. We were dropped there from a helicopter. It was pretty special, and just 12 months after I was told I wouldn't ride a snowboard again.

Making my way across a log on the Kokoda trek in 2011.

Kokoda was tough. But here I'm the lucky one on this 'staircase'. I'm the one not carrying a pack.

Me with Ray Palmer at Isurava after we finished the 96-kilometre trek along the Kokoda Track.

At the end of the Kokoda trek, with all the guys after the memorial service we held at Isurava. In the background hang the photos of all our deceased. Scott Palmer's photo is the eighth along from the left, on the bottom row.

The memorial at Isurava. The black granite pillars are inscribed with the words 'courage', 'sacrifice', 'mateship' and 'endurance', representing the values and qualities of the Australian soldiers who fought along the Kokoda Track. I think they also represent the underlying values of the Australian soldiers I was lucky enough to fight beside.

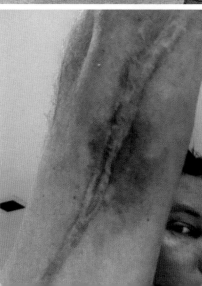

Snowboarding, too, comes with injuries. This is my tricep after an incident at Smiggins in 2012. It hurt a little, but by then my definition of pain had been rewritten.

The world-famous Escadaria Selarón steps in Rio de Janeiro, Brazil. On our trip in 2012, I was determined to get to the top of the staircase. It apparently had an impact on the somewhat eccentric artist, Jorge Selarón, who came down and allowed Tisha and me to have a photo taken with him, something which we heard didn't happen too often.

With Tisha on Anzac Day 2013. Proud.

While I was in hospital, the money continued to come in and was stacking up, so I started to build a portfolio, and I thought I had instantly gone from a stock-market pleb to the next Warren Buffett. Researching the stock market provided rare satisfying moments. I believe that your mind gets used to achievements or milestones. For me it used to be the 20-kilometre run I did of a Sunday or knowing that I had gone as hard as I could in a session on the pads at the kickboxing gym. Being able to play the stock market gave me goals to reach for even from bed, but my achievements ended up being less about my skills and more about the timing of the market.

In January 2008 my portfolio got chewed up and spat out. It was a very good lesson regarding eggs and baskets. The $30,000 I had built up from my three months in Timor shrank in front of my eyes — around 60 per cent in two days. I can remember sitting on the computer while visiting my parents on the Central Coast for holidays, and wondering why I hadn't followed the advice on stop drops, a stock-market term meaning where you would consider a sell price for what you are prepared to lose off a share. Even more, I wondered what had caused the stocks to plummet. Now in hospital, I had boatloads of time to research such things as the subprime market and try to prepare for the next, as yet unseen, crash.

Stocks and the emergence of social media are what kept me sane. And possibly also the truckload of pain relief. This stock-market research was also my first step towards eventually understanding that I would not be a soldier anymore. It was a thought that was hard to hold on to, like every other thought. At this stage I was experiencing a

151

phenomenon that I described as my five-minute memory. I would be telling a story and not be able to remember places, names and other details. Then, like magic, when I was in the middle of my next tale, the name I had been looking for would suddenly come to me. This was great at the start. It's that awesome feeling you have when there is something you are sure you know but can't remember and then you suddenly hit on it. I got that relief not just daily but hourly. That great feeling lost its effect soon after I began forgetting the names of nursing staff and doctors, or when I was reading up on stocks and forgetting information I had just researched. When my mates came in and asked the standard, 'What have you been up to?' I would tell them I'd been looking at stocks, but then couldn't recite any of the details. At least my money was performing better, though. When I was injured, in 2009, our stock market took a good turn, for most of the blue chips I had been paying attention to anyway.

I think my interest in the stock market also gave the army bosses who visited me some comfort that I could perhaps go into business when I got out of hospital. It was a good fit. I had always been interested in money, and because my awareness level as a soldier was so highly attuned to everything — you never totally switch off — I had the type of alertness that could serve me well in business. I know now about what is called a SUDS level (Subjective Units of Distress). It measures your arousal, and mine had been at 7/10 for years.

DR ANDREW ELLIS

I was always thinking about how to get the best for Damien, and thinking of how to cheer him up when he was cranky and shitty. When he had challenges like infections, I wanted to help him deal with it, and I'd seek out different opinions for him. One of the big things I thought about was Damien's rehabilitation.

I had this guy who was Special Forces, a lot like an elite athlete, and also quite wild — full of energy. He didn't take rubbish. If he didn't like what somebody had said, he'd say, 'They are no good for me,' and he'd move on to someone else. I thought, how are we going to rehab a guy like this, with all those injuries, and give him the best possible outcome? We didn't need to figure out just the best prosthetist, but also how to get him the best rehab when most facilities mainly cater to 70 and 80-year-olds with joint replacements.

Defence has got a good rehab program for less severely injured patients, but at the time they were still learning how to care for more severely injured patients. Things were in place in a policy sense, but the reality was a bit clunky. So we had to think about what we should do, and where we should do it. We had a lot of discussions and I spoke to a lot of different rehab doctors about Damien's special needs. The rehab facility had to be somewhere used to looking after people with amputations; it had to be somewhere with a hydrotherapy pool; and a place that would still be accessible to his parents, who lived on the Central Coast. We thought Lady Davidson would be just the place. It's an ex-Defence hospital, and the corridors are full of pictures of diggers and nurses from past wars.

But it proved to be a challenging choice for Damien, particularly as the nurses were very strict on procedure. Here was a young bloke, with a beautiful girlfriend, and he wanted to get out and do as much as he could, as quickly as he could. He wanted to push boundaries and push the envelope and had a goal to be up and walking in 12 weeks. Everything was slow, plodding and a bit rule-bound in his rehab at Lady Davidson, though, so he ran into a bit of conflict over that. I did a couple of visits up there to speak to them, asking them to pull back a little bit and give him what he wanted, assuring them he would be OK.

We were worried, though, because he was doing things on his elbows, basically using his arms as legs when he shouldn't have been, and then he got a bone infection, which slowed things down further. It just added to his frustration. We were saying, 'Mate, you can't use your arms like you want to use them.' And he couldn't. He would still have elbow issues five or six months after his wounding. It was a long healing process.

15

When I left North Shore Private bound for rehab at Lady Davidson, even though I had no legs, I didn't feel like a disabled person. That wasn't me. I was never a huge fan of the rehab hospital because in my mind I was still a commando and did not belong there. I considered rehab an unfortunate hurdle. The hardest thing was that everyone around me wanted to help, but in my head I didn't need help. I didn't need anyone's handouts. I was still me. I was really struggling to find the place between who I was before the incident and who I was now. My brain was slowly catching up to the reality, and even today I don't think it has caught up entirely.

I had a tough time with the occupational therapists. I used to kickbox with a mate at least three nights a week, surf four days a week, and occasionally play golf with the boys on the weekend and stuff like that. And on a Sunday, if I was bored, I would run from Randwick to Bondi and back, a 20-kilometre run, just for something to do. Mentally I was still at that level of fitness and I was still that guy. Then a therapist came into the picture, one who was used to treating older people. The therapist just wanted me to do a little bit of therapy, but I would argue: 'No, I don't want to do this.

I want to do this and this and this.' I've never responded too well to being told no, and we would have some serious wrestles over this.

At Lady Davidson I had a half-hour session each day to learn how to walk again with my prosthetics, and was taught by someone who didn't have any experience dealing with the type of knee I had. Their expert was apparently away at the time. In the rehab room, they had a floor-to-ceiling punching ball, and even though I had an infected elbow, I just went in and hit the ball; I could still move my arm. It was the type of thing I had always done when I was working out. I'd warm up with a speed ball, move on to a floor-to-ceiling ball, kick a bag and then go into the weight room. And while it was a bit different now, mentally I was still Damien, so every time I went into that rehab room I would hit that floor-to-ceiling ball while I was waiting for other patients to finish on the walking rails.

'I'm sorry, you can't use that piece of equipment,' I was told the first time I did it.

'Excuse me?' I said, disbelievingly.

'You can't use that piece of equipment, there is nobody here in this room qualified to supervise you using that piece of equipment.'

Still stunned, I said, 'I used to warm up for my gym sessions by running from my house down to the gym at Randwick barracks. There I'd use the speed ball, the floor-to-ceiling ball, kick the bag a few times, and then go and start lifting weights. And now you're telling me I'm not qualified to sit and punch a floor-to-ceiling ball? Are you fucking kidding me?'

'Did you just swear at me?'

'Yes, directly. Are you serious? Are you kidding me?'

The lectures didn't stop me. I did it every time I went in there, and most times I was told I couldn't.

I knew they were all trying to do the best thing they could for me, and were only trying to help, but I needed more, and I wasn't willing to budge.

One particular night, though, I went from zero to hero at the hospital. The staff apparently weren't too happy with one of the senior people there for some reason. Anyway, I worked out I could do rehab in the gym by myself at night. The hospital's gym shut at 6pm each night, the lights were turned off, and no-one would be in there — perfect, that's when Damien goes in and trains. Happy times. No-one could say, 'You can't use this,' or, 'Don't do that.' So I would go in there and walk between the bars, and try to get used to my prosthetics by myself.

I felt I was looking skinny and needed to build up again, so one night I was sitting in there, doing bicep curls, when I heard a voice.

'Excuse me, you can't be in here. You need supervision to be in here.'

I replied, 'OK, that's cool. Do us a favour, go and grab someone to supervise me.'

She then changed the tone: 'Clearly you are not listening to me. You cannot be in here.'

As soon as I heard that tone, I thought, fuck you. I put the weight back down, turned around and said, 'Don't you ever fucking speak to me like that again. I didn't speak to you like anything. I'm not making a statement, I'm giving you advice. Don't ever fucking speak to me like that again. Now, go fuck yourself.'

The next day, even nurses who weren't too happy with me because I'd been a little standoffish with them were coming in and saying, 'Wow, we heard you met her and put her back in her place.'

Everyone who knew about it was really, really happy. All of a sudden, I'd told this woman they couldn't tell to fuck off, to fuck off. She was probably more worried about the lawsuit that might have happened if something had gone wrong in the gym and I can understand that now, but I just wanted to get going again, and half an hour a day wasn't going to do it for me. That was a tough time and I started to lose heart with training, something I thought would never happen.

Lady Davidson was frustrating in other ways as well. Being the thoughtful, go-beyond girl she is, Tisha booked us a night at the Shangri-La on Sydney Harbour for my birthday on June 3. But the staff at the hospital were not too keen on the idea. They wanted me in my bed by 11pm. It was my birthday, though, and my girl had booked a restaurant and hotel for us. She had been through enough and I wanted to get out of there, so we stowed away for the night. It was gorgeous. Sydney had a laser show on at the Opera House and it all felt so surreal. It was good to feel I was being an adequate boyfriend after being stuck in hospitals for what seemed like forever.

Upon our return to the hospital, I was called into the manager's office and informed that I was to be checked out for not being in my bed the night before. A heated exchange followed. I attacked her management skills, accused her of failing to care enough about her patients' wellbeing. I left and decided to stay at Tisha's until she saw the light, which happened the very next day. The response from the other staff was amazing and it seemed I had turned from frustrated problem child to common-ground saint with them, and I loved it.

From the first moment I spoke to my occupational therapist, I made it very clear that my main concern was being able to drive a car because of the freedom that would give me.

With one of the first payments I received from the army after my incident, while I was still in Lady Davidson, I bought an Audi A4, which was an amazing feeling. It was my dream car. My sister was driven to her wedding in an Audi A4, and Dad took me for a ride in it. I thought it was spectacular. When I worked myself to a position where I could go and buy one, I didn't hesitate.

It just made sense to me. Before the incident I had been driving Dad's old Mercedes, but I thought instead of doing all the modifications on that, why not get my dream car and do the changes to the Audi.

A few weeks passed and I started to get a little mission creep, which is like when you are so prepared, you over-prepare for the start of a 'mission': in this instance, driving. I decided to find the occupational therapist I thought was in charge, and ask her what the hold-up was. When I found her, she advised me she had forgotten about what I had said about driving and there was nothing I could do anyway.

This infuriated me, mainly because it felt like the occupational therapist was not held accountable for failing to do her job. If this was done where I worked, she would have been in for a treat involving being very uncomfortable and cold. But clearly in the occupational therapist industry, this was not the way things worked.

Eventually I got things moving, and two weeks later I was introduced to the driving instructor who would teach me to drive with hand controls. The entire exercise was not too complicated; compared to driving an RHIB in the pitch black and stopping alongside a vessel, or matching its speed on the water, it was fairly straightforward. The driving instructor gave me the rundown and said that a good driver would only need one, possibly two lessons. This gave me the glimmer of hope I wanted, and to the best of my memory the introduction went well, with the instructor not having to touch the brake. I felt really great about the fact that I could drive, but I was met with the statement: 'You are really good and I think we can get you ready in nine lessons.' He hadn't even had to do anything for me and now he was saying he needed that long to teach me. He explained that I could have two lessons a week, which to me was entirely too long. I felt it might have been a case of tapping the bottomless pit of Department of Veterans' Affairs money.

During my second lesson, the instructor said he was going to show me something. He jumped out of the car to prove that my blind spot hadn't changed. He got back in and said, 'So, I figured you would get something out of that.' It was a huge relief to know that my blind spot had not changed in the 10 years I had been driving. From that day I decided I was going to have mysterious illnesses on my lesson days, knowing that my test was already booked in.

This didn't sit well with my occupational therapist and we had an intense argument in which I ended up calling her unprofessional. I asked whether the first aspect of her job involved assessing her client properly. I was a driver of Special Forces vehicles, who was driving a Special

Reconnaissance Vehicle at the time of his incident. This didn't seem to make her budge. She remained focused on the fact that I had cancelled my lessons. We yelled at each other for a while and I hung up.

On the day of the RTA driving test, I had to do a mock test, and then a quick drive with the occupational therapist, who would give the whole thing the go-ahead. I passed the mock test with flying colours and then we picked up the occupational therapist. She jumped in and was clearly still not too impressed by our recent argument. She began to have a conversation with my instructor — not including me — about whether she should give the test the go-ahead. I think perhaps this was an attempt to express her dominance after I had insulted her about her professionalism. So we both felt insulted — all square.

I interjected to ask the driving instructor, quite directly yet carefully, whether, in his professional opinion, given that I had just passed the mock test, he thought I was ready to have my driving exam. He responded with something about traffic conditions, and then decided we were going to do another mini mock test first. He turned to me and said, 'The occupational therapist is in the car — are you feeling the pressure?' I thought about RPGs (Rocket Propelled Grenades) being fired at our cars, the sound of rounds whizzing past, and said, 'Are you serious? I've been shot at.' His face dropped and the wave of my words seemed to hit him.

Then came the test, which I also passed with flying colours, although once back in the RTA waiting room I ran into another problem. Making small talk in there with the instructor, he asked me about the hand controls I was putting in my own car, my beloved Audi, and I responded with the name of the European design that I had chosen. He said I could not legally drive a car with those kind of controls unless I was taught. I asked if he had ever seen controls like that, and he hadn't. So in essence we both had the same level of qualification.

I was so frustrated that I needed a laugh in the RTA, so when I approached the counter I crossed my eyes. One thing my experience has taught me about human nature is that if something is noticeably different about you, most people find it's impolite to stare. So the first look at my eyes would likely be the last and no questions would be asked. I enquired about variations in hand controls if I wanted to drive, say, an Audi in Europe. I was informed that I would be licensed for all of these classes and that in fact it would have been easier to be licensed with those European-style controls. My cross-eyed licence picture was priceless, until I got sick of security guards and doormen asking me about my eyes and how I got them fixed.

For me, being in a wheelchair was an emasculating experience, although I know people don't mean to make it that way. When I was still in hospital, my parents took me out to a Mexican restaurant and I had to go in a wheelchair. We got to the door and there was a step to get up into the restaurant. Because my arms were still in plaster, I couldn't manoeuvre the wheelchair to get myself in. I said to my brother-in-law, Andrew, and my dad, 'You are the only ones who can do this.' But the lady from the restaurant was saying, 'OK, we're going to have to get him up here,' and I was arguing, 'No, no, don't touch it.'

But she insisted: 'No, it's OK, here we go — wooo.'

Wooo? A middle-aged waitress going 'wooo' at me in a restaurant, are you fucking kidding? But I was trying not to show the family how much it bothered me. Again, I realise now that people just want to help but don't know how, and they also don't consider how it might make you feel as the one being helped.

Through the recovery process, Mum was always cautious of anything that could go wrong. In particular, sometimes when I walk, and this still happens today but rarely, one of my prosthetics doesn't do exactly what I expect. This can be caused by uneven ground or little things like that, but it ends up with me thinking my arm is like Kelly Slater's during a massive cutback, but really it looks like a drunk losing his balance, with arms flailing everywhere. Mum being Mum would always worry and stick her arms out ready to catch me. This created a problem. It's like someone watching a beginner on a snowboard. Those who have experienced it know what I am talking about. The snowboarder is taught this: if you think you are going to run into something, focus on your line, the path you are supposed to be heading. If you think 'tree … tree … tree … TREEE', it's like a magnet and you will go towards a tree. It's a similar thing with Mum holding her arm out helplessly. God love her, there was nothing I could do to convince her to stop. Figuring I would be fine and could balance, I decided it was best that she just walked in front of me, which she made no argument against.

She is gold.

During my early recovery I met a really good guy named Bill Rolfe, who was the Repatriation Commissioner then. Bill lost both legs below his knees in Vietnam. He's just the nicest bloke, and one of the first things he said to me was, 'You are going to have to have a really good relationship with your prosthetist.' At the time I didn't fully comprehend the gravity of what he was telling me, but it was only a matter of time before I would understand the importance of his message.

At first it was all new for me and I always blindly trusted the prosthetists and never questioned anything they did. At this stage, too, early on in my recovery, my brain was in no condition to be processing the information I was taking in and the things I needed to do. I had problems with the first prosthetist I saw, though at the time I had no idea that my problems weren't universal issues. I thought I would get all the respect in the world from my prosthetist because of everything I'd been through and my background in Special Forces. But all I was given was a sales pitch about 30 years of experience he had tightening legs. At the time, I thought that seemed good enough. In hindsight, my assessment of the situation isn't the same.

I guess I just assumed that I would be well looked after, and I was told by the military that I was getting the best treatment from the best people available. Everyone swore to me that this was the case, including the prosthetists. Looking back, I can see it was the kind of line people threw at me without thinking. Defence really didn't have great treatment plans in place. It's not surprising because they hadn't had to deal with my type of injuries since Vietnam, with the exception of one or two from Iraq, from what I understand. Over time, my prosthetics proved to be a source of so many problems and so much frustration for me.

Having no legs does come with some advantages, however. I never have to worry about itchy feet, stubbing my toe, cutting my toenails or struggling to find the perfect-fitting shoe. And there are various tricks I can do with my knee. I'm pretty sure I'm one of the few people in Australia who can stand at a bar and have one foot facing forward and one foot facing backwards. Sure, wearing the prosthetics was painful, but I put up with the pain from the start, because there was nothing more important to me than feeling normal. My brain at that stage hadn't dealt with the fact that I had any type of injury. I was still Damien, and I just wanted to be as normal as humanly possible. That included walking around and doing simple things that most people do every day.

It hurt. But I didn't think about how much it hurt or how hard it was, because I didn't know any better at that time. Even though I was frustrated at the pain while it was all going on, it was only later that my anger at some of the prosthetists really started to come to the forefront.

I struggled to walk on some of the prosthetics, but I was told consistently in the early stages that I was the problem, not the treatment or the prosthetics. It was incredibly tough because I was trying to describe sensations I was experiencing for the first time and had nothing to compare the pain to. The legs were uncomfortable and difficult to operate. I needed a walking stick to move at all. But I wasn't even thinking properly about it at the time. I had a single-minded goal to be there on the tarmac, standing to meet the guys when they returned home from Afghanistan. When there is something that matters so much to you, you would do anything to achieve it. They could have given me 20-foot stilts, and I still would have got to where I needed to be. That was my focus.

I had a great relationship with the rehab personnel from Defence, though, and there was some back and forth between us at the time about the things I should have been able to do but was finding impossible. They would say, 'Well, we have to get that core of yours working.' I would reply, 'I'm balancing on one leg and it's behaving like it's walking downhill. My core could be as strong as an Olympic wrestler and I still would have no control over the knee bending.' The response: 'OK, I will come and have a look.'

I continued to communicate my frustrations, and alterations were made regularly. Unfortunately these tweaks led to one of the most embarrassing experiences I have had post injury. I was walking through a restaurant for dinner with my gorgeous girl, Tisha, and my prosthetic socket snapped, causing me to fall crashing to the ground. No matter how thick your skin is, you feel emasculated. Another irritating experience I had with a prosthetist was when I walked out of his office, having just been in to have alterations done to my 'walking legs', and was carrying my 'snowboarding legs'. I was on such a high as I had these new legs and was about to experience a new-found freedom on the snow. Being a smart-arse, though, the prosthetist said as I left: 'Don't be surprised if you don't get further than 10 metres.' If I could stomach seeing the guy, I would love to race him on a snowboard now.

Soon after the restaurant incident, I had a prosthetist from Melbourne look at the socket design. He explained that he hadn't made legs using that design for 20 years, which partly infuriated me, but also gave me hope that the path to walking 'normally' again may be less painful than I once thought. So, after a brief consultation with Defence, I was on a plane to Melbourne. It's a tribute to the ADF that they were willing to pull out all stops to improve their casualty management. I was so happy with the solution we came up with that I rang the prosthetist at least once a week for several weeks, explaining how I thought he was a magician, calling him Copperfield and Houdini.

Although my situation was unfortunate, and so frustrating initially, I did manage to achieve a new outlook on prosthetics and that affects the advice I now give others. But the sad fact is that if a less assertive person was treated the way I was, they would not be walking, and I hate the thought of that.

The socket is the most important thing. If someone takes the time and effort to make that correctly, it becomes the basis for a good prosthetic. Underneath the socket are all the different working parts that suit the individual person. Each part is designed for different purposes. It's anything but a 'one size fits all' system, and when prosthetists do not understand that, it's very disappointing.

I also had problems with my feet. I didn't get a choice of different types of feet from which to pick the ones best suited to my needs and conditions. I only got what I was given. When I went to the United States much later on, I noticed they had a much bigger selection to choose from because of the sheer number of amputees over there. When I went to a clinic there, I was offered the option of new sockets, and the choice of four different brands, and different styles of feet. In Australia there are fewer options to work with because we don't have the same market. Amputees are given a foot and then after eight months the prosthetist will ask if the foot is good, and if it's not, they say, 'Maybe we can get a new one.' It's a different world here.

Things are much better for me now because I know how to describe the problems I am experiencing, but I have had my moments. At one point, I bought a particular leg because I was told it was the latest and greatest technology available. It turned out to be a trial item and I was one of its trial monkeys. It's now discontinued. Those sorts of experiences left a bad taste in my mouth. While prosthetists are not all the same, it's frustrating to have to think twice about the people you naturally assume have your best interests at heart.

16

The guys from my unit were finally about to arrive back from overseas, and as I had wanted and planned, I was going to be there, standing on my two new legs only 12 weeks after the accident. It had been a battle at times, but when the day arrived, I forgot about all the frustrations, struggles and arguments I had been through to get there. I remember walking in to meet the plane that afternoon with the SOCAUST, Tim McOwan, and he was really happy. The whole time during my recovery, whenever we came into contact, he was super stoked about the progress I was making. And now here I was, the most seriously injured soldier since Vietnam, who had managed to be up walking again only six weeks after the incident, standing there, waiting for my guys.

I remember looking down a long tunnel to the plane. I had stood back from the SOCAUST and his entourage of three or four people, but he looked over at me with an extremely fatherly grin and waved me over. He pointed his hand at the ground as if to say, 'This is your spot here.' He moved his entourage and anyone else out of the way, just so I could be there. One of the first things the guys would see when they came out was me standing there. That made me feel amazing as well. The SOCAUST, a Major General, had moved out of his position and waved me over with a smile that said, 'You deserve to be here.' Even with all the pain I went through to be there, this moment made it 1000 per cent worthwhile.

I was looking down the tunnel, and the next thing I knew, the guys started coming out. I could see their faces lighting up. I could see the excitement on everyone's face, even guys who weren't great mates. It was all worth it, I thought. This is going to make at least a couple of them get that little bit of extra sleep and hopefully they will let go of something that may have bothered them since the night it happened. No matter how tough you are, the reality of the incident was pretty traumatic. It would have been for anyone. It took a while for the guys to open up, but later on, when they did, they told me how helpful it was to see me there that day.

I've got respect for all the guys I was lucky enough to work with, and I look up to them. That respect is mutual, and it comes from the heavy and reliable teamwork ethic in Special Forces. Every single person who got off the plane shook my hand. There was a procession of people as they slowly came out. Some gave me a little hug, had a joke, and when they'd all got off my entire team stood behind me.

These are the guys I look up to. I was lucky that in my role I got to work with guys I idolised, because of how well they do their job and how well they operate under duress. So seeing the pride that they had in me as they stood there behind me, with me, was a moment similar to when your dad looks at you and says, 'I'm proud of you.' To have people who you respect so much give you that amount of respect … It was really one of the most powerful moments I have had in my life. It was an awesome feeling.

I had no preconceived idea of what it would be like that day. My full focus had been on getting to that point, rather than thinking what it would be like. I honestly thought I owed it to them, and that was all that mattered. So apart from being powerful, it was also extremely gratifying. I also made it to Marshy's wedding up in Newcastle. I knew I would. When he asked me to be his best man before I went away, I was so proud. There was no way anyone could stop me standing by his side, no matter how much it hurt. I did end up having a walking stick at the time, but I was still standing, and from what I remember, I did a fantastic best man's speech. It was gratifying to be able to be there for him and with him. Not even running over a bomb was going to stop me from doing that.

After conquering my two most important goals, I had to face the reality of what came next. What was going to be my thing? I was not the same guy anymore. It was a time when I really started to question myself, and I would spend a lot of time thinking about being a commando, and what that now meant for me. What was next? I didn't have a next. I'd put myself in a position of not knowing what was going to come next. Reality hit me when my company eventually deployed again. That drove everything home in a big way. I wanted to be that guy again, but how could I? I had worked so hard for 12 months just to get into the program, and I had been in the army for five years, and now all of a sudden my boys were redeployed and I thought, what the fuck do I do now?

Could I be a soldier? A real soldier? The Chief of Army, Ken Gillespie, had been kind enough to tell me I definitely had a job with the Defence Force, but would I be able to become a commando again? I eventually started to look at possible degrees and other ways I could make an impact in a different industry, but it soon became apparent that I would have to give my recovery a bit more time. When I tried to write an essay, I could not concentrate for longer than five minutes.

I also started bridging courses to try to make up for what I'd missed at high school. These courses attracted a variety of people, but my fate was sealed when, in front of an impressionable group of youngsters taking a second bite of the cherry, just like me, a woman in her late 40s explained how she was sure that Australia was selling uranium under the table to someone and the government knew who. Not surprisingly I took offence to that, knowing we have competent agencies keeping a watchful eye on that sort of thing. And more to the point, how would an operation that large go unnoticed? So I piped up and asked, 'Who are we selling it to? And regardless of who you think it is, wouldn't it be a breach of every trade agreement in existence?' The lecturer stepped in before she had a chance to respond and said, 'Everyone is entitled to their own opinion.' But what if that opinion is fantasy?

I understand that different points of view are as valid as your own, but some impressionable kid is going to take what that woman said way more literally than it should ever have been taken. Instantly, conversations I had had with girls in pubs — generally girls who were studying at uni and had a boatload of knowledge about headlines bastardising wars — came flowing back. They were happy to put their point across, but when I would highlight that, in my opinion, uni students should be seen and not heard, they got upset. With that, my course was over.

During the recovery stage there is a lot of learning to do and I was forced to learn new things. Whether it was getting told I wasn't good enough, or getting told I was never going to ride a snowboard again, or that it would take 12 months to walk on prosthetics, every time I hit an obstacle I simply broke it down. I took bite-sized pieces, and got through it. That was what I learned to do all the way through the recovery process and it's something I still do today.

I changed my approach to problems and, believe it or not, my current ability to approach problems was improved and refined by the adversity I went through and everything that surrounded it. It's all about turning something like that, which might seem like a hurdle, into a positive. I think that might be the secret to it all. Let's face it, no-one ever has a gold-plated run, regardless of what it looks like from the outside. Life's hard work and it's all about getting through the tough periods. For me, there have been loads of them, and I've made shitloads of mistakes along the way. But I would always take responsibility for myself, assess the situation and move forward. I would always work out a way forward, and not worry about looking backwards at what was behind me.

Hospital was basically a baptism of fire for my philosophy of strong self-belief. I approached it by knowing that I could do what I dreamed of doing, rather than by saying, 'I might, possibly.' 'I might' insinuates doubt. If you know you can do something, you approach it with face-off confidence. You approach it in a completely different way than if you have doubt in your mind. And in my experience, that confidence makes a hell of a difference.

Since my accident I have been lucky enough to meet some important people and truly inspiring leaders. Quentin Bryce came to visit me while I was in Lady Davidson, and a great picture of the two of us was taken, with her giving me a hug. I was going to send it to her on Valentine's Day. It would have looked perfect in a heart-shaped frame sitting on her desk, but I figured it might have been mildly inappropriate, given she is the Governor-General.

Prince William was another great leader I got to meet during the course of my recovery. He came to Holsworthy and met a group of us who had been injured overseas. He is tall and strikingly good-looking in person. That day I was the first person he spoke to, solely because of my proximity to the door he walked in. But he had done his homework about my situation and stood and had a chat with me for a good while. We spoke about my trip to London at the end of 2009 when, to try to reward Tisha for her unwavering support, we went to Europe, and how great it looks when it snows in London. Then we traversed back to talking about my injury. He said something that made me quite proud, but at the same time it was something I wished everyone who dealt with me would think. He said, 'So you were walking in six weeks?' Then quite humbly he added, 'I would expect that from someone who does the job you do.' This was a huge thrill for me and I will always remember Prince William as a great guy.

Then we proceeded to photo time. A couple of the boys were standing off behind us and I figured they would be looking, so I pretended to squeeze Prince William's arse.

174

At that exact moment, he switched support legs and placed his bum cheek in my hand. With a smile he said, 'I think someone might be touching my arse.' I looked at him with a shocked smile and mustered up: 'I am only human, mate.'

Another great experience was when I was lucky enough to have one of my mates from basic training, Steerie, take me to watch the fight between Danny Green and Roy Jones Jr. We had organised it pretty quickly and I knew that Steerie's coach was coming — a bloke who had represented Australia in judo and been around the fight scene for ages — so I was very happy to go there with them, not to mention how fantastic it was watching Greeny TKO Jones Jr in the first round. It was the loudest thing that I have ever heard. It was awesome.

After the fight I asked if we could sit down for a while in the lobby of Acer Arena so that I wasn't wrestling with crowds on my way out. Everyone — there were about eight or 10 of us there — looked at each other with cheeky grins and said it was fine. At that stage I got the drift that something was up. We sat down like the fight fans we are and spoke about the stellar performance Green had put in. Before I knew it a bloke had walked up to us in a black suit with a tag round his neck. He shook Steerie's hand, then he smiled, walked over and shook mine, saying, 'Damien? Follow me, mate.' I looked at the lads with a knowing smile, and they all looked stoked. We then proceeded down to the dressing room and were led in. The room was full of media and a bunch of other people. I was happy enough with just being there. Then Greeny walked out in a towel and his management said, 'OK, media, that's it. We will need you to leave unless you are a close friend of Danny's.

Please leave.' And then Greeny looked over at us and said, 'You boys are right!' I thought, shit, this is cool. The biggest fight in Australian history and I am in the locker room of the winner. There was nothing that could have prepared me for the next bit, though.

Greeny walked over to me and said, 'Hey, mate, you're Damien?' I was fucking speechless, that's what I was. We talked for a bit and got some photos, then he asked his manager to grab his walk-in jumper from his bag and bring it over. He gave it to me and said that it was the least he could do. I grabbed him and gave him a hug, and he said in my ear, 'I am not half the fighter you are.' The bloke is pure class. When I was going through a dark period later on, in 2011–12, he sent me a set of gloves, and there is no doubt that along with the jumper, they are getting framed and going straight to the pool room.

I would also meet Chief of Defence Angus Houston, who is another great man who makes you feel like he is your proud, loving grandfather. He has always been brilliant and has an air of calm that surrounds him, which I find relaxing. I heard from the boys who have been overseas with him that he is a bit of a machine. Up at 4am to run and he can run with the best of them. This opinion came from a mate of mine who is a remarkable runner himself and had trouble keeping up with him on their runs at the air base.

I'll always be grateful that my injury provided me with the opportunity to meet these amazing leaders.

DI THOMLINSON

Quentin Bryce is one of the most gracious, genuine and impressive people I have ever met. She asked for permission to go and see Damien at Lady Davidson Hospital, and it would be in her private time, not in her official public capacity. Every day on the website of the Governor-General they publish her diary so that the public can see what she's doing, but her visit to the hospital was in her free time, so it doesn't appear in the records.

Her security went to the hospital ahead of the visit and checked everything out to make sure things were safe, and naturally they paid a visit to the matron. All the nurses then knew something was going on, and that someone with a high profile was coming to the hospital, and they were all having bets on who it would be.

On the day of Quentin Bryce's visit, Pink, the singer, had arrived in Australia, so for some reason a lot of people thought it would be her. Of course we knew who it was and so did Damien, but that was about it.

Quentin Bryce turned up, and was met outside by two people from Damien's unit. They walked straight into his room and her bodyguard shut the door behind him. She stayed there for an hour or so, then her security people knocked on the door and told her they needed to make a move. She just packed up and left after that, which I think left a few of the staff a bit dirty because she didn't do the usual meet and greets with them. I thought to myself, ha, Damien's finally getting back at you for all the tough times you have given him.

He got out of Lady Davidson three months to the day since his accident.

17

During my recovery my right arm remained infected and I underwent four operations to attempt to isolate where the infection was, what bug was infecting my bone and then solve the problem. I was told by my first micro-biologist that I would probably need to be on an antibiotic for the rest of my life and at best the rest of the year. Alternatively, I could have a little IV pump attached to me that I had to carry around. I wasn't having a bar of that. This was not the opinion I wanted, so I was going to keep firing them until someone gave me the right answer, which was, 'Yes, we are going to fix it, end of story.' The main problem was that they couldn't grow a culture from the infection and as a result they couldn't work out what would kill it. I was on a broad-spectrum antibiotic for ages, hoping more than anything to fix it, but that wasn't good enough. The bone was basically being eaten away by the infection.

I had to be on all kinds of medications to sort out what was going on with that arm, and the different antibiotics I was on were absolutely kicking my arse. I was taking three separate oral antibiotics and one intravenous antibiotic, as well as my pain medication. They just destroyed my insides. The meds had me scratching my arse to the point where it bled because of the bacterial impact it was having on the body. Everything was just haywire. After the antibiotics, I'd sleep for four or five hours on the couch, then wake up and it would be time to have more.

For the 12 months we were trying to fix this infection, I had a hole in the skin of my elbow that exposed my triceps tendon. Getting it wet was a big no-no. I wanted to do as much as I could to get this right, but salt water was what I was really craving. The whole time, all I wanted to do was get back in the ocean. That's all. I had that open wound on my elbow, though; it couldn't be closed because of the pus coming from where the bone was infected. I still have a hole in the bone from the infection.

I just wanted to go down to Clovelly. I didn't want to surf, I just wanted to get in. I don't care what anyone says, salt water cures everything. But my theory was falling on deaf ears. I told the micro-biologists, everyone. Ordinary tap water would make it worse, too, so I had to wear plastic bags in the shower. More than anything, this infection was an incredibly frustrating experience. After operation number four, Dr Ellis brought in a micro-biologist called Professor Bernie Hudson. He explained that as long as we didn't have a culture grown, we would be just shooting in the dark at the infection. I said, 'Start shooting.' I told him to keep trying to grow samples. I didn't care what they put me on, I just wanted the infection out of my arm.

A little while after we started the process, Bernie came into my hospital room, sat down and told me that they had identified something. It was a type of drug-resistant Staph Aureus, or Golden Staph. He said he didn't like doing this, but would I be happy hitting it with four major antibiotics? I said, 'Just attack it.' This 'attack' involved the four antibiotics: Ciprofloxacin, Fucidin, Romycin and Tigecycline. It's amazing that while at times I can't remember the names of people I met three days ago, I can instantly remember the names of those four drugs.

Tigecycline was an IV antibiotic that had to be given twice daily and this was done for the first few times at a clinic in North Shore Private generally reserved for cancer patients. Being there was an eye-opener for me. I had some great conversations with other people in the clinic, and was given yet another insight into how lucky I was. I mean, I was unhappy about having to take a few antibiotics, but there were people around me who were going through chemotherapy. An ex-girlfriend of mine had had Hodgkin's lymphoma, so I had a bit of experience witnessing how debilitating the drugs used in chemotherapy are.

At that stage I was desperate to be out of the hospital environment. Yet again, the rock-solid Leticia was there with me to save the day and help me administer the drugs. With her Master in biochemistry and my ability to convince doctors that I didn't need to be in hospital, I was set to start treatment at home. During this period I had a pick line that delivered the drug straight to my heart because the chemical was so strong that it would collapse a vein. The only problem with this was that the other antibiotics I was on were affecting my skin's tolerance to the glue that kept the pick line in place, creating burn-like scabs that I am lucky did not leave scars — to this day, I am allergic to bandaids. After around three months, though, I got the great news that the cultures they had grown had been killed off. Soon after that, the year of frustration was over. The infection had finally left my body.

During my dramas with the infection, I developed another problem. My arm was leaking fluid out my elbow and when it was in a cast it got extremely itchy. Frustrated by plastic bags in the shower, and keen to get into the salt water, I convinced my doctor I needed a fibreglass cast. I'd seen Mick Fanning, who had broken his arm, snowboarding in Japan wearing one. I thought he could obviously get in the water with it, so I wanted one, too. I ended up getting a fibreglass cast, but I was told that I still had to cover it with a plastic bag when I showered, defeating the whole purpose. The doctors were just worried about the infection.

Amongst all this I actually fell on the other arm, my left, and snapped one of the plates in it. I didn't realise until the next day when I went to use a walking stick and felt faint again. So Dr Ellis replated both my arms at that time, but still we couldn't stop the right one from leaking. And the itchiness never stopped. Imagine the worst itch you can, and now imagine not scratching it. It was the worst. I tried everything from chopsticks to knitting needles, which I actually found to be the best. I eventually couldn't take it anymore, and, one afternoon, out came the Leatherman. If you are familiar with the saw-like tool on one of these, you can guess how long it would have taken me. Not only was it a tiny saw, but in order not to cut my skin, I was forced to cut in only one direction, not in a sawing motion. Bear in mind that the cast began around my hand and ended at my armpit. After around two and a half hours, I experienced one of the most relieving moments in my life: I finally got a wet washer to the itchy arm.

When Tisha got home from work, she was not as impressed as I was with my handiwork but continued to soldier on and administer my night-time dose of Tigecycline. The doctor then wanted to put the cast back on, but I told him I'd just take it off again and he knew I was serious. So I negotiated that he recast the arm, but in two pieces, with straps that went around it so I could take it off from time to time. Before the split cast I was having major problems sleeping. Sure, I was getting some during the day after my antibiotics, but I couldn't get comfortable at night.

It was getting to me and I remember at one point Leticia was pretty worried that I was addicted to painkillers. She decided to hide them from me. So when I couldn't sleep during the night because of the pain, I couldn't find the pills. I would be in agony at 4am — bone infections are one of the most painful things you could have, and my threshold for pain is fairly high — but I couldn't find my painkillers. She felt bad for me, but she was genuinely concerned. She had never dealt with anyone with chronic pain. She couldn't understand why I was taking them even when I wasn't in pain. I told her it was because I had to keep the pain medication at a certain level in my system, even if I wasn't in pain, because if I didn't, and I took my first painkiller at 1am when the pain started, it was still going to hurt the rest of the night and there would be nothing I could do. It was difficult finding the right balance with the pills.

Tisha was working in the pharmacy then, and she introduced me to this stuff called Restavit, which is an antihistamine. It's a super strong antihistamine. It says on the box: 'May cause drowsiness.' It should say: 'Don't make any fucking plans.' It's amazing shit. I hadn't slept a full night in three months, and then I had a dose of Restavit. Wow. I woke up and felt a million dollars. The feeling of 'I'm awake now' was the most amazing feeling. I couldn't take them all the time or it would have diminished the impact, but they were good for me when I could take them.

From these stories, it's obvious I did get frustrated about a few things, but losing both my legs was never something I dwelled on or something that got to me. What did get to me, though, was when people would let me down. After getting out of Lady Davidson and moving in with Tisha, I had a team assigned to do various jobs and one guy in particular was an externally hired liaison for me. While I tried to be as independent as I could, there were some things I wanted some help with — particularly cleaning. I could lie on the couch all day, get up and make toasted sandwiches, or order in some food if I needed to. I didn't really need anyone, but I felt it was unfair that Leticia would work all day, then come home and have to do chores around the unit.

My liaison was a guy I used to call King Useless. I rang him and said all I want is a cleaner to come around and clean. Not a carer, just a cleaner. The first guy he sent around was a really nice guy. He came in and sat on the couch while I was watching Foxtel. He asked me how I was going and I said I was good. Then he asked if I needed anything done. I said, 'Aren't you here to clean?' He said, 'No, I'm here as a carer.' I couldn't believe it. I said, 'I want you to clean that bathroom, because that is the only thing I can't do.' He had no experience, and it was a waste of time. He came twice and then I rang up King Useless and said, 'Send me a fucking cleaner — once a week.' What happens? The same guy comes back.

I rang up yet again and said that I didn't want that guy to come back, I wanted a cleaner. The next guy came over and asked, 'Hey, how you going?' I said, 'Great, can you start by cleaning the kitchen?' And he said, 'I'm not a cleaner, I'm a carer.' I had just had my intravenous medication and was about to pass out, so I just said to him, 'Don't be here when I wake up.' I woke up and he was asleep in the spare room. But he had tried. He used bleach to clean the bathroom — enough bleach to clean out a sewage plant. It was so strong. It was woefully strong. I couldn't believe this was happening.

The cleaning and communication debacle continued, though. In September 2009 Leticia and I went up to Darwin for my cousin's wedding. My elbow was still open and infected at that stage, but I was sick of doctors telling me what I couldn't do, and there was no way I wasn't going. My logic was: 'What, is it going to get double infected?' Neither of us had ever been to Darwin before and we had a great trip, one that we were both very much in need of.

While we were gone a red dust storm hit Sydney. I knew it would have hit our place, so I called my rehab manager, King Useless, and said, 'Look, I hear there has been a red dust storm. I need the cleaner to come over to my place on Tuesday.' I'd given him about a week's notice just to make sure it would happen. 'A cleaner, not a carer.'

The reason I wanted a cleaner there was because I knew that the balcony would be covered in red dirt, and I was expecting an important visitor on the Wednesday. I rang King Useless on Monday when I got home and he didn't answer. The next day, nobody showed up. I rang again at lunchtime. No answer. At five o'clock I cracked. I called and left a message, saying, 'You are fucking fired. I don't give a fuck. Don't speak to me, or anyone involved in my case again. The reason why I wanted you to organise this clean-up, which for some reason you are incapable of doing, is that Angus Houston is coming to my house tomorrow. I didn't tell you because it was on a need-to-know basis.'

I rang Mum: 'The backyard is bright red. Can you please come down to help me clean up? We have to do this.' So my poor mum and I, mainly Mum, spent hours cleaning. Then Dave, one of my mates from the army, came over, and Tisha did a bit in the afternoon. King Useless eventually called me back, but I refused to pick up my phone. He left a message offering to come and clean it up himself. I thought, dude, you've had a week to organise it. I hadn't told him initially why the clean-up was so important, but I shouldn't have had to. That's what I mean about being let down.

There were some tough times in that first year, but there were also some good times, particularly at Christmas when Tisha and I went to Europe for a holiday. There was a slight hiccup on a stopover in Dubai. At the airport, they refused to let me push my own wheelchair. I said, 'If I'm getting into a wheelchair, I will push it myself.' And they said, 'No, sorry, Sir, it's airport policy that if you are in a wheelchair, we have to have control of it, for insurance.' So there I was in a wheelchair, getting pushed by a middle-aged woman. After that I decided I was always going to have my legs on when I travelled, even if it makes it a bit more uncomfortable. At that stage the doctors still weren't close to sorting out my arm issues, so I had that to contend with, too, continuing with the broad-spectrum antibiotic pills while we were travelling. It was a great trip, though, and it gave us a chance to get away from things a bit. We even spent New Year's Eve in Paris. With lots of walking it was tiring at times, but a truly memorable trip for both of us. Seeing the sights that you have read about, walking through the Tower of London, staying at a hotel which overlooked the Tower Bridge, and all through Europe we basically did the quintessential tourist holiday — the Leaning Tower of Pisa, the Eiffel Tower, the Arc de Triomphe, Sistine Chapel — it was great. So many things you see in 'fantasy land' or on TV and then you are actually there. It was extremely surreal, and a wonderful holiday.

Even though I was in pain much of the time, there were so many different things happening around us that it took my mind off my problems for a brief period. The hardest thing was when I would get back to the hotel room, overlooking wonderful sights, and my legs would be hurting so much I couldn't do anything but lie in bed in agony. That's when I felt bad for Tisha, being stuck there with me. But as always, it was never a worry or concern for her. I wanted to do this for her, take her on this holiday. I thought it was a nice way to say thank you for everything she had been put through — mostly by me. She deserved some reward, and so much more.

DR ANDREW ELLIS

For people who have sustained injuries like Damien's, one of the big challenges is managing the pain and getting off the medication. I know that recently he has been reflecting upon the times when he had a real struggle with pain medication. To me it wasn't so obvious at the time because he puts up a very strong front and also because it's common for those with injuries like Damien's to require some form of medication six, 12 or even 18 months after the incident.

I wasn't writing his prescriptions, so I didn't have a direct view of that side of things, but I'd say struggling with pain medication is a common problem. With OxyContin drugs and things like that, doctors try to keep the patients on them for as short a period as possible, because it's very easy to take too many of them. Young men in general can be more silent and less articulate on things like that and will often say to themselves, 'Look, I'll just have another one.' The drugs can contribute to mood changes, irritability and crankiness, but so can the natural process of recovering from a major injury. All of these behaviours can be linked to depression, but having depression doesn't necessarily mean sitting around doing nothing. It can mean saying or doing things you later regret, or exhibiting behaviours that appear a bit uninhibited, or thinking in a slightly disordered way.

Patients with major injuries are looking to fight their way through a lot of psychological and emotional issues, not just the physical ones. Damien had his career, his body image, his pain, his relationships and his mates to think about. The injury changed him permanently in some way. He'd been through a lot, and now people were trying to tell him what to do, and he must have thought, mate, why are you telling me what to do? What did surprise me — no, what amazed me — was how quickly he was able to get up and walk. That was just like something out of a classic novel. He was just like the cliché of the guy who gets up bleeding off the deck and takes himself to hospital. He was so driven.

18

Even though I was feeling a bit lost with my new circumstances, I knew for certain that I wanted to get back to work as soon as possible. About three weeks after leaving Lady Davidson, I was back at a desk job in one of the army offices, on and off, three days a week. Work was a place where I felt comfortable, and after all the disruptions, I wanted that sense of normal back. It was great to be speaking to the guys and starting to get back to being myself again. I didn't know where it would all lead, and how I would feel about the destination, but at that time I was happy to be making a start on my new direction.

The problem with my plan was that I had effectively taken a punch from three of the world's best heavyweights combined, and I had had a terrible concussion. My brain was still trying to cope with the injury, and it was affecting my concentration and my ability to solve problems. The situation was amplified by various medicines, painkillers and antibiotics, but in my usual defiant way I decided that I was going to try to find a way around the problem. I started by concentrating on share research, just as I had done in the hospital, and then progressed to finding simple songs I used to know on the guitar but which were not coming naturally anymore. It was my love of guitar that slowly started to piece my thinking back together. The problems would continue for quite some time, but gradually I worked through them and my memory and brain power began to improve.

It was my nerve medication that I really struggled with, and that led to some pretty dark times. For just over three years I was prescribed a medication called Lyrica. It is a powerful painkiller that assisted in treating what I would later learn was an 'adjustment disorder', which was like the worst anxiety you can imagine. At the same time my nervous system would be going ballistic. I discovered the only thing that seemed to ease my predicament was a depressant by the name of vodka.

Early on in my recovery I was on ridiculous amounts of medication — along with the antibiotics and painkillers, there were muscle relaxants and sedatives to stop strokes — and, unsurprisingly, I had the shits with every medication. I just wanted to stop taking anything that was in tablet form. Soon after I started working again, I think I began to come to grips with the fact that my brain really had been injured, but I always wanted something else to blame for it. I thought, I'm not an invalid, I can fix anything, so I stopped taking everything all at once.

I had never had a migraine before, but one day at work I had a terrible one. I was getting my arse handed to me, looking at my computer screen for so long, and I was just thinking, fuck, what's going on here? Fuck. A few people could see there was something wrong and told me I should go see the doctor. I went and sat in his office, and he asked if I was alright. I said, 'I have the worst migraine ever,' and he asked, 'Have you stopped taking any medication?'

So I started the list. He told me that I was supposed to wean myself off two of them, and then asked me how long I'd been off them. I told him about four days.

He put me back on a small dose of Lyrica. Half an hour later, on my drive home, my migraine was gone. When I spoke to Professor Cousins about it, he told me that Lyrica is super strong, but that the dose I was on was relatively small compared to what you would normally give someone in a similar situation. He said it is a targeted nerve painkiller which hits a specific part of the brain. I was taking one a day, for however long, and it did make things bearable. What I didn't realise, though, was how much the drug would affect me when I drank.

Of course I was told not to drink with my medication, but my attitude towards that was: well, I'm already the odd one out everywhere I go, and even though I'm proud of the reason why, I'm still the odd one out. I'm not going without a wine with dinner because of nerve pain. And people around me constantly told me, 'Yeah, sure, it's OK to have a drink or two.' I was good until about six drinks in and that's when it could get really bad.

Eventually I realised that Lyrica was the reason I could drink so much even with my small body mass. It doesn't change the effect of the alcohol, but it was affecting my perception of it. I would be able to get four drinks deep and not comprehend how much I had drunk. The simple signs like overbalancing, slowing down and slurring are taken away when you're on Lyrica. It's almost like it offsets the sensation of drunkenness.

The problem with that phenomenon is that not only do you feel like you could drink forever, but the little filter you have when you are stone-cold sober doesn't work. The thing in your head that stops you from telling that guy what you really think of him doesn't do its job. I became obnoxious. I would tell that guy what I really thought. The Lyrica warning says it increases the effects of alcohol. For me it altered the effects. For some reason I reached a point of clarity when I was six beers deep. I would never be stumbling and falling all over the place — at least not until I hit another particular point, well into the night.

Another problem arose when I decided I might need to have two of the Lyrica pills to try and get to sleep. It ended up doing the opposite and kept me awake. The situation could only be helped by going back to the original solution: our Russian friend, vodka. You can see a pattern emerging, though it didn't happen every time I drank.

I hear so many stories of things we did in Afghanistan the day before I got hit and I don't remember any of it. It's an odd feeling to know you were doing something and to not have any recollection of it. I started to get those same sort of blank periods when I had nights out on the drink after the incident. My memory would get to a stage where it was just black, so I would assume that the night had ended there. But really I was awake for three hours after that point, still speaking, still moving and still coherent. People would ask if I remembered certain events that I was definitely physically conscious for, but the fact was, I didn't remember cracking that bottle of wine or having a certain conversation.

I hadn't passed out; I had just gone into a completely different zone or something. I wouldn't stop to think before I spoke. There was basically a point I would get to if I was drunk where apparently my personality just started to change. It was the one time I kind of put away the perfect facade that everything was fine and would start to show the real me. I shocked a few guys from work when we were out one night and it happened.

It's weird and also scary. It has become a bit easier now that I understand why it happens. I have a level I reach when my body can handle being awake but my brain can't handle functional memory. When people from work started to see this in me, alarm bells began to ring. They saw different parts of me come to life when I was drinking that just weren't there when I was sober. Much later, in 2012, I met a guy who has a brain injury, one that was worse than mine, but I still had to ask him questions about what was happening to me and my memories and everything. I really didn't gain anything significant from him in relation to my problems, but I was so desperate to figure out what was going on that I would ask anyone I thought might be able to give me any relevant information.

Later, when my story had come out on *60 Minutes* and was widely publicised, I knew that everyone must be getting the impression that because I looked like I was happy and smiling, everything must be going great. But I would get home and I wouldn't be able to turn off the anxiety in my body, which is a really weird sensation. Imagine having intense nervous butterflies for hours, but for no reason. And there was also the freaky sensation of ants crawling up and down my spine. I went through a stage where I would say I had appointments just to get out of work for the afternoon because I was feeling so wired. I wasn't supposed to drink coffee, but I was drinking a ton a day. Then I'd be going home to a shot of vodka in the afternoon just to be able to calm down. This went on for quite some time, and led me to some very dark times in my life.

It wasn't until more than two and a half years after my hit that I started to speak to a GP who wasn't involved in the military. I hadn't realised that military doctors had to work within specific parameters. What military doctors can and can't do is written in black and white. There is no room for them to move either way, which I think restricts their care sometimes, but the military is a big machine and that's just how they have to work. So, finally, I sat down with Lawrie Ransom, GP, family friend and the guy who'd said sarcastically that I was just what the army needed. I wanted him to break down the medications I was on and explain what was happening to me and why. He gave me an honest and frank opinion because he didn't have to report to a chain of command. He was accountable only to me.

He told me that he would only ever prescribe Lyrica for six to eight weeks at a particular dosage, so I made the decision then and there to stop taking that medication. I think my body had become addicted to it, but I no longer needed it — I could sleep without a nerve drug. As I said, I was told not to drink with this and not to do that, but I just wanted to be normal. Part of me wanted to escape the scenario I was in and be who I was before. But I had to try to manage and it's only really this year that I've felt I've worked out the best way for me to do that.

That period of anxiety was probably caused largely by the painkiller I was on. But the whole experience had taken me to the stage where I would wonder, am I depressed? I haven't felt this way before, is there some way to solve this? Lawrie never said do this or do that. He said that he was not going to give me any medical advice, but he told me what he would do: give me the facts. He was extremely professional about it. He explained what all the medications did, gave me all the knowledge he had, so that I could come to my own conclusion. This was the best way to go about things and I'm still thankful to Lawrie for his effort because it got me away from that drug for a while.

But I began to self-medicate with alcohol. I needed something to level myself out. I explained to the military doctor what I was doing with Lyrica. He started to say, 'You realise …' and I said, 'I don't care — this is the way it's happening.' That was my new approach. I stopped taking the painkiller on Christmas Day 2011, and that enabled me to get off another lot of anti-depressants that were linked to the effects of Lyrica as well.

I dropped all of them and there was one stage where all the drugs were gone. I was on nothing. I was sick of what they were doing to my body, and I thought the best way for me to rid myself of them was by going cold turkey.

It was like being an addict. I could go without it for a week and everything seemed to be fine, but then it would be terrible. Eventually, I would have the cataclysmic fall that everyone was expecting but I, for some reason, didn't see coming. It was still a little way off yet, though.

During the first year or so after the incident, I wanted to get some ink. Dad always instilled in me how much he hated tattoos, just because I think the era he grew up in was not a heavily tattooed one. These days, everyone's got a sleeve. But I wanted to make sure I got something that had meaning for me. Not long after I joined the army I got a tattoo of the Federation Star on my back. The Federation Star is the seven-pointed star that sits under the Union Jack on our flag, and above the Defence Force symbol on our coat of arms. That was to represent my respect for Australia. I wanted to get it instead of the clichéd Southern Cross, which so many people have.

About a year after I was back from Afghanistan I got the Spartan shield on my bicep. This was my sign of respect for the guys I worked with. Our company's symbol was the Spartan helmet. I thought the Spartan shield was appropriate because your shield looks after the guy next to you. The designs of our attacks were based around that idea, and the day I got hit the man next to me protected me. Underneath the shield are the Greek words: 'Anathesis Tois Exatesmenois', which translates roughly to 'a tribute to the proven'. This was my tribute to those guys and what they did. I wanted to get a tattoo that would always remind me that the only reason I was alive was because of the guys. I couldn't write their names, so for me this was the most appropriate thing to do.

In June 2010, not long after I got the tattoo, I was at home at Bondi, sitting on the couch, when my phone rang. It was an officer from my unit, and the news was shattering. He gave me the official rundown and nothing more. There had been a helicopter crash in Afghanistan, and we had lost three guys. There were no names given yet because the families had to be notified and had to give the OK for those details to be released. I knew which guys were over there from that company, though. I had spent a lot of time with them. I had done all of my basic training with them, including the RIO course. That was the first Alpha Company I joined at the unit.

It seemed like time slowed beyond a crawl. I wanted to know who they were. Not knowing meant that for the time being it wasn't three guys, it was the 40 or so guys from that company. Then I remember looking at my phone as it almost leaped up, screaming its ringtone at me. While I wanted to know who had been killed, I still dreaded the phone ringing. There was no good way for this conversation to go.

One of the other boys who was back in Australia had rung to tell me the news.

I heard Ben Chuck's name first. He was the first commando I'd met at Singleton. We'd met on a night out, and I'd spent the rest of the night hanging out with him. We got along pretty well, and when I heard his name now coming down the phone, all those memories raced through my mind in a matter of seconds. Shit, Ben. Then it was Tim Aplin, and the first thing that came into my head was this tall drink of water with the happy, cheeky smile he would always wear on his face. I instantly remembered that one of my good mates, who was close to Tim, would tell me all the funny stuff he did. There was only a split second after I heard each name, but it's like time stopped while those details flew around my head.

Then, bang, he says, 'Scotty Palmer.' All I could think of was the visor he used to wear. Everyone had these different little quirks and Scotty's was the way he used to wear this curved visor. And then there was his dry wit. He would say something like, 'Yeah, this is awesome, great idea,' but with his own Elliot Goblet-style sarcasm. Then I remembered, when we were over there and it had been raining for six days straight, the most consistent rain that the province — and the whole country, I think — had had in 40 years, one of the powers that be decided it would be a good idea if we all went out on a patrol in the quagmire, which baffled all of us. We thought he couldn't be serious, but he was, and Scotty, with this really blank face, looked off into the distance, rolling his eyes, and said, 'Yeah, that's an awesome idea.' I just laughed.

I remembered our Platoon Commander asking me whether I knew what Scotty had done the night I was injured. At that time I hadn't spoken to too many people about it — I was letting people talk to me. I didn't want them to remember something like that if they didn't have to. He said Scotty's car was one or two behind mine: 'Bang, the thing goes off and next thing you know I see Scotty running. He jumped out of a moving vehicle to run to the scene.' What he did was extremely dangerous. Generally, when there is one IED, there are two, or you are about to be ambushed. But Scotty ran up to us straight away and, from what I hear, was one of the first to lay hands on me.

The funerals were a private thing for the families, but we would also have a service at work. There's a board of remembrance now at Holsworthy, but our sole memorial then was a rock that had the names of the fallen inscribed on it. It sat out the front of HQ at our unit, along with the Australian flag, the 2 Commando Regiment flag and what was at that stage the IRR (Incident Response Regiment) flag. Everyone would crowd around the rock and we would have a full military service, and the family of the soldier or soldiers would place a wreath upon the rock.

Those three guys and all before and after them will live forever there and at the War Memorial. I remember the first time I watched a person lay a wreath I thought, how the hell do you look down at the name of your own blood in that rock? It's not like it's a bad ritual — it's a great thing to honour them — but for me it would be such an emotional overload. I remember watching Tim's son, Ty. His family were the last to lay a wreath, and Ty, who would have been around 14 then, walked up to do it. Even though all the families were quite emotional, he had been tough the whole time. But then Ty got three metres from that rock and he just broke down. Everyone there wanted to just bury that kid's head in their shoulder. Everyone may have been wearing sunnies at the time, but I know there were shitloads of wet cheeks.

I almost never thought about how close I'd come to having my name on that rock. The one time I did I was just thinking about what it would have been like for my family. They would have been the ones standing there, staring at it. It was never about me; it was about how it would have affected everyone around me. They weren't just names anyway, they were people, both on that rock and on the Wall of Remembrance at the War Memorial in Canberra. When I visit our War Memorial, I look at all the names and rather than just seeing massive walls of letters, I see people, people who meant something to other people. It humanises the loss. I went to the War Memorial for Remembrance Day 2012 and met a lot of families there. When I was standing in front of our regiment's section of the Wall of Remembrance, I froze. I was holding one poppy and wanted to put it in 11 different places. I had to apologise to the other 10: 'Sorry, boys, but I was 400 metres away when it happened.' I put it by Brett Till's name.

As I walked away from that experience, I realised I was slowly getting further away from a military career. Moments like those also showed me that I might not be as desensitised to trauma anymore. I had started to become more of a civilian again. I began to realise that some of the stuff I had seen and dealt with was pretty intense. It's incredibly difficult to have to deal with losing one or two people who are important to you, but I had lost a bunch of people I was really close to.

A year after the death of Scotty, Tim and Ben, the unit lost another great man, Brett Wood. He was the epitome of a Special Forces soldier — a perfect role model. He instructed me on three or four of my courses. I had done the *60 Minutes* show by then and my identity was no longer protected, so I would get asked to do media stuff from time to time. I got approval to speak to the media about Brett and I was wracking my brain, trying to think of something to say that was worthy of this guy.

How do I explain how good this guy was, what a heavy hitter he was for our unit? It was tough to put in words. In the article, I tried to say something similar to that. He's the type of guy I want to model myself on. I was at Bondi Junction Westfield the day after the article was published, taking my suit to get pressed to go to the ceremony at our unit, and my phone rang. It was one of the toughest guys I had ever met, a larger-than-life character who has the respect of the entire regiment, and he said he just wanted to thank me for my kind words in the paper. What I didn't realise was that Brett had been kind of his protégé. They had been working together forever. Then, while we were speaking, this toughest of dudes broke down mid-sentence. That was moving. And on that escalator, in that packed shopping centre, I, too, had tears streaming down my cheeks. I dropped the suit off, went back to the car, and it took me 10 minutes to move again.

It hits you every time, and often in very different ways. The next time I heard bad news was when Merv McDonald and Nathanael Galagher went down in a chopper crash in August 2012. I wasn't close to Merv, but he was a section commander in the same platoon at 3RAR when I was there and then later he came across to our unit. I can picture his face and his smile, as I can with all of them. I don't know whether it's just the way the brain works but I can see them smiling — that's my instant memory of them. When I heard about Merv and Nathanael (who I had never met), I just lay there at my place at Bondi, thinking. I had this little vision where I was sitting there, almost talking to Merv. I said to him, 'No offence, dude, but I can't do it. You know I'd be there if I could, but I just can't do this one.' I couldn't do it again. I couldn't go to his ceremony. I'm sure with the number of ceremonies he saw me attend over time, he would have understood why I couldn't make it, and that's what I told him that day. I think that might have been a pretty good indication that my time was up as a soldier, too.

19

As I've mentioned, our Chief of Defence, Angus Houston, and the Chief of Army, Ken Gillespie, were both amazing during my recovery, and were really passionate about looking after our wounded soldiers. They started a program called ADFPSP, which stands for Australian Defence Force Paralympic Sports Program. People in the Defence Force are usually so fit and motivated, and their athletic abilities generally translate well into sport. There were quite a few guys in Special Forces who had played sport at an elite level and would have been on the cusp of a career in professional sport had they chosen that avenue.

The ADFPSP launched in Canberra in mid-2010. I attended the launch and was told there would be summer and winter sports camps. I thought about the summer camp, but I wasn't really mentally ready for it because it would have meant wheelchair racing for me at that stage. All the wheelchair and different Special Olympic activities didn't feel like me. I still viewed myself as Mr Invincible Damien, with no limitations. I have a lot of respect for the guys who do it, but wheelchair racing was never a sport I considered. The problems with my arm didn't help and I just don't think I was physically up to doing anything like that at a decent level.

But when I got an offer to come down to the winter camp a couple of months later, I thought it would be fantastic. My whole idea was that I would be able to snowboard again.

I started working with a prosthetist, bought a new snowboard, which I thought would be more forgiving and easier to ride, and in the first week of August I headed to Jindabyne. I was so excited about getting up and snowboarding again. Before my incident, snowboarding had been just one of those things you do for fun. Surfing was a lifestyle, and snowboarding was something I'd do for one or two weeks on holidays.

I love sports where I am standing on something, balancing and moving. It feels great. I had tried getting back in the water and surfing, but it proved a logistical disaster. Just walking the 100 metres across the sand at Bondi was so tough. I would get to the water and be too exhausted for anything else.

I saw snowboarding as a way to get the same feeling I got when I was surfing. But unlike the ocean, a hill doesn't go anywhere, so I could fall down and get straight back up. On the hill down at Jindabyne, lifts would be open from 8am to 4pm, and I could keep going until I got what I needed out of it. But that was all in theory.

As soon as I got there I ran into an obstacle. The Defence Force guy running the show told me that I was never going to ride a snowboard again. Instead, I could come over and sit in the sit-ski. He went on about how they had organised things for me, and he just wanted me to sit in that sit-ski so he could tick a box. Not surprisingly, I blew up. 'Come over and have someone pushing me around in a sit-ski? Wow, how emasculating.'

I have nothing against sit-skiers; some of those I know are actually amongst the most inspirational people I have met. They get so much speed up on those things. But the fact is, it's just not me. I wanted to snowboard again. It was something I had done before the incident, and I was trying to get back to doing as many things as I could from my old life. I wanted to be able to adapt stuff I was doing before so it was possible for me now. I thought that would be one of the first steps towards getting back to being me.

At this winter camp, I had also just met a great guy called Pete Higgins. He had been a top-level coach in the US before moving to Australia, and he was the snowboard coach there that week. I had a word with him and basically he told me to go and do what they wanted me to do that day, and if I still wanted to snowboard after that, I could go with him tomorrow.

As expected, the sit-ski wasn't for me, so from day two I was with Pete on the snowboard. On the first two days I fell down a lot. I was continually getting my arse handed to me, but the feeling I would get from riding 10 feet and then sliding down was something I hadn't felt in so long. I used to surf a couple of times a week at least, and I would do so many other physical activities. This was my first real contact with that old world. From the start of the day, I was on an emotional high, and it lasted right through the entire day. It felt absolutely amazing. For the first time I thought I could really be myself again.

At that stage I was still a bit self-conscious about how prosthetic legs looked. On a snowboard, I had long pants on, and while it might have looked a little odd, I also finally felt I could do something I had done before without having the unintentional pressure from people worrying about what I was doing. It was good for me to be in a world that was a step away from the official, cut and dried nature of Defence, too. I wasn't thinking about things like competing or the Paralympics. There had been talk about the inclusion of snowboarding for 2014, but for me it was about that feeling of being me again. I only snowboarded for seven days in 2010, those five with Defence and then two with Ray Martin and the *60 Minutes* film crew.

The next year, it was really cool to have this recreational thing that was something I would have done before. It's life-changing enough losing both legs; I wasn't going to start saying out-of-character things like, 'Well, now I'm going to become a world champion seated shot-put thrower.' I wanted to do something I was already passionate about and loved doing. That year, in 2011, I met a girl called Jodie Thring down there with Pete. She had incomplete quadriplegia, having broken her neck at C5 in a snowboard accident years earlier. Watching her snowboard on that first day, she just blew me away. It was amazing to watch her — one of those moments where I could believe anything was possible. It's people like Jodie who really prove it.

That was also my first real introduction to the competitive side of the sport. Jodie spoke a lot about her time in the US, training in Utah, where I would eventually land, and how she had spent five years on the adaptive circuit. She was a true pioneer of adaptive snowboarding in Australia. She spoke about the Paralympics, too, and I can honestly say a fire was lit. This could be something I can work and strive towards, I thought. It could give me a reason to train.

Around a year later I had a boatload of leave accrued and was having some dramas at work, so I took some time off and headed to New Zealand with a good mate, Phil Shaw. I had a couple of chance meetings on the trip. On the plane, we sat alongside Tori Pendergast, Stuart Hume and Lincoln Budge, all members of the Australian Winter Paralympic sit-ski team and all heading to New Zealand to train. This coincidence ended up dictating my future goals. The Snowboard World Cup was also on in New Zealand at the time, and there I met three other adaptive riders, all of whom still compete. Meeting them was the first step towards figuring out, hey, there are more of us. Being able to ride a snowboard again was a big thing, but then, when I started to look at some of the things those guys could do and the courses they were running, I knew I had a challenge to aim for. It wasn't slalom, it was boardercross — basically a BMX course on a snowboard.

I had thought, wow, I'm killing it. Then I looked at that course and thought, are you telling me amputees are doing that? Shit, I've got some work to do. It really lit that fire in me. I had fallen in love with snowboarding with Pete Higgins, but this opened my eyes to an entirely new world of snowboarding — one that I had to get involved in.

PETE HIGGINS — snowboarding coach
The Defence Force has an annual thing where they bring a bunch of guys to the snow and see how they go, with the possibility that it could perhaps lead to some Paralympic stuff. Damien was part of that group in 2010, and I got asked to get out there and give him a hand. At the time I was only told there was a guy missing a leg below the knee. I turned up and

there was not one guy, but two, and I thought, oh, this won't be easy. I have the ability to ride along with and support fully the person I am helping, so if they can stand on two feet and we can strap them into a snowboard, then I can ride right there with them and correct any mistakes they make. When there are two people, it's hard to do that. It was interesting that all of a sudden I got this curve ball. And then, of course, one of the guys is missing both his legs, which I'd never seen before or heard of. It's not a common thing to come across in snowboarding, and there wouldn't be very many snowboarders around the world riding with both their legs missing.

Once I got going with Damo and Ian (the other guy), we got all the gear sorted out and started hiking the hill. I always get them to hike the hill just to burn it, and to make sure they are all fighting fit. Damo has trouble walking up and down hills because he's got to throw his legs out in front of him, but he still did it fine. He was a little exhausted at the top of the hill, but he was OK.

We got them strapped in and I usually just give them a lift up on the back edge of the board when they're starting to get their balance. It's called the heel and side flip. It's my way of lifting them up so that I can stay behind them in a position where I can do stuff with them, without wrestling snowboard to snowboard, which would damage edges.

I figured Ian would take off quickest so I sort of left Damo there and started down the hill with Ian. I thought if I got Ian's balance going, he could do some practising while I worked with Damo. I started going down the hill with Ian, but we had all these problems. He was worried that he was going to fall down and all those sorts of things, which is quite natural. By the time we got down the little hill — and I'm talking about just 40 or 50 metres — Damien had already flipped over, got himself up, and gone for a run.

I was impressed, but not really surprised, because just from talking to him in the parking lot, I knew he'd be able to do it. What I didn't know at the time was that he was Special Forces. In hindsight, you could tell the difference between someone who was in Special Forces and someone who wasn't. You can just pick it. A Special Forces guy is someone who has got the desire and the motivation and the physical capability. Whether he's missing his legs or not, he's still got the co-ordination to make it happen. There was a lot going on inside Damo when we spoke, and I could pick straight away that it was going to happen for him.

Once he got down the hill, though, his Commanding Officer for the trip came over and told him he was going to be late for his sit-ski lesson. I said, 'What?' We had just spent 45 minutes putting all the gear on, getting everything going, getting up this hill and doing a run. We were well and truly into this. Damo had just got up on his own, and this guy was saying, 'You've got to get out of all this and get into your gear for your sit-ski lesson.'

I said, 'No, it's OK, leave him with me. I'm pretty experienced at what I do,' and I didn't think that the sit-ski was the way to go.

We did another two runs and Damo was doing a lot better than Ian was because, honestly, with Ian, his issue was a mental thing and it was really too soon after his injury. He hadn't recovered enough. He still had pain, and snowboarding puts pressure on the pieces of bone that are left. If part of your shinbone is left after an injury, that will push really fiercely into the front of the socket of the hard

207

prosthetic, and hurt really badly. Ian was experiencing all of these problems, and Damo wasn't. He had rehabbed himself really well. He was doing great.

His Commanding Officer said to me that if Damien wanted to race on a Paralympic team, he needed to be in the sit-ski because that's the only shot he would have at competing at that level. He spoke about this and that and I thought, honestly, that's probably the way he'll be able to get all around the whole mountain. The snowboard might limit him, so I thought, alright then, fair enough. I was asked to go tell him. So I went over and told him the sit-ski would give him the best shot at becoming advanced at something, getting all around this mountain, and really experiencing the snow. I love the mountains and I just wanted the guys to experience it, but Damien didn't want to sit in a chair. He wanted to get back to the life he knew.

After I told him that, he just threw down his snowboard and stormed off. He did the whole sit-ski thing and I took Ian up the run again. Ian took over an hour to get down the beginner's hill. We had to take a lot of breaks and he just wasn't ready. I knew he wasn't going to hang around for the whole week, and I had a whole week specifically cleared to work with these guys.

I decided to head over and find Damo. I found him and asked him how he was going. He wasn't too keen on sitting in the chair — he didn't like it at all. He was a surfer, had snowboarded before, and he wanted to snowboard now. He said he had done a lot of research and spent time on the internet talking to other disabled vets in America to figure out what legs to get and how to set them up to snowboard. He was dead focused on the snowboarding side of things.

So I put it to him that if he finished out the day in the sit-ski and still hated it, then I would clear things up with Ian and I would teach him for the rest of the week. It would just be the two of us. I sorted it out with the boss. I said, 'It's not fair, I don't care about the Paralympics. This guy needs to get out there doing what he wants to do. It will be better for him mentally and that's the whole point of being here.'

I was pretty impressed with his development over the next couple of days. I 'carried' him through the first run and for the second run I just helped him through the tricky parts. There are parts where I helped him through, and then when it opened up, I just let him go and it went really well.

He would be going down a hill a little bit out of control, especially because he's snowboarding on a pair of stilts, and he just had to try to figure out the feel of what was going on down underneath those stilts, and early on there was nothing he could really do about it. He already knew how to snowboard a little bit and he knew how to surf. The funny thing was that his method of snowboarding prior to meeting me was a really amateur thing. He had all the bad habits in the world, a total punter. I explained to him how to look at the mountain and how the board performs in relation to the hill, by tipping the board onto the curved shape of the board and letting that form the turn rather than kicking your tail around and trying to skid straight down the hill. Once he understood how to arc the board, things really took off.

The goal on the second day riding with him was to go the whole run with no falls, riding without my help. He didn't achieve that goal on that second day. He always had at least one fall, sometimes there were three or four. Every time he just about had it, there would always be one fall. On that day, I gave him a ski pole, which he could drag in the snow to help him get friction and pressure. Also, if he stopped, he could just sort of lean on it. That worked well, but he really took off again when I took the ski pole away.

On Thursday morning, the third day snowboarding, he didn't fall at all. When we rode the chairlift, I would have only one foot strapped in to the board, but he would ride the chair with both feet strapped in. At the top he would hop off the chair and start going down the hill while I quickly stopped and strapped in my back foot, pointed the board down the run and took off after him … and I couldn't catch him. It was pretty special to see him doing that. Everything was just fitting together for him and it was so rewarding to see him doing it and enjoying it.

There was one particularly funny incident. When you are snowboarding, it's more comfortable to ride the lift with just one foot strapped in, so you can sit square in the chair and your snowboard hangs behind you. If you strap in both feet, your snowboard is crossways in front of you and it's a little more awkward to sit in the chair, especially if there are a few people in the chair, and then the board hits everyone else's stuff. There were only two of us at all times anyway, and I'd explained to the lift operators that he had lost both his legs and that we were in the process of teaching him how to get on the chair. The first ever chair ride we took, though, we tried with only one leg strapped in and I pushed him along with his other foot just standing on the snowboard. I pushed him through the line and then we got to the gate where you go through and wait for the chair to come up behind and scoop you up. When we went to make that little manoeuvre, his unstrapped toe had slipped off the board and hit the snow, dragging his foot off the board altogether. The snowboard kept gliding but the planted foot was now not moving at all, so he does the splits. And because he's on prosthetic legs, he does the splits at the femurs.

Oh man, the looks on the faces of the people behind us were priceless. As his pants were rolled down to his boots, nobody would have known he had prosthetics, so it must have looked to them as if he'd just broken both of his femurs. The lift operators were in shock, diving for the stop button.

Damo was just laughing and we picked him up and got him on the chair. After that we started strapping in both his feet. We had some fun run-ins with lift operators because they are not allowed to let anyone up on the lift if they have both feet strapped in. It's usually a punk-arse kid trying to get away with something funny, so the lift operators really jump on it. I always explain what's going on beforehand, but the lift operators would still jump on us, telling us that we couldn't do it that way. We've even had lift operators dive on Damo's foot while the chair is coming and try to unstrap him quickly.

I've had to fight them back, actually grab their hands and pull them off his binding and say, 'Do not touch,' only to have them run over and stop the lift so we could have another major discussion. Things have changed a lot since then: Damo's now independent with his new snowboarding knee and he's worked out how to get onto the lifts by himself. He doesn't need to be pushed and doesn't need both legs strapped in, and that independence was a big thing for him.

That first week, though, was pretty special for both of us and we shared the same outlook on things. It wasn't about which sport he would be better at from a Paralympic viewpoint, it was about him reconnecting with what people with two legs do.

That's where the mountain is so special. Every day magic happens in the mountains, so it was just great to get him up there. On the Thursday, he told me, 'This is the first time since my accident that it feels like I've got legs again,' and honestly, I knew exactly what he was feeling.

No matter what, he still has nerve-endings in the stumps and they feel the leverage working on those prosthetics, and as soon as you start to bend and flex the board into the snow, arc those turns, and charge down the hill at speed, it doesn't matter whether you're missing a knee or an ankle or a foot or a toe, you feel your body leaning into those corners as if you are on a motorcycle. If you can picture that, it doesn't matter what you have got underneath you. We all use equipment. I use boots, bindings and a snowboard. He just uses boots, bindings, a snowboard, prosthetic legs and connections (the connection point between the socket and different items in the leg). It's all the same thing. As soon as you start actually getting it all flowing, and the riding is happening, it's an incredible feeling, and I know exactly why he would say he felt like he had legs again.

I found out only on the Friday that he was Special Forces. He told me he was a commando, and that *60 Minutes* were doing a story on him; they were on their way down and wanted to film all day on Saturday. Even then I didn't know his last name; he was just Damien to me.

As for the Paralympics, honestly, after the first two days, I wouldn't have thought he would do much more on a snowboard than just kick around the bunny hill, but I also had had no experience with a double amputee. On that

Thursday when I would start the run not even 20 seconds behind him and couldn't catch him, I knew he'd be able to ride everywhere. And the Friday was crazy. We were on all the intermediate blue runs. In one week he went from no hope, to riding everywhere. What he does now continues to surprise me. Well, he doesn't really surprise me anymore. I just sort of squint my eyes, grin, nod my head and go, yep, there he goes again. He's on a whole other level.

Now that the Paralympic side of snowboarding has taken off, we specifically focus on analysing what Damien needs to do and then give him challenges and tasks to get there.

When he's riding with challenges and tasks, it puts all the lights on inside him and he really steps up and does it. It's almost funny, because one thing I always tell an athlete is, 'Look, you've done six runs in a row, just hammering it, trying to do this, trying to do that. Why don't you go up and take a free run and just enjoy?'

Damien comes straight back at you and says, 'Look, I don't really enjoy a free run, I'd rather have tasks. I don't want to do it for fun — I want to do a task.'

He always wants to stay focused and keep improving. It's not even the improving; he just loves having a challenge put in front of him. It's the commando in him and it's him in the commando — the two are so intertwined.

20

When I was initially asked to do something with *60 Minutes* in mid-2010, I didn't expect too much to come of it. At that stage I was still a protected identity soldier. But during my first week in the snow with Pete Higgins, I was told that the crew from *60 Minutes* would be coming down to film me for their story on wounded veterans. It sounded cool and I was happy to be part of that. I just assumed that the mask I wear when I snowboard would cover my face when they filmed, and if I was interviewed, I would probably just wear the same mask.

But I got a call from the unit a couple of days before the visit, saying that the story would now just be about me and one other guy. Then I got another call telling me it was going to be a story solely on me. I wondered whether anyone had cleared the whole thing security-wise. I was so grateful for everything Defence had done for me. If I had a problem, my unit had solved it. I guess I was kind of the prototype case for the unit to work out what needed to be put in place for my type of injury. I was happy with that, though, because it meant that the next guy in my position could have some things done better, and the kinks would have been ironed out. Not long before the interview, I was told that my protected identity would be lifted and I'd do the story as Damien Thomlinson. The reality that my identity would no longer be protected and the impact that would have on my role as a commando naturally hit me, but I thought the message I wanted to get across was more important.

I saw the *60 Minutes* opportunity as a really good outlet for me to try to change people's attitudes about soldiers in Afghanistan. We are people. This is what we do and you are the people we are doing it for. Ironically, the people we do it for are the exact same people who ask you whether we should be there or not. At that stage, too, the war and our efforts weren't well publicised, and the public only got information about Australians in Afghanistan when a picture of a guy who had been killed in action appeared on the news. I wanted to help promote the good work that our unit and the SAS were doing over there. Nobody asks for thanks, but at the same time their commitment and sacrifice shouldn't go unrecognised. Those dudes are often doing superhuman things.

To have Ray Martin, one of Australia's most respected journalists, doing the interview was also a plus. I'll admit I was a little wary. Sometimes the press want to push a political message more than anything, so it was in the back of my mind that they could turn what I said into propaganda. I was also aware that everything I said would reflect on my boys, my unit and the Australian Army, so I was conscious the whole time of how the boys would react when I said stuff, and how it would be interpreted. I spoke from my heart about the way I wanted people to view them and the response was fantastic. Overwhelming and brilliant. I didn't just hit one person with the message, I hit a large group. I hadn't been too interested in watching it on television, but my parents were keen as and were stoked to come down to my unit in Bondi and watch it with me. In that instant I went from having no identity to being in the spotlight. It was an odd feeling. I had an online chat session with viewers for an hour or so after it and the number of emails that came in made me proud that I had got my message across.

To me, this is what the guys deserved. Although I had to give up my protected identity, it was more important for me to help get some respect for what those faces behind black stripes do in the dead of night, when people are at home, sleeping in their comfy beds. Those guys are the guys who kept me alive. If I had my way, I would stand on the top of the highest mountain on earth and tell everyone how proud I am of them, and this might have been the next best thing.

What I really wasn't ready for was the number of offers that started rolling in because of the story. People wanted me to talk at their conferences and do things with the Commando Welfare Trust, which had just started up. I was asked to speak to groups of school kids and was offered other motivational speaking gigs. I had never viewed myself as a leader. I was a soldier. It was odd having that new level of exposure, and going from never being approached by strangers about anything, to having my email inundated with people wanting to chat. Not to mention the offer of a book deal, which at that stage I wasn't ready to write.

I went from being a soldier forbidden to say anything, to suddenly having a microphone in my hand in front of 300 people, and I enjoyed the change. It was something I liked doing and I had really strong motivation for speaking out, especially for the Commando Welfare Trust, because at that stage there wasn't the same support in place for the children of our guys as there is now. The publicity and exposure I was getting became a tool we used to push the Trust, which looks after the families of the deceased and fills some of the gaps when it comes to the income those families miss out on due to injury or death overseas, helping with both initial emergency funding and then long-term financial requirements.

It was overwhelming at the time, but the best thing about it was the great feedback from the unit, and the great feedback from the army's leadership. The boys were really stoked about it. They felt appreciated, and that was what I was going for.

While things changed at work, things at home continued to be a struggle. Despite my smiling face when I spoke to people at various functions, or the facade I maintained at work, I was still battling pain problems and frustrations, particularly with my prosthetics. It all wore on my relationship with Tisha. When I got back from Afghanistan and was in hospital, I actually asked Tisha a couple of times, 'Why are you still here?' I certainly wasn't saying I didn't want her there, and I wasn't trying to get rid of her; it was just that, like a lot of people at the time, I was surprised that she would put her hand up for something that was clearly not going to be normal, and not going to be easy. It would have been understandable if we had been together for years, but we were still in the honeymoon phase of our relationship. We had only started dating less than six months before I was hit.

Of course knowing the Tisha I know now, and the type of woman she is, it doesn't surprise me one bit that she was there when I got home and stuck around through some incredibly difficult times, harder times than I would ever ask anyone to go through. But as expected, the tough times took their toll, and eventually cracks started to form. We split up in late 2010. Looking back on it now, I can see how she was slowly getting depressed. Tisha was in the hardest position of anyone. After my stint in rehab we moved in together, and there was so much 'getting used to things' for both of us. It would have been difficult enough with just the frustrations of getting used to my prosthetics, but then add to that the bone infection in my arm, the subsequent surgeries, the problems sleeping and the pain medication — it all had a major impact on Tisha. It wore us both down.

I still wanted to be independent, but everything was exhausting, so I also wanted Tisha to be doing things for me. As I mentioned, she was getting depressed, and that affected her motivation levels, so she couldn't keep up running around for me. I was basically couch-ridden when that arm got re-infected, and I was on that boatload of antibiotics. I could walk places, but I'd sweat my arse off, become exhausted, and would have to lie down and sleep afterwards. I wasn't very self-sufficient at home. My legs early on would hurt so much to wear that just standing would be painful. I couldn't stand in my kitchen to cook food more complicated than a sandwich, so there was pressure on Tisha to make dinner when she got home from working all day. I knew how tough that was, but I couldn't really do a lot to help. At the start it was just so painful to do things with the prosthetics, even simple things like going to the shop. I obviously wanted us to be a happy couple and a normal couple, which meant staying tough no matter how much I was hurting. But gradually, that chipped away at our lives.

Slowly, because things were so hard for both of us, we reverted to being quite selfish, and there was probably a lot of resentment, too. It was a pretty natural reaction, but it meant that Tisha and I became more like brother and sister than boyfriend and girlfriend. I know this is going to sound really, really selfish, but there were times when I was feeling exhausted and I'd get a message from Tisha and just couldn't think of anything nice to send back. I was in so deep a hole, feeling very ordinary and just not healthy. I might have missed her with all my heart, but there was nothing I could do to tell her or show it.

Because I was so distant, I think more than ever she wanted to feel that she was wanted and needed. We didn't have that physical side to our relationship happening, either. My body temperature was going through the roof because of the infection and we couldn't hug each other or anything like that, because there was always something that was hurting. Not being able to do that normal relationship stuff started to make the whole thing feel like a chore. It chipped and chipped and chipped away at her, until there was no more to chip away.

In the end, it was very depressing seeing each other, so we ended up going our separate ways. I think that decision made me want to become more like the guy I used to be. That Damien didn't have too much trouble walking into a bar and convincing a girl what he and she should do that night. I thought maybe this was a way for me to go back to being that guy.

TISHA

I had never lived with a boyfriend before Damien. When he left Lady Davidson, he didn't want to move back in with his parents on the Central Coast and he didn't want to have a carer, even though they said he needed one or at least someone to live with. So, while he was still in hospital, we spoke about it and he asked me if I wanted to live with him.

And I said yes. I was visiting him every day and I was with him every day already, so we moved in together after he got out of hospital. It was a difficult period for Damien. He was starting a whole new life and had a whole new situation to deal with. He had to adapt to having no legs, not being able to move his hands properly, and he was dealing with the problem of his bone infection. After we moved in together, he had several surgeries on his right arm, too. He was home, but back and forth from the hospital.

They were big adjustments for me as well. It was not only the fact that this was the first time I had lived with a boyfriend, I had also moved in with someone who had a wheelchair. We both tried really hard to make things work and it did work for a while. We lived together for maybe a year, but it was really getting too much, especially psychologically, for both of us. When the accident happened, I just dealt with things, but once he was out of the hospital, we had to try to re-adapt to normal life, and that wasn't easy.

I would have my breakdowns and he would have his. It got to a point where it was too much. We were living together, but we weren't boyfriend and girlfriend. I was a carer. We didn't mean to have it happen that way, but it ended up happening. During some arguments he would tell me that I was like his best friend and I would say, 'I don't want to be your friend, I want to be your girlfriend.' Because of his surgeries and all the medicines he was taking, I couldn't get anywhere near him. I couldn't touch him or hug him. He would be sore or itchy or wouldn't be feeling well because of the pain. It wasn't for a week or a month; it was pretty much the whole time. It was extremely difficult for both of us. I was taking care of him, but there was no intimacy.

We got to a point where we respected each other a lot, and liked each other, but we knew we couldn't take it anymore. I moved out. I said I'd find another place and that we could still try to be boyfriend and girlfriend. I thought we could go to the movies, have dinner and those sorts of things. But even that didn't work and we decided to break up. It was really hard in the beginning because I couldn't help thinking about all we had gone through and everything that had happened. We had a story together. It seemed like such a waste to let it all go. But although I felt that way when we first broke up, at the same time I knew I had had enough.

I should have looked for counselling and professional help from the start. People asked if I had someone to talk to, but I kept saying I was fine. I wasn't. After we broke up I went to a psychologist and had some counselling and that helped me get through that period as well. Talking to someone also helped me to digest a lot of what had happened before we split. I had had a lot of weight on my shoulders, and it had been really hard to process and understand a lot of things I hadn't even realised were happening.

I don't think he had the best of times when we broke up. As far as I know he went downhill instead of going up, but I think ultimately it was good for him. We had a little bit

221

21

After the *60 Minutes* program aired, that was it. I was out there now. No more protected identity, no more pseudonyms and no more having to hide what I did or who I was. The only thing was, I was still a commando — once a commando, always a commando. I had suddenly become the public face of the unit, and through the Commando Welfare Trust, I was able to help many others by showing that you can still smile and have a positive outlook, even if you had been through something as bad as I had. I could personally lend whatever support I could to the families of those who make the ultimate sacrifice for their country.

This wasn't something Defence ordered or suggested I do, it was just something I felt was appropriate, given the circumstances. Hindsight tells me now that maybe I wasn't totally prepared for it mentally, but it was something I felt strongly about. The way I saw it was that I had a unique opportunity here: families could relate to me, because I was one of those guys … I still was a commando. And I couldn't say no to things like that, either, regardless of how hard they were emotionally. Helping these people in any way I could was the least I could do. I had so much respect for my fellow soldiers, but also for what their families go through.

When a soldier is killed, quite often he leaves behind kids who will never see their dad again. That's heartbreaking and I feel the same as the next guy about it. The only difference was that I was in a position to do something for them, and sadly I've been in that position a few times.

When Scott Palmer's dad, Ray, organised a tribute rugby match in Katherine in the Northern Territory where Scotty came from, I was able to say a few words about Scott and what he had done for me when I was hit, how much I appreciated what he did to save my life, and how he deserved to be remembered by everyone as the hero he was.

It was a wonderful day, and I have a vivid memory of the fundraising auction that was held. I bought a few things, too. Tim Aplin's mum was there — all the families of the guys who were killed in the chopper accident were up there — and during the auction I could see someone was bidding against her for a painting she wanted. I walked over to her and said, 'Forget about it, we've got this.' The bidding went into the 1000s, but I didn't care. It wasn't about money. She was solid through the whole thing and then, when I'd won it for her, she turned and looked at me, and I just said, 'I did it for Tim.' Bang, she was bawling on my shoulder.

The shirt I wore that day is hanging in my wardrobe. I haven't washed it, it's still got the lipstick stains and makeup near the collar from her face on my shoulder, crying. I just wanted to do something for one of my mates.

I became a bit of a trusted point of contact for the families of my unit, and on one occasion I got an email from the mother of a guy I had trained with, Mason Edwards. He had done two deployments to Afghanistan and was killed during a live ammunition training exercise in late 2009. I was asked by his mother why his name was not on the Wall of Remembrance at the War Memorial in Canberra.

How could I respond to that? I said he should be remembered as a hero, but unfortunately the way the military works is black and white. The problem was the word 'operational'. His name is not on the wall because he was not killed in 'operational service'. I explained it was a similar situation for the families of the soldiers who were killed in Townsville in a chopper incident years back, but that was no consolation. I personally thought it was unfair, but there was little I could do.

It gutted me enough knowing that she was never going to see him again and the thought of not replying was never an option. But those little things, plus the regular funerals, had me asking myself how long I could take it.

I put an extraordinary amount of pressure on myself. I was dealing with my own emotional stress at the time, and I don't know whether I thought that dealing with other people's problems was a good strategy for me or not, but at that stage it was too late. I was that guy. I was the guy they could speak to, someone who had been there, where their son or husband or brother had been. When I found I could keep giving something and it was helping people, I just kept doing what I was doing. I wonder now if I just didn't want to look at my own problems at that time.

While the feedback had generally been positive from the *60 Minutes* program, there were some who weren't that impressed. A few of the older heads wondered how I was still a Special Forces soldier. Firstly, there was the rule that no Special Forces soldiers are permitted to have their identities made public, and there was also the fact I was still being employed when I could not make the running requirements for an ECN-079 Commando, therefore making me unfit for employment in the eyes of some.

I was back working in the Development Cell, which deals with developing and procuring equipment, five 'flexible days per week', less than two years after I was injured and having only just rid myself of a bone infection that had had significant impact on my ability to function. I was one of the forerunners in the ADF's upgrade of its systems for injured soldiers. I was one of the prototypes in a way. Unfortunately there were parts of the system that have to be reactive. We were doing our best to make them proactive, but it's a complicated job, especially because everyone is such an individual that trying to find a 'one size fits all' is very difficult. The outdated policies are still being upgraded, although they have improved significantly in the years since my injury.

I found it hard to balance being a spokesperson of sorts and a full-time soldier. I was doing talks to assist the Trust, which was a great experience, but some of my leadership increasingly viewed it as if it was for my own benefit. They were intent on having me make up all the time I spent away from the office. It was frustrating to be thought of in a bad light at work when I was still coming to grips with the fact that when I walked in front of a crowd they were looking at my legs. They weren't judging my bad taste in shoes, or my odd choice of jeans, they would just notice there was something not quite right going on. All anyone in the office saw was the smiling face and the extra liberties I was getting. They didn't see how hard it was for me to stand for an hour and a half, with my legs hurting so badly.

I would still have to smile because that was the person they wanted standing there in that suit, accepting the cheque. Many people in the army just saw me smiling and assumed I must have been having fun. Things were tough, but the last thing I would ever do was let anyone see it. I was having problems with my prosthetics, but I didn't want to speak about it at work. For me, it was still about showing no signs of weakness. And it was also about getting the message across, which was more significant and more important than any pain I was feeling.

I had a Warrant Officer who was obsessed with the power that the chain of command gave him, and he thought I had a blatant disregard for his authority. But since I had access to offices that most diggers in the army would never be able to walk into, I was able to exercise the option of getting things done more efficiently and occasionally bypass him. I can see how this would be threatening for someone who had had to clean out urinals with Brasso during the beginning of their career, but I just wanted to do anything I could to assist in the care of our injured, even if it meant skipping a step in the chain of command. After all, at that stage, Special Forces made up only two per cent of the army yet accounted for 52 per cent of casualties and 48 per cent of our deceased warriors.

Around that time, those in charge began to ask me the question: 'Do you want to be a public figure or do you want to be a soldier?' My answer was soldier. But what kind of a soldier was I going to be? The whole question baffled me as I had been asked to do two jobs: the PR side to help brand the unit, as it had just been rebranded from 4RAR Commando to 2 Commando Regiment and they wanted that name more widely known, and a full-time desk job. Then I got a phone call from one of the army physiotherapists, Rowena English, asking why I wasn't coming down to the ADFPSP winter camp after my success the winter before. I knew there was an issue because I hadn't even heard that I wasn't going. I felt the now familiar wave of anxiety rise up in me. I walked down to the Executive Officer's office and asked him whether the unit was no longer supporting the program to find aspiring Paralympians. I remember him looking at me nonplussed. He said he had forwarded the message about my entry to this year's camp, and I believed him.

So I went to visit the Major running the Development Cell, to see if he could shed some light. I got along with him really well. He had been a good mentor to me, and had helped manage my situation. Naturally, though, he was very busy so he would pass things down the chain, and in this case, it became clear that the instructions about my participation in the camp had been held up somewhere.

So I walked into the Warrant Officer's office, where I was informed that the event, in his opinion, was a 'funzie'. It was clear to me that he had copped a tough time at some stage of his career, and felt it was his duty to pass on the favour. I couldn't let it go unchallenged in this instance. The previous year I had travelled to San Diego and Canada with one of our Colonels on a trip aimed at building bonds with foreign forces and to get some guidance about improving our rehab systems. I thought I would write the Colonel an email now. I explained that while I was completely in support of the ADFPSP program put in place by Angus Houston (CDF), my unit viewed it as a 'quote — "funzie"'. Because I wanted to show that I was learning very quickly about this chain of command thing, I CC'd the Warrant Officer in on the email. I let out a quiet chuckle to myself and, after speaking with a few other disgruntled soldiers, decided I was proud of the fact that I had just picked a fight with a WO.

I guess this was all part of the process of learning that I had to go in a different direction. The WO walked into my office about an hour later, fuming. He took his sunnies off and said with great seriousness, 'My office!' At this stage I removed my jacket and thought, well, if it comes to it, I will go down swinging. So I followed him in and he barked, 'Where do you get off saying things like that to a Colonel?'

I stayed calm and with a hint of a grin said, 'Sir, can you point out anything in that email that you didn't say in your office?'

'That's not the point! You went outside the chain of command!' he shouted.

I thought, yes, I did, but at that point it just wasn't a priority for me. I came back at him with, 'Sir, as I said, what did I send that we didn't discuss? I don't understand why you would say something to me that no other ears can hear. I enjoyed the camp last year and have been looking forward to it all summer. It makes me feel free and is one of the few times my body gets past walking pace. What's the problem with it? So I wrote to the Colonel who had dealt with me before, and relayed what I believed to be your opinion. Where am I wrong, Sir?' I knew this would leave him in an awkward spot. It was one of my moments of clarity through my brain injury, thank God.

I didn't get to do the program that year, but, as I mentioned previously, I immediately put in a leave application, which was granted, and I flew to New Zealand to go snowboarding

229

with my friend Phil Shaw instead. What I didn't realise, though, back in the WO's office that day, was that the lads from the surrounding offices were piled up near the door to hear the 'debate', knowing full well that I was fuming and wouldn't be holding back. They also knew the intricacies of my situation. These guys knew that my company had been redeployed, which will change the way you look at your ringing phone for the rest of existence. The redeployment also took away the guys who knew people who could influence things on my behalf.

The camaraderie is something that will live with me forever and it is so much easier to forge from the lowly rank of Private than in higher places. It's really difficult to explain. I would spend every day with these guys and then we would end up surfing, drinking and chilling together. It had become clear to me over time that I was going to have to balance out my relationships with guys from work and civilians. Also, the attitude that went with work didn't really fit into the civilian world, which was growing nearer daily. But the beret and work was my career. I loved that place. So many there went out of their way to do good things for me, especially in those first two years.

Ultimately, Defence were good with the amount of time they gave me to make a decision about what I wanted to do, and they gave me every option possible. I wanted to be a shooter. I didn't want to be retrained as a clerk. I didn't join the army to become a clerk. I joined to become a commando. That was the goal and it was all I wanted to do. But reality was ever kicking in. It was a happy idea for me to redeploy, but then I wondered what I would do over there. Chances are I'd be sitting in an Ops Room, writing logs on a computer or something similar. It made it difficult to see where my future was headed.

DR ANDREW ELLIS

I remember when I did my interview piece for *60 Minutes*, Ray Martin asked me, 'Would Damien go back to work as a soldier?' I thought, now what is the difference between Damien's expectations and the reality? What is the medical, grounded view versus Damien's aspirational view and personal drive? What does he want to do and what can technology really help him to do?

He wanted to go back to being a soldier and he wanted to go back to being 'normal', which meant going back overseas. I knew that he would never do that in terms of what the military regulations said at that time, and with the fitness levels you need to do certain jobs in the army. I must admit I was interested to see how adaptive the army could be for a guy like this. I had seen how adaptive they were in America, where they have a lot more resources. There have been stories of soldiers going back after losing legs. But I felt the reality was that he could go back and work in the Operations Room of a Fort Operating Base, and plan the conduct of operations and man communications. They could give him a rifle and he could participate if he had to, but could I see him — as they say in the army — with his house on his back, and all bombed up with a rifle and weapons, going out and marching 30 kilometres? I didn't really think so.

But when Ray asked me that question, Damien was sitting in the back of the room. It was clear that Ray wanted me to say, 'There is no way he is ever going to be a normal commando again,' and Damien was eyeballing me and waiting for my answer. I remember looking up at him and thinking, I'm not going to dishonour your aspirations with my doubts on what you can achieve, because you have amazed me so much already. Although I held the view that his continued service in the Defence Force would be limited by how the Defence Force could employ him, I knew that Damien would not be satisfied with being a recruiting clerk or something similar.

Commandos can't step back from what they do, or have done, very easily. And Damien was a youngster. If he had been older and less aspirational, he probably could have gone back and helped in the army reserves or something like that, but that's not him, and it wasn't in the spirit of the level of elitism he was at. I could see the time coming when Damien would have to face things, but I was never going to put up those barriers to him. It was not the right time; it would not have been helpful to him. It would just have been another way of the system saying, 'Stuff you, mate, you know you are destined to fail in this.' There was no point, so I didn't answer the question.

22

I had been asked two or three times by Defence if I would think about walking the Kokoda Track. They wanted to show the world how good military rehab was, and I was insulted a bit by that, because I basically did all my own rehab. The army were great and offered me everything they could to help, but I did it all my own way. Besides that, the Kokoda Track is 96 kilometres of fucking torture. It's not the City to Surf, which might have been achievable. So I said thanks but no thanks.

Around that time, in 2011, I also met Brian Freeman, a wonderful guy who was an ex-Captain from my regiment, though before my time, and also the honourable man who takes injured soldiers and the parents of our fallen heroes across the Kokoda Track to aid their physical and mental rehab. I know that 96 kilometres of hills sounds like a paradoxical approach to improving your physical and mental state, but it does help. From time to time Brian gets celebrities and dignitaries along on some of the treks, too. He is also the guy who discovered the lost battlefield in PNG. But still, the idea of Kokoda didn't appeal to me.

Then one night I went along to have a beer and a bite and see a few of the guys from Alpha Company who had been seriously injured in the chopper crash of June 2010. I didn't know them all that well, and those I did know I only knew from passing in the mess and on training courses. We were sitting down having dinner when Ray Palmer, Scott's dad, came up and we started chatting about Brian's trips to Kokoda. I didn't really anticipate what he was about to ask me. Ray told me that Scott was going to get out of the army after what ended up being his fatal trip to Afghanistan, and that one of the things they were going to do together was walk the Kokoda Track. Wow, that hit home hard, like being doused with icy water, showing me again the price families pay. Ray was elaborating on it and saying how much he still wanted to do it. Part of me knew at the time that, while Ray was really proud of what Scott did, Kokoda was a bit about Ray wanting to prove to Scott that he could do it, that he could live up to the guy Scott was. Then he dropped the bomb on me: 'Look, I obviously can't do it with Scott. I want to do it with you, Damien. Will you do it with me?'

It took me five, maybe 10 seconds, before I said, 'Yes. Definitely.'

I didn't really think at that stage about what would be involved. I didn't care. I wasn't thinking about 96 kilometres of pain, I was thinking about the fact that when I did it, Ray Palmer, who deserved it, was going to sleep a little bit easier each night. To me that would be worth it. Scott would have done it for my dad, anyone else in the unit would have done it for my dad, so I was doing it for one of theirs.

Probably foolishly, in the couple of months leading up to the trek, I didn't really train too hard for it. To be honest, I thought I'd be able to wing it. I was a commando and I had confidence in myself. I did a little bit of training as it got closer, but I have a solid threshold for pain, and I thought, whatever it is, I'll get used to it. I was enthusiastic about the trek, though, and my enthusiasm was boosted even more when the organisers told me I would be able to promote the Welfare Trust on a TV special that was being made around the trip.

The message I wanted to get across was that everyone goes through hardships but we were doing this to gain exposure for an organisation that helps Special Forces soldiers on the eastern seaboard of Australia with their fight through tough times. To me that was the focus, rather than questions about whether we should be in Afghanistan, which the journalists with us seemed to be preoccupied with. At the end of each day, when everyone was exhausted, the journalists would ask the guys questions like, 'What did you think about your mates dying?' Have some fucking respect, is what I thought. If they want to tell you, they will tell you. Those journalists had no right to ask questions like that. It was upsetting for me and many others. For me it was also a good learning experience in dealing with media, but it kind of took a little bit of the lustre off what turned out to be a really good trip.

Kokoda is such a source of Australian pride. We sent over a bunch of reservists who anticipated that they would need to take their golf clubs, and they ended up being part of the biggest fighting withdrawal in our country's history, stopping a Japanese advance that could have basically given them the gateway to Australia. That's one of the things you get a sense of when you walk that track, especially with someone like Brian taking you. He is so knowledgeable about it, giving talks at different spots. At places like Brigade Hill, he talks about the battles that went down, what happened, and what our guys had to go through in light of the limited experience and training they had. As I looked at the terrain around me, I gained a new respect for them. They weren't really ready to fight at that capacity, but they did. They fought like Australians, thrown in the deep end. It's a cliché, but a true one: like American logistics and German engineering, we have Australian soldiers.

Being there was motivational and eye-opening. I hadn't read too many books about Kokoda and what our soldiers had done there, so Brian's stories were great. I also found out my pop had been stationed in New Guinea, on one of the bays, though he didn't actually fight on the Kokoda Track. Getting back out into a bush setting and sleeping in a sleeping bag again felt good after so long. The night before we were to start the walk, though, Ray and I decided to have a drink together, a few beers for the boys, and a good talk. We had a great time and drank a ton while we were doing it, but our therapy session, which lasted until 2am, wasn't the best idea. We got up at 5am to start walking arguably the hardest 96 kilometres we'd ever do.

Even after the first day, where we only walked from 9am to 3pm on the track, I was hurting. I was struggling and trying badly to rehydrate myself. Ray rang his wife Pam, and I hate laughing at this, but he was so serious on the phone to her: 'Geez, Pam, I think I've done the wrong thing. I know we are doing this in Scott's honour, but I think I've killed him. I think I've killed Damien.' He had tears in his eyes at the time. But by day three my body became conditioned to it, and I woke the morning of that third day ready and pumped.

It was eight great days. I remember turning around at different stages and seeing Ray carrying one of my legs while

I operated like a tripod on one leg and crutches. I would turn around and see him struggling along with his pack on, sweating a treat, but powering through. Ray also had his brother-in-law on the trip and three days in I got to pass down a tiny bit of commando knowledge to him. He was basically saying, 'I don't know whether I can go on, my knee hurts …' I sat down with him and said, 'Look, mate, this is the time you should live for. It's a time when you are about to find out a lot about yourself.' He said he wasn't quitting. I told him, 'I know you're not. All I'm saying is, when your body sends that message to your head that you are done, that you have nothing left, that it's all you can give, you still have 50 per cent at least left in your tank, you just have to dig down and find it. You can do it, mate, we can do this.'

This was a way of thinking we took for granted when we were pack marching at training. We knew that every single time we pushed a bit further, a bit harder, we were basically re-engineering the way our bodies viewed how much energy they had left, and how much further they could go. Ray's brother-in-law came to me on day seven and he was powering. He thanked me for our chat. It's that kind of moment that motivates me and reminds me I can go that bit further, too. That I have way more left.

At the end it was bloody hard and the pain levels were extreme, but it was a great feeling being able to do it with and for Ray, and the group we were with. There were about 45 injured soldiers on our trek. A bunch of guys were engineers from 2CER in Brisbane and you won't find a better group of soldiers. I have an enormous amount of respect for the job they do, sweeping for mines with their guns down and protecting the platoon of the company that is behind them, just as Brett Till had done, defusing his last IED two weeks before my incident.

We held a service at Isurava Memorial and I gave a speech. I think it was the best speech I have ever given. It wasn't scripted, but I had thought about what I wanted to say. I really wanted to pay tribute to Scott and let Ray know how proud I was. I also wanted to tell the engineers how much I appreciated the work they do.

Brian Freeman worked extremely hard to create that Soldiers Kokoda program, and it's a great and inspirational thing. Ray Palmer has gone on to become a mentor for wounded troops and families of fallen soldiers.

And I got to meet General Peter Cosgrove at the end of that trek, back at the hotel. That was a highlight. He has some of the greatest stories you are likely to hear. During one of these magical stories of far-off lands, I drifted away from the fact it was General Cosgrove, the former Chief of Defence, and after one of his punch lines I said, without thinking, 'Aw, bullshit, Cozzie!' I will never forget the look on his face — that of a man in no way used to a Private addressing him like that — or the fact that he will always remain Sir or General to me now.

I hadn't meant to be disrespectful, it was just something I would have said to any of the boys who had just told me such an 'out there' story, but back then my judgement wasn't always the best. And I had a long way yet to fall.

I went back to Kokoda in 2012, not to walk it, but as a guest with Angus Houston, to see parents of soldiers who just got caught up in the numbers game, and to see how much the families get out of it … That was when those treks made the most sense to me.

23

I hit rock bottom by the end of 2011. Something had to give, and it did.

Leticia and I had broken up, my prosthetics continued to cause me grief, I was still struggling with medication, my anxiety had become an enormous problem, and I was now having dramas with a few people at work who thought I was only there for the good times — for public performances and trips to the snow to work on my snowboarding. The irony was that at work the main reason I was copping shit was because I was putting on a brave face, but even so, I wasn't willing to let up. I think some people, too, wanted to see weakness in me. They thought there should be weakness there, so where was it?

I had a diary to help me remember appointments at that time, and I found a piece of paper in it one day that was from the anniversary of Tiananmen Square. I remember I had torn that picture out of a newspaper. It was the shot of the man standing in front of the tank. I think in some way that symbolised the way I felt about the battle I was facing. Because of everything going on, I was basically self-medicating with alcohol. At work, it would get to lunchtime and I would start to get that sensation of things crawling on

239

my back and up my spine. It was a horrible feeling. I couldn't sit still, yet I couldn't move, and I couldn't concentrate on anything. These were all symptoms of adjustment disorder, a precursor to post traumatic stress disorder, which as yet I was unaware I had.

I might get home at 1pm or 2pm, and have one or two shots of vodka straight away to try to calm my system down. I was still wrestling on and off with Lyrica then, too. At my lowest point I was drinking a bottle of Russian Standard vodka a day. There was an absolute shitload of it going down. Not when I was out doing things, only when I was alone.

There were times when I thought things were going well when they really weren't. Principles I had had my whole life started to waver. I was on anti-depressants and opiates, and all I could think was: I don't know at the moment what my system wants, but it's not food. I was completely confused about what my body was asking for and what I was craving. I had no idea at that stage. I told the psychologist I was seeing that I thought I was exhibiting basic drug-seeking behaviour. I don't know where I got that term from, a movie perhaps, but it seemed to tick the boxes and describe what was happening to me. I had an Audi A4, a two-bedroom unit 100 metres from Bondi Beach, and great friends who were a fantastic help through the entire thing. Everything around me was so perfect and I didn't know what was missing.

I knew I had to change things. I looked in the mirror, saw myself and thought, whoa, things really aren't going as well as you let on. That brave face you put on in front of people, being that guy you feel you have to be, it's not working out for you. Deep down I knew I was living too hard. But

I couldn't stop. I love dressing up in suits and ties, always have since I was young, and I'd go out to accept a cheque on behalf of the Welfare Trust, then go back to a hotel room in agony. My prosthetics were still hurting badly, but I would never let that show in public. After I took them off in my room I would shower, sitting where a normal person would stand, and then slide on my arse to the toilet. I would numb myself with some type of alcohol, before eventually falling asleep, and in the morning I would rediscover, again and again, that Lyrica was the world's only hangover cure. I also tried different things like retail therapy and gambling to try to fill that craving I had inside.

I was completely self-destructive, and I had begun isolating myself, too. One exception was Freddo. I can't count the number of times we spent just sitting on the couch at my house, chewing the fat, talking. There was no hiding from Freddo, and he saw so much of it.

At one point during my self-destruct phase I got so fiendishly drunk at home I apparently started yelling — at nobody. Subsequently, I found myself speaking with two paramedics and three policemen. Somehow, my elbow had been cut and was in a bad way, though I did not think it was ambulance worthy.

Apparently I refused to get in the ambulance and through my drunken stupor was presenting a logical argument about how they could not legally remove me from my premises unless I had committed an offence. I thanked them for stopping by, and thanked who I thought was my mother but was really my next-door neighbour. From there I was sedated and woke up in the back of an ambulance strapped in with a paramedic putting in an IV line.

Again I fell into a deep sedation and came to at 3am, in a hospital bed with the straps they tie lunatics down with lying by my side, though not engaged. I proceeded to check myself out of hospital, walked out into Darlinghurst and hailed a cab to take me back home. I then scaled the 10-foot gate to get back into my sanctuary and get some sleep.

The downward spiral for me was becoming uncontrollable. As we approached Christmas 2011, it happened. I hit rock bottom.

Throughout that time, the strange thing was I had people looking at me as a motivational figure, someone who had all that strength in adversity, but while I would be talking to them about that, I would be internally crumbling under the load.

And while this was happening to me, I was trying to do it all — deal with media, maintain my life in the military — all the while dealing with the stress of not having a defined direction for my future. I didn't know what I was going to do. I didn't know whether I could be a soldier — a commando — again, and the thought of never being *that* guy again was hard to accept. It was what I had really wanted and loved doing. It was me. It was who I am.

Truthfully, I was just lost and was trying to find myself. I kept asking my mates, 'What do I do?' Guys would say, 'You inspire me by showing that it is possible to cope.' That was great, but I needed something to inspire me, so that I could keep going. My motivation was starting to wear thin.

For someone who had always relied on doing whatever I needed to physically, to now coming to grips with the reality that my specific physical ability had been reduced … it left me in an enormous, unknown place.

I also felt I noticed changes. At the beginning everyone in the army was really understanding of everything, but then the more you try to show them how well you're doing, and the more 'normal' you appear, the less tolerance there is to the situation where you might need that little bit of help or leeway. So effectively I had become my own worst enemy. I wondered why everyone was all of a sudden becoming less tolerant, but the fact was it was just my mind slowly starting to break down.

I don't think I realised at the time things were crumbling. I was just hell-bent on self-destructing, which was exactly what I was doing. I wasn't ready to acknowledge that a problem was there. I was too busy looking for the solution. It sounds counter-intuitive, but it's really relatable. It's an odd situation.

Looking back on it now, I think about the idiom of making a mountain out of a molehill. Even if things are mountains, it's a lot easier to break them all down into molehills, and deal with them bit by bit. It's less daunting to do it that way than to try and face one massive issue, and climb out of one very dark hole, which was how I did it then.

In hindsight that's how I should have handled things, and I never even contemplated it. I was just searching for the one solution to all my problems. It was a massive spiral, but I learned from it.

In the end, I had to find my way out of that funk. The first step is looking at that guy in the mirror and asking if something is wrong with what you see. Ask who are you trying to convince that nothing is wrong. Reach that stage and you are at a point where you can truly believe you can get out of it.

It had been some time coming, but over Christmas 2011, I plummeted.

I never contemplated suicide. To me that was selfish. I had so many people in my life who had done so much for me. And anyway, I couldn't let something like this get the better of me.

It did reach its lowest point, and one night I called Freddo and asked him to come down from the Central Coast. He didn't hesitate, and the next morning we cruised straight up to the coast.

It's true what they say about hitting rock bottom — there's only one way to go from there. Having to call Freddo showed me it had reached that point. The more I thought about a solution, the more I came to the conclusion that it was my stubbornness and defiance which had got me through adversity so far. Those qualities were also what had got me that beret in the first place. I needed to come to grips with the fact that those were parts of me. It wasn't being a commando that made me become me. I was always me. It just harnessed abilities I had. Now, what I had to do was use those abilities to look for ways of dealing with my problems. When I made that realisation, it took a huge weight off, and my self-confidence began to return.

It was the same with everything I had been successful at. It was me being me that did it. From then I changed my approach to problems. For those first few years I had been approaching problems as a commando, which is only one version of me. It was essential to find the confidence to approach everything that got put in front of me as Damien, using all my skills, abilities and opinions, rather than thinking about what the military had imparted to me. If I'm myself, I'm going to be successful in what I do.

There are different stages in your life that shape who you are, and sometimes you need to get your arse kicked to turn things around to your advantage. Realistically, if I hadn't had the group of people around me that I did — my mates, some of the guys from work, people from the Welfare Trust, the great old veterans I met and spoke to along the way, fantastic people like Leticia and my family — I don't think I could have come out of it. Without them, there is really no telling where I would be today.

They are the real reason I am where I am. I can try to take all the credit, but I'd be lying. I remember one day, during a particularly dark period, I got a call from a legend of Australian sport, boxing trainer Johnny Lewis, who I'd met during a Soldiers Kokoda dinner. I'd missed his call, but got his message. I was in my apartment, and at that stage was so depressed that all I could do was sit and stare at my coffee table in my lounge room. I couldn't concentrate on anything for longer than 10 minutes. When I looked at my phone, I noticed that it was on silent, so I checked it, and saw there was a missed call. I dialled 101 and listened, waiting for some shit from work to come down the line or some other depressing thing, but all I heard was the voice of Johnny Lewis saying, 'Damien, I was having a bad day and all I did was think of you and my day turned around. Thanks, mate, I just wanted to say that.'

With that I broke down on my couch and wondered how some people can be so callous and others give so much without knowing it. Moments like that helped me get through that dark place. People around me gave me a boost

245

when I needed it; they were the true friends who were there when things got tough.

FREDDO

Particularly early on, most of what I saw from Damien was positive. He wouldn't allow others to see him going down a negative path, despite what he may have been doing at that time privately. He might have been thinking about some problem he had all week, but he wouldn't discuss it; he would just say, 'This is bullshit,' and that would be it. There wouldn't be a two-hour conversation about it.

But if you don't actually get it out, then you are suppressing it and it comes out in other ways. Even if he put on a brave face, over time in the army, having to do that consistently for everybody, every day, was always going to take its toll. It was as though seeming like he was alright was his job. That's what hit me. The guys he was working with weren't even thinking about what Damien was going home to, and when he was cracking, where was the support? It's like the army just thought, this guy is doing well, so put him out there and show him off. Where was the safety net? There was none.

Then it all came back to family and friends. We were the ones who had to pick up the pieces. I think his really dark times came out of a few different things: being the face of injured soldiers, his own injury situation, his home life at the time and a few other bits and pieces. All these things accumulated and led to him doing anything he could to escape the reality. That's what I meant before about the problems surfacing in other ways. I could tell if he was or wasn't doing well pretty much by his reactions to situations. The fuse just got shorter and shorter. He was still positive about everything, he never stopped and said, 'Woe is me,' but he would act much more erratically, and he had no patience for anything.

During that time he was very distant as well and disconnected from everybody. He would say he'd meet up with you and then wouldn't show. I went from getting phone calls at least once a week to not getting called for a couple of weeks at a time. That's when I would know that something was a little bit off. He was at one time hitting the booze hard, and mixing it with his nerve drug.

Then I got that phone call from him, in late 2011. He basically said things weren't going well and can I get down there. He was lost and didn't really know what direction anything was going.

I'm glad I got that phone call. It's the phone call you don't get you have to worry about.

24

Getting back to the coast and being with family and friends was exactly what I needed, but I also knew some things in my life had to change. The army decided they needed to be proactive with me now, and I was told I had to be diagnosed to see if I was suffering from PTSD. I agreed to check into a clinic on the outskirts of Sydney, but it wasn't simply to see if I was suffering from PTSD; I also wanted to have my alcohol and substance abuse treated, although the army didn't know that.

I checked into the clinic in January 2012. I knew it had to happen, but it was a terrible feeling going there to start with because I felt like I was being institutionalised in a crazy house. Over the two weeks I spent there, I had to try to solve my problems and work out ways to cope with things. In the end, I worked out more solutions to problems by actually recognising they were problems.

The prosthetics were the root of my problems. I had thought I should be able to trust people's opinions, especially experts' opinions, on stuff. I didn't like the fact that I had to rely on someone else, but I thought that I couldn't do anything about my problems with the prosthetics because this was their field. I have never liked to rely on anyone but myself. Things that are out of my control get to me, and that was something we identified in the clinic.

It was strange being there. I was in a hospital-style room, with two to a room. There were a couple of old Vietnam vets, and some former police officers with some serious, serious issues. I might have hated the clinic itself and the concept of being there, but I ended up loving the people. I met some really good people there. We had these groups where you would sit down and learn about the different parts of post traumatic stress, and the people I was with were open and willing to learn from each other, and the two weeks ended up going very quickly.

I didn't show any signs of PTSD. The problem is that once the ADF catch wind that a soldier has PTSD — which I am still confident that I don't have — they cannot only no longer deploy, but will be rehabilitated and removed from the army. The thought of that was a bit much after the year I had just had. So I played the game and spent a lot of time reading books about PTSD to ensure I would be able to answer relevant questions appropriately. I then successfully convinced two psychologists and a psychiatrist that I was not feeling any of the symptoms of PTSD.

The clinic turned out to be the best thing that could have happened to me at that time. I basically had a clean slate to look at the way I was going about things on the outside. I didn't think rage was that much of a problem. I could get around and do things in society without too much hassle, but when someone made things tough for me, or when other people's actions had an adverse influence on me, I found it harder to deal with. Looking at this issue made me reassess who was around me. I spoke to Freddo and my family a lot, and I even started speaking to Tisha again.

That was when I realised I really did love Tisha, but that I had to change the way I spoke to her about things. If I was having trouble with something, I had to say so, and if I did that, she would be fine with it. Before realising that, I just assumed she would wonder, what happened to the invincible Superman I used to date? The approach I took in the clinic was the start of me really being Damien again. I revisited the way I dealt with problems and decided I was going to deal with things very differently. Rather than drinking myself out of trouble and into trouble, I would try to find another escape that wasn't bad for me.

I think everyone has those escapes they use to relieve the weight of their problems. My problem-solving used to involve exercising and working out, a long run, or surfing. I just had to find different things that I could use to put my head into. Snowboarding is my thing now, obviously, and when things aren't going well, I think about planning the next trip or I work out to make sure I'm strong for that trip. Or if the opportunity is there, I go snowboarding.

I had a guitar with me at the clinic and that was a great release for me at the time, too. I'm not a talented musician, but I have a great time and I love playing covers. At the end of one particular day at the clinic I felt bad because I could see other people were visibly distressed, even when we were in groups, having talks. People were dealing with some really difficult things, and I felt bad that I had it so easy. I'd already worked out what was wrong, what I had to do to fix it, and what was causing me problems. I wanted to add a little bit of fun for the guys at the end of our group talks, and funnily enough it also allowed me to deal with something. I like being a showman, the centre of attention, I always have, and I said to everyone, 'I'm going to just do a sign-off,' and I started. The only song I can sing and play guitar to at the same time is Denis Leary's 'Asshole'. I'm tone-deaf like my dad, but that song is one where key isn't an enormous issue. I thought, this is fantastic and will lighten the mood, so I sang 'Asshole' and it was the best rendition I've ever done, and I even had two or three people chiming in at the chorus.

Seeing that group of people, with their variety of significant problems, walking out that day with huge smiles on their faces, all singing 'Asshole', was really satisfying. It made me feel like I was helping people out again, but on my own. This was nothing to do with anyone or anything else but my desire to help others, which I've always had, and now it shed light on another of my problems. While I loved helping people out, I realised the stress that came with maintaining my public persona was starting to weigh on me. It was becoming really, really hard to handle.

And at work, two schools of thought were still competing against each other — was I a soldier or wasn't I? Defence were telling me I couldn't have the best of both worlds and I felt like they couldn't have the best of both worlds with me, either. I thought about what I wanted to do with myself, yet again. I was still coming to grips with my ambition to be a commando having been wiped from existence, but I did decide now that I wanted to deploy again. I wanted to be the first double amputee to redeploy into a combat role. I was confident I could do it. At that stage the options were to be a sniper or a mortar man, and I would naturally have to do the courses required, as I wasn't currently qualified for those things. I would stop doing all the media events and PR, and focus on what I wanted to achieve. All of a sudden I felt like a soldier again.

As I mentioned, I spoke to Tisha a few times while I was in the clinic, just to ask her some questions and get her feelings on a few different issues. I was trying to piece together the way my brain had reacted, how I had been ignorant of how hard things had been for her. During those conversations, the good thing was that she didn't have to worry about whether she was going to upset me with her responses. She could tell me how it really was and not feel guilty about what she was saying. She could be open and honest.

We made an agreement when we started talking not to take it any further than that. We could be friendly with each other and I thought that was great. I've ended up hating most of my ex-girlfriends, so it was good to have one that ended on good terms. When we sat down together, the main thing I wanted to get across to her, because I thought she deserved it, was that it was all me; it wasn't Tisha who had been the problem. She had done a tough job during those early times. We'd missed the honeymoon period and the simple things that a normal relationship has when it's building. Now, we had a month-long period where we got to speak to each other really openly about the things we had done and said during the months after the incident. We were both able to approach things differently and say, 'I didn't like this,' or, 'I didn't like that.'

She said I had been the worst boyfriend ever. I said, 'What? I took you to Europe, we had New Year's under the Eiffel Tower, we got to stay in great hotels, I gave you fantastic presents. Why am I the worst boyfriend ever?' She said she didn't care about hotels and all that, but when it came to girls, she said, 'You are the biggest flirt. You flirt with every single girl you meet.' I argued with her assessment, but she said she could easily prove it. So we went to a wine bar in Bondi just to grab a glass of wine after dinner, and I thought I was just being polite to the waitress there but Tisha said, 'See, you just did it.'

What did I do? Smile? I told her I had always been like that since I was a little kid. I always smiled at people like that. It's just what I did. When I got home, I rang Freddo and asked him if he thought I flirted with every girl I met. He said he knew me, so no, but that he could see how people might think I was. That was one of the things Tisha and I got out on the table. It led to a discussion about what happened after we broke up. Tisha fell into a depressed state where she didn't want to do anything. But now she had joined the gym, was running, had changed her diet, and was in a perfect space. The way I saw it, we were both in a good space. The worst of things had passed. We knew each other really well now, including what ticked the other person off.

'How would you like us to finally have the chance of just being a normal couple?' I asked after our month of reconnecting. We hadn't been a 'normal couple' and that was something we identified during that month. There was obviously still that bit of fire between us and we still shared a good sense of humour. We ticked all the boxes again for what we were looking for in someone, plus we'd already ironed out the things that take normal couples ages to iron out. She was apprehensive, naturally, but I think she was

253

comforted by the fact that we kind of made a pact after that. We were going to recognise the things that upset the other person, and if things weren't going our way, we would be open and honest about it. If one of us was doing something that inadvertently affected the other, we could really talk about it, in a helpful way. In our time apart, we had learned to discuss things and not argue, which is the basis of any solid relationship.

It was good, too, that at the start I got to tell her I was looking at redeploying. I explained it all to her, what was involved and why I wanted to do it. I told her it was going to take a lot of work, that I might be away, that it would hurt, that it would take sleepless nights and there would be periods, once again, where we couldn't contact each other. The amount of effort I went through the first time around would be multiplied tenfold by having no legs. It would be inherently harder, but that's what I wanted to do because I thought I still had it. Mentally, I thought I could do it.

If she was going to run, it would have been then, but she didn't. She said she'd be right next to me while I did it. It was good to have someone I had confidence in, and who had confidence in me. And after more than a year apart, having each been through other relationships, she was pretty shocked when she came around to my place after we started seeing each other again and I still had those coasters, from the first night we met at The Rose, with those first words of Portuguese she taught me written on the back.

TISHA

I would be lying if I said I had no hesitation about getting back together with Damien.

But the signs I saw were extremely positive. The time we had spent together, the talks we had had, all the problems we had spoken about, were all good things. He was more mature and a bit more centred, more thoughtful about things, and calmer. There was a big difference between the guy I had left and the guy I came back to. And that was the only reason why I said, 'OK, I'll give us a second chance.'

He was still having problems at work early on after we got back together, and I must admit there were times when I went home and wondered whether he had really changed or if he was falling back into the way he used to be. I didn't want that to be my life again. What also made things a little difficult was that amongst my family and my friends, none of them wanted me to go back to him, because they knew everything I had gone through before. They said, 'It's your decision, but we don't want you to suffer.'

So I was actually going against everybody to be with him again, and I wanted to prove — I wanted him to prove — to everybody that he had improved and things would be better this time. My mum was a bit worried when we got back together, but as she said, 'Darling, the worst is gone. I think what you both went through before was the worst, so now it's good times. You will still have ups and downs, but it's good times from now,' and that's pretty much how it has been. We do have ups and downs, but even the down times are different now. The way we talk about things is different, even the way we argue.

There are not the dark holes anymore. We respect each other so much and we love each other. It has definitely been an interesting ride. But I think it's only the hard times that

25

A bonus of my decision to try to redeploy was that I would be able to get the type of prosthetic support I wanted and needed. Not only would I have Defence on my side, but a prosthetist was going to have to live up to that high standard as well. I would need specific parts, and higher level pieces of equipment. I needed to know without doubt that I could be supplied with those bits of equipment if I was serious about deploying again. To be the person I wanted to be and the soldier I wanted to be, I needed my prosthetics to be working well.

Prosthetics are expensive, but the prosthetist I had then said they could do it, and Defence said they were backing me. It all seemed full steam ahead. I got support from my unit and started the rebuilding process. I put myself under the pressure of achieving what was not thought possible at one stage. My training started with an Image Capture and Transfer Course and was followed by a Mortar Course, which I can proudly say I am the only double amputee in the Australian Army's history to have completed. This four-week course, in February 2012, was done down at Pukka (Puckapunyal), and it was my first taste of being back at work, proper work, besides a few shooting sessions on the range.

Pukka is an experience. As commando units are operationally focused, we had usually been saved from some of the finer points of war-winning military maintenance as long as we kept our shit together when it came to doing our job. Having a bit of freedom with things such as shaving, hair length, blousing pants and choice of boots makes a big difference. The boots thing is an important one for a commando, because we had to walk massive distances with tons of weight on, and that's a lot harder with bleeding feet. But Pukka is a whole other world. Seasoned veterans of training camps were quick to point out shortfalls in my uniform maintenance. The positive thing is that I knew this was the case and could suck it up.

Because of how skinny my legs are, I couldn't blouse or fold in my pants. One Captain had to swallow his words as soon as he started uttering them, when he watched his victim lift his unbloused pants to reveal metal legs. I could see the horror in this guy's face, and decided it was not worth causing a scene. The other boys thought differently. They were fuming that I had been pulled up about it, but I reminded them that we shouldn't rock the boat. Pukka is run a specific way to achieve specific goals. Discipline and regimented behaviour are really important to the running of things. Every Special Forces soldier knows this is how the place works. When you go there, you're expected to cross the t's and dot the i's. You accept that that is what it will be like. And the last thing I wanted was for my unit to draw heat. I didn't want those at Pukka thinking: awesome, another group of guys from 2 Commando Regiment coming down, let's make their time here difficult.

At one point, we got a visit from the Regimental Sergeant Major of the Army. I positioned myself at the back of the group during the visit and as he began his speech I was shocked to hear the words, 'So where is this Private Thomlinson character?' I thought for a second and said, 'Uhhh, he's off sick, Sir.' Thankfully he had a great sense of humour — of course soldiers don't get sick days. He then told me how motivational he thought I was and how it helped his drive. Meanwhile my back hated what I was putting it through and my legs were starting to scar up a bit from my prosthetics, but it was the means to an end. It was all about getting me back on the ground.

After the successful completion of that course, I ran into problems with my X2, which is the prosthetic knee I wear. It's an amazing piece of technology called a microprocessor controlled joint, which has gyroscopes and sensors in it to help it adjust to terrain and sense where you are in your gait cycle. The joint at the knee had blown out from the force of me landing on it during a mortar drill. I had done the action quickly with little regard for my fragile prosthetic joints. This process was all part of putting the prosthetics through their paces and testing what my legs could handle. Unfortunately the doctor from work, a new guy who had taken over my case, was more interested in the bill to fix the thing than in investigating how it had happened.

I tried to explain the fact that prosthetic conversations were like my kryptonite and caused a fair bit of angst and distress for me, because of the simple fact that while you can change a tyre on your car when it is flat, you don't always require your car. You walk everywhere and I was in no way ready to sit in the wheelchair which I spent my time in at home. The prosthetic knee was expensive, around $140,000, but defiant as ever, I tried to make the point that I relied on this thing to walk, and do my job, so it was relevant to everything I did. His attitude was baffling, considering what I was trying to do, and had done.

I recall having another conversation around that time with a Warrant Officer about me having to remember I was a soldier. I replied, 'I am quite aware of it every morning when I get out of bed. Or get in my wheelchair to go for a piss.' I can remember the WO's face when I said those words and he came to the realisation that there was more to me than just the brave face. Though in essence he was right: I was not ready to jump through the hoops that were necessary in order to be a soldier. But in my mind I was a soldier, wasn't I? Hadn't I proven myself? Was my relentless anxiety a sign of weakness? These questions would all be put to rest when I finally decided my future was not where I thought it was, and that I really could manage my recovery without being a commando. Don't get me wrong: I will be a commando for life, but for the sake of the melon on my shoulders I needed to fall back into the civilian way.

Ultimately, there was one incident that made me choose to walk away from the unit I held, and still hold, in such high regard. It was in Tasmania, and I had just competed in the Targa rally to raise funds for Legacy and the Commando Welfare Trust, and to raise awareness of the Trust and the unit. For the entire time I was under the impression this was a charity event, rather than an army event. Despite my decision earlier in the year to stay out of the media spotlight, for the sake of charity I had spent a heap of time on radio and doing TV interviews talking about this 'fundraising initiative'. I had spoken at the Castrol annual conference to secure Castrol as a sponsor and in the spirit of the event decided that the black-tie dinner after the rally was the best time to break my three-month dry period.

I drank a fair bit. My language may not have been entirely in check that night, and I was told by the Sergeant, the driver and creator of our rally team, that it was time to shut up. During the rally, I had been growing increasingly annoyed with the way he'd treated the team and the people who were donating their time and effort, getting worked up and extremely upset if something was not done the precise way he wanted, and upset if something was done and didn't work, and it was never his fault. So now, while my recollections are a bit vague, I think I responded along the lines of, 'Go fuck yourself, I am sick of your shit.' Apparently he then asked me to leave and I provided much the same response.

I didn't understand the gravity of the situation until we got to work on Monday and his first words to me were, 'You are in a world of hurt, my friend.' I thought, fine, he is still upset, but I am sure we can have a quick chat and all will be good. I was miles away from the truth. After training that day I was kept back. I thought he must just be putting it on for the boys. Once again, that was not the case.

Sitting in his office, he said, in a frustrated way, 'You had better stand!' At that stage our Company Sergeant Major, who had been friends with the Sergeant for a decade, came in and told me that I was being charged with insubordination and failing to comply with a lawful command. It shocked me that this Sergeant, who had also been drinking at this event that was in no way related to the army, could have me charged.

This set off an emotional chain reaction. The screws had been tightening as I waited for my punishment, and now I was slowly breaking. Not only had I done all the PR work with the car rally, but this guy had stayed at my house for a week last time I was overseas. What was his problem? What followed was my first experience of major depression. I still had my rocks Leticia and Freddo, but this experience was finally one push too far.

During this period I explained the situation to psychologists and a psychiatrist, who all agreed that it was unnecessary for me to be punished by the Sergeant who had triggered my outburst. However, my CO at the time decided that it was in everyone's best interest that I was left at the mercy of that same man. I personally think that it was extreme mismanagement. The CO's primary job is to manage people. He knew that the Sergeant had a serious personal issue with me, but he still thought, let's leave the punishment in his hands.

When it came to my punishment, I was given 'Restriction of Privileges', four days confined to the base over two weekends, on the trot. Generally, when that punishment is handed out, it would start at 6am on the Saturday morning and finish at 4pm on the Sunday afternoon. Mine started at 4pm on the Friday, and finished at 4pm on the Sunday, effectively taking away my entire weekend.

During that time I would be assigned all manner of jobs at the base, and while this punishment might not seem too bad, the first weekend I was there was Mother's Day weekend. Part of the punishment was that I could have no entertainment or access to phones, including my own, which was confiscated. Again, this might not sound like a big deal, but Mother's Day was a significant day for me. With the deaths that my unit had suffered, and my growing status as

262

a public figure, I had spent a lot of time with families of my dead brothers, and I had had at least three mothers crying on my shoulder over the loss of their boys, my mates.

Thankfully the Sergeant who was having to enforce my punishment was empathetic to my situation. He wasn't happy with it, but he couldn't argue with it. He could see how upset I was that I couldn't even ring my mum, and then I spoke about Scott's mum, and we made an agreement. His way of doing it was that he walked out of the office and said, 'Look, I'm just going up here, I'll be about 10 minutes.' Wink, wink! I rang Pam Palmer and wished her a happy Mother's Day and I rang my mother up, but to me it wasn't good enough. I wanted to see my mother on Mother's Day. I had put her through so much, and she deserved better.

I hadn't slept for three nights, rehearsing the speech I gave in the office of the Company Sergeant Major. I wanted to get it right. I owed that to Mum.

'Look, Sir, I have given this unit and the Australian Army two legs, three years of recovery, years of my family's anguish, their time and effort, to make sure they are there for me. I have given everything I can. I have had three different mothers crying on my shoulder over losing their children. I have responded to an email from Mason Edwards' mother about why he's not included on the wall of the War Memorial as best I could. It wasn't an officer official answer; it was a personal one. You want to know the one person who fucking misses out on Mother's Day? My mother. Hasn't she been through enough? Hasn't my family been through enough?'

Up until that point, while I was annoyed and frustrated by the excessive punishment, I had kind of shaken it off.

Furthermore, the Sergeant and the Captain in charge of the entire punishment cycle had decided that I would be required to write formal apologies to the other guests who'd been at our table on the night of the dinner, including the director of Octagon, who runs the event, and Glenn Ridge, who had been the master of ceremonies. In response to the written apologies, I received four replies expressing the opinion that my behaviour was not what they would have considered out of line and 'definitely not worthy of a written apology'. Glenn Ridge, who I had had a great time speaking to that night and at previous events, sent a written reply and a personal email saying that he hadn't even noticed and was looking forward to seeing me at the next event. The director of Octagon thanked me for speaking at his company's event and explained how grateful Octagon was for my involvement.

While these responses showed me that my work for Legacy and the Commando Welfare Trust was not going unnoticed, the severity of the army's punishment made me feel like all the effort I had been putting into promoting the great work our unit was doing suddenly meant nothing. The work I had done for the Welfare Trust meant nothing to the army. The work I had done with that rally event meant nothing to the army. I was getting my arse kicked ruthlessly.

During my punishment I was isolated from just about everything, which is mentally challenging enough, but I'd also been reduced to a wheelchair because my back was so painful, and that's a big deal for me. It was one of those things that chips away at you. The tasks I was given were tasks you would get a whole platoon to do over two days. I had to perform a technical inspection of the flotation devices we use — all 45 of them. For me to be doing that by myself meant lifting crates from above head height on prosthetic legs, then running through every single one, checking serial numbers and serviceability tags. It's a big job and it wasn't the only big job I was handed. I had to go through all of our image capture and transfer equipment. I missed one thing when I was doing it, and as a result I had to go through all of it again. It had taken me three days to do it the first time.

And then I had a Sergeant and a Captain asking me why I was incapable of doing the 'pedestrian tasks' they had given me. I was honest and told them I did everything I was physically capable of. For them to belittle me when I had done my best was humiliating. By the end of it my back was in agony, so much that for a few of those hours I was reduced to working in a wheelchair, which was something I hated to do. And why was I put through this? Because I had embarrassed a guy who was being an arsehole to people who were raising money for a charity, Legacy, which to me was the focal point of the event. I have no words to describe how little respect I had for him.

It was at that exact stage that I thought, I am done with this. There is something seriously wrong with these guys and somehow they have the backing of the CO. I thought about the apologies I was getting from the boys when they were made to give me pointless tasks. I thought about how hard it was when my company deployed back to Afghanistan, and the anxiety of hoping my phone didn't ring to inform me that I would be attending a ramp ceremony to carry one of my mates home.

Tisha and I had been back together for a month or so, and it had been going great guns, but then this incident happened in Tasmania and it all started going downhill at work. She tried everything to get me out of that hole and both of us knew drinking wasn't going to help. It was very frustrating for her and we were sliding back into old patterns. She came to me after a three-week period of shitty behaviour on my part and basically said that if I kept it up, she couldn't do it all again.

While I had spiralled to what I felt was rock bottom a few months earlier, what I was now going through was the worst time since the injury. I never sat up for nights on end in hospital, stewing over something, like I was doing now. The dramas with the prosthetics had made me angry, for sure, but this entire situation gutted me.

My CO came up to me one day towards the end of the punishment and said, 'G'day, Damien, you're looking great.' I turned my nose up at it. I wanted to say, 'Go fuck yourself,' but I was scared I'd be tied to a pole and whipped. I just said, 'Look, Sir, I don't know what the fuck you want from me, or what you are trying to achieve.' He looked at me with a puzzled, concerned look on his face, which made me realise he didn't know exactly what was going on down our end. He asked me what I meant, and I told him everything. I said it felt like some people just didn't want me to succeed. I was a broken man. I told him I'd been back with my girlfriend for a month, and she had already given me an ultimatum that she'd have to leave if I didn't get my shit together. And I didn't blame her. If I lost my girlfriend after I had worked so hard to convince her to give me a second shot, I wouldn't be able to take it. I said, 'That's blood that won't wash off your hands.'

I also told him that it had got to the point where I had spoken to a lawyer friend of mine and asked him if he wanted to be part of the biggest discrimination case Defence had ever come up against, and he was chomping at the bit to represent me. I only said that to give a sense of how serious I was. It wasn't a threat, I was simply stating that I felt what they were doing was unfair, but I have no doubt our conversation about the potential of a case had an impact, as suddenly after that, the chains got lifted. The next day I got into work and all my punishment was over. I instantly said I wanted some leave. I got granted seven days' worth, but I had to report to work every day for 'my personal wellbeing'. I had to rock up at 9.30am every day, check in, say hi, go to the gym, then go home.

The worst of my anxiety disorder was peaking again. I hated it. I wasn't willing to take any medication, though, because I was convinced it wasn't helping. My back felt like it was infested with ants again. When I drove through the gates at work, it became unbearable. When I got inside, I didn't want to spend time there. I didn't want to see anyone, even my good mates from the unit. I didn't want them to come up and say hi because I couldn't bear talking to anyone. I sat there thinking, this is it, time to knuckle down and focus on what's happening and beat it. It took me three weeks of wrestling with it to do it.

The Sergeant who had a chip on his shoulder continued to make it all harder for me. I nearly lost it in one of the last talks we had. When he told me, 'Commandos are selected, and you hope for particular attributes,' I had to stand up and walk out of that guy's office. I could see what he was insinuating and it took every ounce of resolve I had not to make things worse. And I had shown that resolve countless times and in countless situations. I had dealt over and over again with situations of extreme duress. I purportedly break a rule at one social event and this guy starts telling me about commando attributes? I couldn't believe he represented the army's leadership. It didn't reflect well on the promotional system.

I don't feel that what happened to me represents how the army deals with problems. There are inherent issues with the army judicial system and there have been for a long time. What I discovered in this instance is that the system is not really based around fair trials. If an officer wants you charged, it will happen, even if he had also had a few drinks and the case would have been thrown out of a civilian court.

There were a huge number of people who showed utter contempt and disgust at the way that situation was handled. The number of apologies I got from mates who saw me getting hosed was testament to the fact that this was not normal. Guys kept saying, 'You know, mate, this isn't coming from me,' and, 'Fuck, there is nothing I can do, dude.' Those comments spoke volumes about how unusual and unnecessarily humiliating it all was.

At the start of that year I had had every intention to redeploy. I had done three courses, and as I said, I was the only double amputee in the Australian Army to have completed that mortar course. But even though I had all the heart in the world, I just wasn't able to approach the job the same way anymore. I wondered how I could deal with the job when I had this overwhelming anxiety. Could I do it mentally? The blow-up with the Sergeant had rammed things home for me. Finally, I realised it was time for me to be selfish and walk away.

26

I put the wheels in motion for my discharge, but for some reason I came up against resistance, and my decision was not being taken as seriously as I thought it would be. It seemed to be considered a bluff. But by no means was it a bluff. During the process they told me, 'This is it, you realise if you sign this, you can't come back. You get a lot of help in here.' I couldn't feel a lot of helping going on at that time.

In the to and fro that followed, I discovered that the CO did not want me to leave with a sour taste, which was probably wishful thinking. That being said, I never felt negatively towards my unit. I am proud of my time there and what the boys do and stand for and the thankless way they go about their job. The way they deal with loss and the general shoulder-to-shoulder nature of the regiment are amazing. I wasn't about to let a poor leadership decision change that view. The process of discharge took six weeks, and the whole time I kept thinking, yeah, I can do this myself. That's what everything since my accident had taught me.

I was thankful for everything the army did in those first two years. But the latest incident had taught me that I couldn't rely on them anymore, and I didn't need to. I had the ability to succeed for myself. When the discharge was finalised, it didn't feel strange or sad. It was like I had been carrying a bus full of families, fallen soldiers and injured guys, and for that brief moment, I got to put it down.

As I mentioned, at that stage I didn't even want to drive through the gates at work. That's how bad it was. Knowing that I never had to do that again was a huge relief and I felt like I was once again the master of my own destiny. Being out of Defence has empowered me with the ability to control what I do. It was great not to have to think: I can do whatever I put my mind to, so long as I then convince this guy, who has to convince this other guy, who then has to approve it and then has to make an excuse for it. I was now in charge of myself.

I knew how much I had given, and now all I wanted was to spend just a few months of my life thinking about me and what I would do next. I wanted to plan for my future with Tisha, and prepare for the fact that, heaven forbid, there will one day be little versions of Damien running around, being the pain in the arse I was. I wanted to give my imaginary family the same opportunities my parents gave me, and the same opportunities the Welfare Trust wants to give children. It still feels like a selfish decision, I can't shake that, but I won't forget or stop working for the amazing families I met.

I didn't go back for a final farewell. My issues with hierarchy had almost cost me my sanity.

It was a disappointing end to my career. I loved the job, and I loved the vast majority of people I had worked with.

I was offered a plaque, but replied that I'd feel better if someone said, 'Look, we made a bad decision.' And that was as far as it went.

I didn't do what I did for a plaque. I did it for the boys, and I don't need a plaque. I've got the one thing I wanted, and I think I earned, which is my beret.

Would I still be there if that drama had not happened …? I feel that without a doubt I would be. It is sad that I didn't get to deploy again. It's depressing that I tried my arse off from the start of the year to prove myself and tick all the boxes. In the end, maybe some people above me just weren't honest enough to say, 'There isn't a position left for you here, Damien, so you're discharged.' Instead, I had to pull the pin myself.

I've spoken to the CO since then over coffee, and to me it sounds like if we all had the chance to run through the entire situation again, we would all do it differently.

Leaving the army has been like being born again. I could suddenly be human again. I could get upset by shit, cry if need be and not think I was showing weakness. It gave me the opportunity to step back from things, and I noticed that even the way I spoke to people changed. My emails got a lot friendlier because suddenly I had to be polite in the real world. In the army it's cut and dried. It was good for me to get used to laughing again, too. I'd been worried about leaving that military world, but the one I stepped into wasn't that bad. All I had was me and my reputation. I couldn't fall back on being a soldier. I think I grew more in the two months after I discharged than I did in the previous three years.

When I did sign the last of my papers at the base, I was driving out on my way home and I got a call from Pete Higgins, who had been so instrumental in keeping me on track through snowboarding. He wanted to let me know that

Sochi had accepted snowboarding into the 2014 Paralympics, and at that exact moment I had it in my sights ... the next thing, the next chapter, my next goal. Now I could focus fully on snowboarding. I could use everything I had learned about my approach to challenges and apply all the good things I had learned in the military to a sport. It's another uphill climb, it's inherently tough, it's an incredibly difficult road to success, but for me, that's perfect.

FREDDO

I'll be honest. When he first got injured, I thought that within six months Damien would be out of the army. I didn't understand why they weren't pensioning him off. I didn't think they would want him around, walking past soldiers looking at him and thinking, wow, that could happen to me. Even before the accident, I never thought he would be a soldier for life. If he hadn't got injured, he could have been deployed six or seven times, who knows?

But when he was injured and relegated to office jobs, I knew he definitely wouldn't stay. He loved that life before the accident. Being a commando was a lifestyle, not a job. He was getting paid five times as much as a regular soldier, he could grow a beard, didn't have to strictly report to anyone, and there was an air of secrecy around it. You couldn't say this, you couldn't say that, it was almost like a spy thing. After taking all that away, he would just be like any other soldier, an Average Joe in terms of the military, and that's a hard thing to accept.

Look, there were a lot of positive things from his time back in the army after the accident. You can't bag them, and at the end of the day it is a system that has to work. Where he is now and what he has been able to achieve is a result of the financial support he received, and that is a real credit to the system. If his injuries had happened in a car accident, it would have been a totally different situation right now. They got him to such a good point physically, but I think the emotional side and the mental side were more of a struggle.

We would speak a lot during the dark times and towards the end of his time in the army. He was angry, especially about the way the disciplinary situation was handled at work. Obviously I wasn't there, but the feeling I got from talking with him was that the army were keeping him around because he was doing such good things with his charity work. He was almost the pin-up boy for recovery. 'Meet this guy, meet that guy, shake this guy's hand,' and people saw him and thought, I want to donate. But that perfect pin-up persona is not the reality. In my opinion, some soldiers don't come back, and some come back with a very different personality type.

It was hard for him to decide to move on from the army, because it was such a big part of who he was. I wouldn't try to talk him in or out of anything. That's not the way to go with Damien. What I was trying to do was suggest that there was life after the army, because I saw lots of things being detrimental to his mental health. He was clashing with people and there was a lack of support. Snowboarding came at a perfect time. Once he focused on getting out, that's where the snowboarding really came in. There was something else there, he had another option. I've read a lot of biographies, and many are stories of downs and ups, then downs again, and while he has had some tough times, most of his story is positive and I hope that comes across. If what happened to

Damien had happened to the bloke next to him, or the bloke behind him, this story would have sounded very different. I don't think there are many people like Damien. He's gone beyond survival, and that's remarkable, really.

DI AND STEVE THOMLINSON

Di: When we went to Canberra for a wounded soldiers event in April 2010, Ken Gillespie, the Chief of Army, said that the way it was with regulations, they could give Damien two years to stay in the army and see how things went, but they were basically prepared to give him up to five years. I think at the end of five years, it was going to be a case of them saying, 'No, that's it, no longer.'

Steve: I think they humoured him with his aspirations of wanting to deploy again. His two strongest supporters were the Chief of Army and the Chief of Defence, Angus Houston, and when you have supporters like that, you don't get too many arguments. As soon as they both retired, I think reality set in. I don't think Damien would have been suited to an alternative role in an office. It was inevitable that he was going to leave the army, it was just a matter of when.

Di: I think he enjoyed doing all the things to help the profile of his unit and the Welfare Trust, but only to a point. There were expectations that were ridiculous. He would be in Brisbane doing something for them, then he would come back and they wanted to fly him to Melbourne that afternoon, for something else. It's a tough schedule for anyone. The thing was, throughout all that, they only ever saw the good side of him. That's what he was like — he'd put the front on. But he uses so much energy just doing things we wouldn't think twice about. The fact is, it takes 80 per cent more energy for him to walk than a regular person. Of course he gets tired and cranky and irritable. Quite often he would get home from work and he would really be a crumbling heap.

In his unit, the CO and Regimental Sergeant Major have to move on every two years, so the ones who were there when the incident happened were replaced at the end of 2009, and then another lot got replaced at the end of 2011. Those new people then wondered why he was getting special privileges and being flown to Brisbane and Melbourne.

Then he had the falling-out on the Targa tour, got severely punished and that was the end of it. One thing I know is that he's nowhere near as stressed now as he was in the army.

Steve: Snowboarding coming along gave him something else to focus on, so I think it was fortuitous, but then again, if it hadn't been snowboarding, he would have found something different.

TISHA

When the time came, I really wanted him to leave the army. Up until then he had been training so that he could go back again to Afghanistan, and I was fully supportive of that. It was what he wanted to do. I respected that, and I knew that before we got back together, but deep in my heart, I was worried about him going back, and I didn't want him to go. I honestly don't like to think about what that end result would have been like. If I had had to face it, I would have, but while he was training it was just something I avoided.

I think a lot of his problems with the army were behaviour problems. I said to him, 'Look, the army is great to prepare

275

you guys to go to war and do what you do, but they are not great at knowing what to do when you come back.' When he decided that he'd had enough and he was leaving, I thought it was the best decision he could ever make. I said, 'I'm pretty sure your life will be so much better, in so many ways from now on.'

But I was obviously also worried because he had been in that system for so long. Going back to Afghanistan was his life goal. I said to him, 'Is this really what you want? I don't want you to regret leaving the army or feel like you can't do anything else because you're not a soldier anymore. What are you going to do from now on?'

Even though I raised concerns, I was trying to convince him it was the right decision, too. I was sure there would be something that would come up and straight away he had that call from Pete Higgins about snowboarding in the Paralympics. I thought, perfect, that's what you can do.

It was not only another focus, it was something physical, and he needs that. He needs to be active and focused on something. It is amazing to see the difference between Damien in the army and Damien out of the army. There are still things we have to work on, but he's so much happier and there has been a big shift in his behaviour. While he was in the army he was always very angry, anxious and aggressive. Ever since he left he is more relaxed and calm and is becoming more like a civilian every day. That transition from a commando to a normal citizen is a big leap, a huge jump, regardless of the situation, but he took it, and I think he's happy he did.

27

My years in the army were the most remarkable time of my life, but it was now over. I needed to pour all of my focus and energy into my next goal. Armed with only a snowboard, I was going to represent Australia on a different battlefield, the slopes of Sochi in Russia at the 2014 Paralympics. Years earlier, when I desperately wanted to become a commando, I learned that nothing worthwhile in life comes easy. Making it to the Paralympics would be another major challenge, but one I felt I could accomplish.

My snowboarding ability had improved dramatically since that first winter camp with Pete Higgins back in 2010. I had put in for my discharge and was now being left alone until it came through. During that winter I was able to head to the snow and work on my riding, and each time I trained, I felt I was improving. But, as so often is the case, hurdles suddenly pop up to make the journey that little bit more interesting.

I was still in the army when something happened which would have an effect on my preparations for Sochi even after I had been discharged in September 2012.

While training in the snow that winter, I lost my voice in the first week. I was training one week on, and one off, for six weeks. I gave it my all, to the point where I was pretty much out of commission for the weeks in between, needing tons of rest and a healthy diet. By the end of the trip my voice wasn't getting any better and I still sounded like Marlon Brando in *The Godfather*, mixed with a dash of Darren Lockyer. Because I was still in the army awaiting discharge at that time, I was ordered to see the doctor at work instead of going straight to an ear, nose and throat specialist. I had to wait a week to see this army doctor, but I went along with it, saw him and got a referral to see a specialist.

I kept extremely quiet about it with the doctors from work but proceeded then to fly to Brazil with Tisha for a wedding in late July, about six weeks after losing my voice. It wasn't a bad place to go for a two-week trip. I love Brazilians and their culture. They are such happy people and love to party. The problem was that I could feel my health slowly deteriorating and could only stand having one or two beers before my body wanted to shut down. It was at that stage I started to question why I had had so much trouble recovering and why my voice was still husky. During my training at the snow I would ride from first lifts at 8am until 11–11.30am, and when we got back to the lodge, I would go to sleep for two hours. I put this down to not having the best level of fitness, though I couldn't understand why my fitness wasn't improving. When we returned from Brazil, I had a scan done, after which I then got the wrong phone call at the wrong time.

Ever since my coach had told me about the Paralympics in Russia I'd had one goal: to represent my country one more time. In doing so I wanted to show how thankful I was to all the people involved in my recovery, whether friends, family or strangers. I wanted anyone who had witnessed one of my alcohol-induced rants to be proud of how far I'd come with their help. I was packed up and ready to go to the snow to get classified, which is when adaptive athletes have their level of impairment assessed to get assigned a factor of handicap, to attempt to create a level playing field on the course. It was then that my phone rang.

It was the doctor at work, saying he had news for me. 'Damien, you have a cyst in your chest the size of a golf ball.'

I responded, 'Well, it's going to have to wait. It's been there a while, so it must be stable.' I was lying through my teeth. I would have tried anything to make sure I could go and get classified.

I tried arguing some more, but the doctor won out: 'That thing bursts and there is no telling what it will do.' So I made the necessary calls to coaches, management and everyone I could to make sure this wouldn't change my trajectory too much. All were supportive and understood my disappointment.

The cyst was located between my trachea and oesophagus, and the chest specialist explained how they were going to have to collapse my lung, cut through my back and separate ribs to remove it. He asked when I would like to have the operation done. I smiled and joked, 'Yesterday? It's pretty much day surgery, isn't it?' It turned out to be the most painful surgery that I had ever had. I spent around three months recovering, and as soon as I could I started training as hard as I could to strengthen my back and core, to get them back up to the stage where I could ride again.

The next hurdle came after I had left the army and was fully focused on improving my skills and successfully qualifying for Sochi. I got a call from Pete Higgins telling me the International Paralympic Committee had announced there would be no factoring system used for snowboarding at the 2014 Games.

PETE HIGGINS

When we first started training together, being a double amputee wasn't a disadvantage for Damien. The sport was run by the World Snowboard Federation, and they had a factoring system. They would classify an athlete into a certain disability bracket and there were nine different categories, and then there were sub-categories within those depending on the athlete. Once all the athletes for a particular race were in their categories, a time penalty would be given to the least disabled and a true benefit to the most disabled. So they would take your raw time and then multiply it by this factor and that's how they would determine who had won.

We'd been focusing on Damien's training so that he could compete in this system, then after the winter of 2012 in Australia, the sport got taken over by the International Paralympic Committee. They did not like the science and the numbers or anything that was involved with the factoring that came out of the World Snowboard Federation. It was a tough phone call to tell Damien that they had deleted all factoring. It meant that he could still compete, but they would not be factoring for the 2014 Sochi Paralympic Games.

They chose to do this because they didn't feel the science was up to their standard, and I think that is sort of fair enough, but it's bad luck for Damien. The Paralympic Committee has also now said that the minimum disability is missing a foot above the ankle. That means Damien now has to race against guys who are only missing an ankle, and first past the post wins.

That's a really tough one for Damien, because the longer your stump is the better leverage you have and the equipment and gear they make nowadays really does perform like an ankle joint anyway. It will be a hard fight to make it into that world, but I'm not discounting him.

DAMIEN

This was a huge disadvantage to me. Before then I thought it was going to be difficult just to get to Sochi. That announcement was like a door slamming on me. But nothing is impossible. At least I still had a shot to qualify.

In January 2013 I went over to the States to train with Team Utah in Park City, with the aim of qualifying for the Paralympics. I had organised the trip through Travis Thiele, who does a lot of work in New Zealand with adaptive riders. Travis is extremely passionate about snowboarding, and has been doing it for 13 years. He was part of the movement that started adaptive snowboarding. In Utah, I learned more in a week of riding with 27 other adaptive athletes than I had worked out for myself in three years of snowboarding. It was amazing. It would be four months before I returned home.

Things were going really well. I had blown away people who had been in this game for a long time. Not only could I snowboard, I could do it well. Some of the adaptive snowboarders blow me away with what they do, but they look at me and can't believe what they're seeing. It's pretty motivational to feel like I'm part of that club. Hopefully, the factoring system will be back in place for the 2018

Paralympics, so that everyone has a fair shot. If so, I am confident I am going to be very successful, judging by the feedback I've received.

At the moment the guys I'm racing against are so much better than me. They are astronomically good riders, of varying degrees of impairment. I'm the only double amputee on the international adaptive snowboarding circuit who is an above knee amputee as well. There are people missing one foot, or one leg, and there are some doubles, but they are all below knee doubles. In the car park at the snowfields, every time I strap my board, some American will go out of his way to say, 'Man, you ride with that? Dude, that is badass.' Early on, in one competition I participated in, people could see my back leg was above knee, and when they found out my front leg was also gone, they couldn't believe it: 'Are you serious, you're a double?'

Being a double amputee is a huge challenge. There are obviously different ways that the two prosthetics interact with each other that makes the arrangement a lot more complicated than dealing with one normal leg that can adjust any way you need it to. The reality is that I just don't have as many points of adjustment. Because I only have one knee, I have got to have everything wired tight to make it work. In addition to that, my back has to make adjustments where my legs can't. It's tough. Compared to all the guys who aren't missing as many limbs and joints, I'm pushing shit uphill, but it's kind of fun fighting out of a corner. That's me.

Eleven days into training in Utah, my L2 vertebrae gave way on a 30-foot kicker — a ramp — and the result was a stress fracture to my back, and another trip to hospital. A broken back, that was something new. I thought that now I had broken or injured every part of my body. They told me to take things easy for six weeks. But I figured that that was just a doctor's guideline. Really, I'd be ready to be out riding again in three and I was determined about it. It was just a broken back. Shit, I'd lost legs. This was nothing. Seven weeks after the injury, I was riding in my first World Cup event, in Slovenia.

I did get my arse handed to me, though, and it was the toughest two days on the mountain that I have had since I started snowboarding. The course was incredible, but I finished it, and that's what matters. It's all about the old commando trick: whenever I think I have given everything, I know I have more in the tank and I keep going. I'll know I'm finished when I pass out or when I'm stretchered off, and even then … I never give up.

If I'm fortunate enough to win a gold medal one day, which is what I'm striving for in 2018 — when, hopefully, they let the factoring system in again — I'll be thanking the amazing people who have helped me along the way, just as I thank them for where I am today. My family, my mates, my beautiful Tisha and so many who don't even know how they've helped me.

Driving over an IED in Afghanistan changed my life in so many ways, and the date April 4 will forever be etched into me. I remember the first year that the anniversary rolled around. I was still a little sick and injured. I had a bit of money then and was thinking about all these things I could do, like having a massive party. But when I spoke to Dad about it, he suggested that we all just get together and have a quiet dinner. I thought that sounded like a really good idea. So we sat down, had dinner and I don't think we even really talked about the incident all night. We didn't reflect on it too much at all. The date is also my sister's wedding anniversary and I think we'd all rather celebrate that.

It wasn't until after the *60 Minutes* episode that I thought much about that night in Afghanistan myself, and that was because I felt I got a lot of attention and accolades then that I wasn't worthy of. I didn't save my own life. All I did was decide that I was stubborn enough to want to walk again. I remember around that time I posted a message on Facebook that said: 'To the amazing people who saved my life, the faceless warriors who people never hear about. All I can do is thank you for what you did for me. It was a life-changing experience, and thanks to you guys, I get to have a life.'

Any time I featured in the media after that *60 Minutes* show, I would have people walk up and shake my hand and say thank you. I don't feel right being thanked. It's not me; it's those guys over there doing it for us all. Thank those guys. All I am doing is walking again.

Our troops continue to sacrifice so much and they don't ask for anything.

What I can say is, Australia, please, it's our job as a nation to back these guys up. Remember, they are human. When they fall, let's be the arms that catch them. Regardless of whether you personally think our soldiers should be in Afghanistan or not, these guys are away doing things that we don't have to see, so that we can live the perfect life that we have here. That is their conviction: for you. Please, respect that.

The fact is, war is bad. War is dog shit and I haven't met anyone who wasn't a complete psychopath who enjoys the idea of war. I've been fortunate enough to travel a lot and there is no place I'd rather be than Australia. I'll vouch for why they call it the lucky country, and our troops who go to war are only over there to help keep this place as great and as lucky as it is.

When I sit here and think about it, I would say 99 per cent of my life has been an absolutely brilliant fairytale. The other one per cent involves the points at which I tried to ignore reality and it ended up hitting me in the face. The dark times have taught me that I have the ability to deal with the one per cent and now I am confident about that.

Things are always going to be hard in some respect; the trick is learning something from the hard times. That way you can always be better prepared for when the next one hits you in the face. And using that philosophy, I reckon if I ever run over another roadside bomb, I'll be fine. I'm prepped for it now.

ACKNOWLEDGEMENTS

The complexity of particular situations you have read about in this book looks entirely different in hindsight and every time I think about these situations, my respect and gratitude for people involved simply grows.

The entire experience regarding my injury changed my outlook on life and the importance of the support network I had, from family and friends to surgeons and nurses. It is indescribable. Thinking about the way you all carried yourselves and acted in such a complex situation, both physically and emotionally, has helped me grow so much as a person.

I have been so fortunate to have been surrounded by amazing people who shared the highs and lows of a situation of extreme duress, people who stuck by me through times that were incredibly hard, people who I have laughed and cried with. To some of those I also offer my gratitude for kindly giving their time and agreeing to contribute to this book.

To my mum Di, dad Steve and my sister Naomi, simply … thank you. This may be the end of the book, but I'm sure you know this is not the final chapter.

To Tisha, my rock. People speak to me about overcoming adversity. I think they should speak to you.

To Freddo … it's all about the stories!

To Corporal B — never above you, never below you, always beside you.

To Dr Andrew Ellis, I thank you for being a tribute to the values of the Australian Army. You encapsulate the mateship and care principles of the Australian Army.

And to Pete Higgins, the man who believed in the fire in my eyes. It is going to take a truckload of snow to ever extinguish or dull that fire.

As I have written, there are numerous people who have played a role, be it major or minor, in my journey since that night in Afghanistan. To you all, I say thank you.

Uncle Ray Ray and Auntie Pam Palmer — I love you both.

The crew from RSL Soldiers Kokoda.

Jodie Thring — an inspiration on the snow.

Ray Martin — one of the most genuine and sincere people I have met.

Nat Briskey — a friend in and out of uniform.

Mick and Shaz Slateral — you both know why!

Chris Ransom — not only a skilled translator but an inspiring friend.

Scott Steer — mates forever.

Danny Green — I will never forget the moment after the Roy Jones Jr fight in your locker room and what you said. You are a legend, mate.

Johnny Lewis — you made a call to me which turned things around. I will never forget it.

Steve Pilmore — for my introduction into the world I was going to be treading into and for your constant support.

Bruce Parker — your Christmas phone call got me through some dark times and I will always look up to you.

Rueven Savitt and the staff at the Skinny Dip Café in Bondi — for helping the evolution continue.

Marv (Chris Marsh) — who has great ears for listening and can pose.

The team at Richardson & Wrench at Bondi Beach (Ian Wallace (Wal), Jason Taylor and Keiran Speed) who helped immensely with my adjustment to a new apartment, and to Wal and his mate from *Bondi Rescue* for getting me back in the water on a board again.

All Sorts Fitness and Jacky Wu — a refreshing approach to dynamic functional training.

Team Utah and the National Ability Center, Utah, and their coaches.

Travis Thiele — a great coach who taught me a lot and really works hard to promote his athletes and adaptive snowboarding.

Those at Disabled Winter Sport Australia for your time and patience.

Lawrie Ransom — who said what I needed to hear.

Dr Ben Cass — for somehow putting my elbow back together.

Bernie Hudson — for finding the bug in my arm and killing it.

Chloe Butcher — amateur hour. Haha. A friendly face and notably skilled nurse.

ACM Angus Houston (CDF) — you are a constant inspiration. Thank you for your time and inspiring words.

Captain JP — from me and my family, thank you.

Major General Ken Gillespie (CA) — your approach to our wounded was, and still is, inspiring.

Sue Turner — thank you for making things happen and being my point of call in some trying times.

Captain Goldie — for bending rules for my benefit and putting your own head on the block, and to everyone else who did the same.

David Wolf — who has supported and assisted my evolution.

Michael Cowley — for helping me piece the whole thing together.

And finally, my thanks to the Spartan Warriors of Bravo Commando Company Group from the 2nd Commando Regiment, for keeping me here, both before and after.